THOUGHTFUL SOCCER

The Think-First Approach to Playing and Coaching

by Russell Carrington

story illustrations by Stan Waling

REEDSWAIN *Publishing*

**Library of Congress
Cataloging - in - Publication Data**

by Russ Carrington
   Thoughtful Soccer
      The Think-First Approach to
      Playing and Coaching

ISBN No. 1-59164-016-4
Lib. of Congress Catalog No. 2002100429
© 2002

All rights reserved. Except for use in a review. The reproduction or utilization of this book in any form or by any electronic, mechanical or other means, now known or hereafter invented, including xerography, photocopying and recording, and in any information storage and retrieval system, is forbidden without written permission of the publisher.

Editing
Bryan R. Beaver

Front Cover Illustration by
Stan Waling

Printed by
DATA REPRODUCTIONS
Auburn, Michigan

Reedswain Publishing
612 Pughtown Road
Spring City, PA 19475
800.331.5191
www.reedswain.com
info@reedswain.com

ACKNOWLEDGEMENTS

Several people helped this book along. Players from two travel teams, the St. Mary's Sweepers and the St. Mary's Settlers, helped develop many of the practice activities. Richard Broad, the director of Middle States Soccer Camp, supported my ideas in a camp setting. Tony Waiters, World of Soccer, provided player images for the original draft. Three people looked the book over, and gave helpful feedback: George Lidster, Jack Greely, and Roy Porter. And my sister, Sue Carrington, offered countless writing suggestions.

Were it not for my son Jesse, there would be no Thoughtful Soccer. He gave me someone to coach, and convinced me that Thoughtful Soccer works.

Finally, this book is dedicated to my niece and soccer friend, Grace Carrington. We were looking forward to working on soccer together before her death in a car accident on January 22, 2001. She was nine years old.

Table of Contents

Foreword: The Story of Thoughtful Soccer v
Introduction: Great News for New Coaches 1

Part One: Organizing 9

1. Practicing the Thoughtful Soccer Way 11
2. Skills Gentle to Strenuous 19
3. Smart Shooting 31
4. Dribbling With Variety 45
5. Secrets of Possession 55
6. Practicing Possession 61
7. Organizing Flexibly 75
8. The Match, With Values .85
9. Stepping In to Teach 91

Part Two: Coaching Soccer's Parts 99

10. Seeing the Parts 101
11. The Offside Rule, With Care 111
12. Preventing Goals 121
13. Winning the Ball Back .135
14. Defending With a System 143
15. The Four-Roles-In-One Keeper 159
16. Breaking Through to Score 173
17. Breaking Through With Combinations 181
18. Breaking Through Defensive Systems 193
19. An Option Approach to the Restart Part 203

Index 219
About the Author and the Artist 225

FOREWORD: THE STORY OF THOUGHTFUL SOCCER

How could a latecomer to soccer, who began as one of those *parent volunteer* coaches, have something to say about the sport? Well, I was a latecomer for a reason. There was no youth soccer where I grew up. I learned how to coach through baseball, football, and basketball.

My only soccer experience came from PE classes, in junior high school and college—until I found an adult league with low playing standards. I had always been a thinking kind of athlete, but I found soccer's thinking side a mystery. There were no firmly established positions, and players could run where they pleased. The action was continuous, with no huddles or timeouts for calling plays. Soccer seemed like a free-for-all in which thinking had no place.

> **Soccer seemed like a free-for-all in which thinking had no place.**

After playing a few years, I began to grasp soccer's thinking side. That grasp proved shaky, though, when I was pressed into coaching my son's team. Like most seven-year-old soccer players, mine were disorganized. They fought with teammates for the ball, and booted it forward aimlessly. They bunched around the ball as it moved toward one goal and then back toward the other.

I wanted my players to spread out, and to pass the ball quickly. But yelling such instructions was futile, and lecturing didn't work either. My players were thinking the wrong way about soccer. What was the right way, and how could I get it across?

The available soccer books weren't what I was after. Usually, they offered a few chapters about skill—how to pass, dribble, and shoot—and a few

FOREWORD: THE STORY OF THOUGHTFUL SOCCER

about practice activities. The thinking side of soccer was either left out, or in soccer-speak. Maybe the authors got it, but I didn't.

A coaching course might have helped, but I didn't know about coaching courses. I began accumulating my own ideas and practice activities outside the coaching establishment.

Learning on Their Own

I couldn't teach my young players the body mechanics of passing, dribbling, or shooting, because nobody had taught *me*. But coaching involves managing human behavior, a topic I had studied as a social work student.

A behavior principle called *response generalization* applies directly to coaching. A soccer coach wants responses learned in practice to generalize, or carry over, to the match. A few secrets make this possible. For example, the practice situation should resemble the match situation. And players should get as many tries as possible in the practice situation.

> **A behavior principle called *response generalization* applies directly to coaching.**

With my young players, I applied such secrets to shooting practice. I realized many different shots could arise in a match. A shooter might be dribbling the ball or receiving it. A received ball might be rolling, bouncing, or flying through the air. And either foot might be required. If my players were to score in the match, they would have to practice all these shots.

I began spending fifteen or twenty minutes of each practice on shooting. We'd work on three shots in one practice and three in the next, and eventually return to the first three. The shooting went quickly, and players got many tries at each shot. I organized the shots and served the balls, but gave only one instruction: "Put the ball in the net."

I still use this shooting approach with all age groups. A player usually struggles with a shot at first, and then has a little success. After several practices, the shot is much easier. And within a season or two, the player has made the shot in a match. When the ball ends up in the net, nobody complains about body mechanics!

The Power of Rules

I first realized the power of special rules when my players were nine. Weary of yelling and lecturing, I began cracking down with two scrimmage rules. If a player booted the ball forward without looking for a teammate, I blew my whistle and gave the ball to the other team. I did the same if two teammates fought over the ball.

The new rules worked where talk had failed. Rather than booting the ball aimlessly, players began looking up before passing. Teammates no longer fought each other for the ball. And the same changes could be seen in our matches. Only once did a player confuse our scrimmage rules with soccer's real rules. When an opponent booted the ball forward aimlessly, young Amanda scolded the referee for not calling a violation!

Over the years, I continued using games and rules, rather than talk, to develop soccer players. To stir up enthusiasm, I gave the games catchy names, like *Ride the Bronco* and *Run the Gauntlet*. Eventually, we had a game for every part of soccer. And we played the same games from practice to practice, season to season, without tiring of them.

A Sport of Options

Options entered my soccer vocabulary when my players were ten. I was a decent coach at the time, but my understanding of soccer thought was still limited. I began wondering how a team can keep the ball for long *if the ball always goes forward*. Wouldn't a turnover or a goal occur within fifteen seconds? If a team had the option of passing forward, back or to the side, could the ball be kept more easily?

> **I began wondering how a team can keep the ball for long *if the ball always goes forward*.**

I tested the theory with a few scrimmage rules. Before scoring, a team had to complete at least one pass back toward its own goal. Adding a rule that limited players to three touches, we had our first Thoughtful Scrimmage—*Three-and-a-Drop*. Next, we developed *Side-to-Side*, in which the ball must be moved from one side of the field to the other.

These options worked like magic! As the ball moved in different directions, players began spreading out. They also began thinking together and communicating. And they were finally able to keep possession of the ball. Our scrimmages became less like track meets and more like chess matches.

If the option of going forward, back, or to the side was good, other options must be good as well. I began watching professional soccer more closely, and saw options everywhere. The player with the ball might pass, dribble, or shoot. The pass might be long or short, on the ground or through the air. And many different dribbling moves might be tried. I was convinced that soccer is a sport of options.

PART II: TEACHING SOCCER'S PARTS

A Great Way to Teach

Developing outside the soccer establishment hurt me in an important way. Until my players were thirteen, I hadn't worried about playing the *teacher* role. I was an organizer, counting on my games and rules to do all the teaching. As a result, I couldn't be sure my players were learning what I wanted them to. And the learning was taking too long.

I finally took a coaching course, and was shown a great way to teach soccer.[1] The instructor started a soccer-related game quickly, with little talk. When he saw something that wasn't right, he froze the action and stepped onto the field. Then, he pointed out the problem, walked through a solution, and shouted, "Play on!"

> **I finally took a coaching course, and was shown a great way to teach soccer.**

What clever behavior management! A negative behavior could be interrupted, and replaced with a positive behavior. The teaching style didn't have a name, but the interruptions were called *coachable moments*. I began calling them COMOs and using them to make my own points. No matter how complicated the idea, a COMO can make it simple.

From Phases to Parts

Years of playing and watching soccer got me thinking about soccer's parts. Players run wherever they want to. The action is non-stop. No two situations are the same. How can players respond to these situations intelligently? Maybe players *group* the situations!

My behavioral theory of soccer went like this. All the situations where an attack is possible can be grouped together. So can the situations where an attack *isn't* possible, or when the ball is about to be lost. Each of these groups calls for different responses. Soccer players read the situation, decide what group it belongs to, and respond accordingly. By grouping situations, players think together as a team!

Suddenly, soccer seemed like a machine, with interdependent parts. If a team can't keep possession, it will always be defending. And if a team can't break through the defense, it will have no finishing opportunities.

Phases allowed me to watch soccer more insightfully, and to figure out the problems. I gave up on the word *phases*, though. It makes a simple sport seem complicated. And the parts of soccer don't really flow in a logical sequence. They jump around, and get jumbled together. Now, I just call the parts *parts*.

It Works!

In the county where we played, our style of soccer was unique. While other players rushed the ball forward, we moved it back and to the side. While other players relied on speed and brute force, we moved the ball to open spaces. And we were more considerate of our opponents, rather than charging into them or hacking them down.

Our approach required thought, and allowed us to be thoughtful toward others. *Thoughtful Soccer* was the obvious choice for a name.

Thoughtful Soccer *works*—as a way to play, to practice, and to develop players who love the sport. That's why I wrote this book.

---

[1] I learned about the coachable moment teaching style at a D license course offered by the Maryland State Youth Soccer Association. Graham Ramsey was the instructor.

INTRODUCTION: GREAT NEWS FOR NEW COACHES

The Intergalactic Sculpture Party

The astronaut families stepped from their spaceship, unsure what to expect of the planet's inhabitants. But although the Zoobies were obsessed with sculpture, they were really quite friendly. They even scheduled a sculpture party for the astronaut children, who were to bring their best representations of the Zoobie planet.

INTRODUCTION: GREAT NEWS FOR NEW COACHES

The children were understandably concerned. None of them had a clue about sculpture *or* the planet. Their parents found a Zoobie web site that offered a sequence of courses: Play Dough Zoobie, Intermediate Zoobie Sculpture, and Mastering the Zoobie Figure. But the banquet was a week away, and only the best sculpture would be accepted!

In desperation, the parents visited the local library and checked out a book of sculpting games. These games revealed the secrets of Zoobie sculpture to all who played. The games were also a great deal of fun, and the children began playing them around the clock. Soon, the children were creating Zoobian plants, Zoobian wildlife, and even the Zoobian figure, with its three eyes and four legs. The children were the life of the sculpture party!

The parents had three problems. They couldn't picture what Zoobie sculpture should look like. They had no method for teaching their children. And they had little time.

New soccer coaches face the same challenges. If you haven't played soccer a great deal, you won't have a picture of what it should look like or a method for teaching your players. You could take a sequence of coaching courses, but that might take years. If your players are to keep up in the soccer world, they need help right away!

Thoughtful Soccer resembles that book of sculpting games. It provides a picture of what soccer should look like, and a method for bringing that picture to life. With Thoughtful Soccer, you can help your players right away, even if you've never played. A *picture* and a *method*—coaching soccer really boils down to these two ingredients.

> **A *picture* and a *method*—coaching soccer really boils down to these two ingredients.**

The Thoughtful Soccer Picture

Your picture of soccer provides a goal to strive for, a way to evaluate what's going well and what's going poorly. Can you close your eyes and visualize what soccer should look like? If not, you don't have a clear picture.

New coaches often start out with a thoughtless picture. They visualize fast, aggressive players rather than smart players. They see the ball going straight to goal every time, for quick scoring attempts. They picture soccer that's very predictable.

The key to the Thoughtful Soccer picture is *unpredictability*. Players might pass, shoot, or dribble. They might move the ball forward, back, or to the side. And they might attack quickly or advance the ball patiently. Observers, as well as opponents, can't predict what's going to happen. That's what makes Thoughtful Soccer so enjoyable to watch.

The word *thoughtful* captures two meanings. First, it describes soccer that is filled with thought. Players constantly think, organize, and communicate. They rely on cunning and deception, not just speed and brute force. Second, it describes soccer that is thoughtful toward others. Players play safely, and win the ball fairly. They respect teammates, opponents, and referees.

Don't think that Thoughtful Soccer is passive, or that winning doesn't matter. Players are encouraged to go aggressively to the ball. What's discouraged is aggressiveness toward others. And although safety and respect are more important than winning, they also contribute to a winning effort. Players with those values avoid costly fouls, yellow cards, and penalty kicks.

The Method Taught in Coaching Courses

Once you have a picture in mind, you need a method for getting players to play that way. Your method consists of all your practice activities, scrimmages, and teaching strategies. If your picture is the goal, your method is how you reach the goal.

The method taught in coaching courses has a very *instructional* flavor. Coaches are supposed to instruct players on topics like dribbling, shooting, and defending. An entire practice might address one topic, and the activities follow a logical progression.

> **The method taught in coaching courses has a very *instructional* flavor.**

A progression for dribbling might look like this:

- Players practice different dribbling moves without competing
- Players try the moves in a one-versus-one game
- Players compete in a small-sided scrimmage where the rules encourage the dribbling moves

INTRODUCTION: GREAT NEWS FOR NEW COACHES

- Players apply the moves in a scrimmage where regular soccer rules are in effect

Every soccer coach should learn this method at some point. The activities progress from simple to complicated, from artificial conditions to the real thing. In just one practice, you can turn a team weakness into a strength. And the carry over from practice to match is impressive.

Here are the challenges. The method assumes you have a clear picture of what you're after. It requires a good supply of activities and progressions. And what about practice time? If you have only one or two practices per week, and cover only one topic in each one, you'll have trouble repeating topics. For new coaches, might there be a better way?

The Thoughtful Soccer Method—Organize!

The Thoughtful Soccer method places organization ahead of instruction. The coach organizes various practice games, and keeps the practice moving. The games get at the important parts of soccer. The same games are repeated from practice to practice. And each practice is similar.

That's great news for new coaches! Organizing requires less soccer expertise than instructing does. And you don't need a sophisticated picture of what soccer should look like. As you organize practices, your picture of soccer will gradually take shape. Instructing can then play a larger role in your method. In the meantime, though, your players will keep improving.

But shouldn't every practice address only one theme, using a logical progression? Coaching courses might give that impression. But progressions are just one way to develop soccer players. There's nothing wrong with covering all the key areas in every practice.

> **There's nothing wrong with covering all the key areas in every practice.**

Where's the Stuff on Body Mechanics?

Someday, you should learn to teach the body mechanics of passing, dribbling, and shooting. You'll get this in a coaching course, but not here.

Why? In tennis and golf, players *must* be instructed in the body mechanics. There are many ways to hit a tennis ball or golf ball. Without technical instruction, players are unlikely to develop effective strokes and swings.

Soccer is a little different. There aren't so many ways to pass, head, chip, or shoot a soccer ball. And most of the incorrect ways fail miserably. After thousands of touches on a soccer ball, players usually stumble upon effective ways.

Here's an example. Chipping a ball into the air requires certain body mechanics. Approach the ball from the side, get the instep under the ball, and so on. Instruction in these mechanics can speed up the learning process.

But players can also learn to chip by facing a challenge, such as a barrier to chip over. After fifty tries, the chips will make it over. And after a thousand tries, the chips will be pretty accurate. What Thoughtful Soccer lacks in instruction, it makes up for with tries!

That's more great news. If you don't understand the body mechanics yet, you can still develop skillful players . . . by providing challenges and tries!

What About the Developmental Stages?

Developmental stages play a big part in some coaching models. Players are believed to mature in stages, and each stage requires a different method. Six-year-olds are coached one way, ten-year-olds another, and teens another.

That would be *bad* news for new coaches. You'd have to be trained in several different methods. And by the time you learned one method, your players would be ready for the next one.

But new players and experienced players, young players and adult players, have much in common. They all need many repetitions in the important areas, and they all like to have fun. With Thoughtful Soccer, a practice for young players is similar to a practice for college players. Once you've got the method, your players won't outgrow it.

> **But new players and experienced players, young players and adult players, have much in common.**

Skill Versus Thought

In most coaching approaches, skill comes before thought. New players work on passing, dribbling, and shooting, while thinking is postponed to a later date. That might seem logical. How can you think about something you can't even do?

INTRODUCTION: GREAT NEWS FOR NEW COACHES

Don't believe it! Soccer thought is easier to learn than soccer skill. New players are more used to thinking than to controlling a soccer ball. And they need thought as much as experienced players do. Thought reduces the amount of skill required.

In Scene 0-1, a player is dribbling toward goal, and three opponents are in the way. Most new players will try to dribble past all three. But the new player who understands Thoughtful Soccer will spot the teammates to the side and rear, who are uncovered. Passes to uncovered teammates usually succeed, even if the passing skill is shaky.

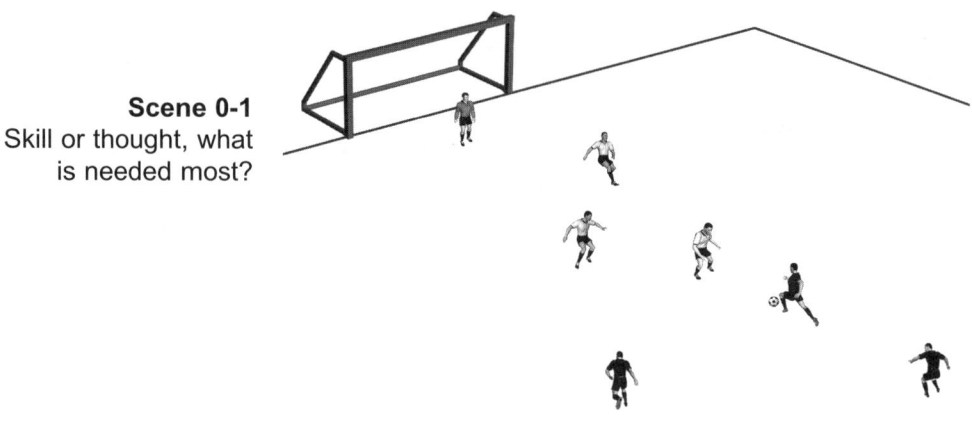

Scene 0-1
Skill or thought, what is needed most?

With Thoughtful Soccer, your players begin thinking right away, regardless of their skill level. That gives them an edge over thoughtless opponents. And they don't go for years thinking the wrong way.

An Overview of the Book

A new coach's first task is to organize effectively, the subject of Part I. Chapter 1 provides tips for organizing practice. Chapters 2-4 show how to work on skills during the first half of practice. And Chapters 5 and 6 show how to scrimmage during the second half of practice.

You won't always have the perfect practice facility, or the ideal number of players. You'll have to adjust your practice to the situation. Chapter 7 shows how.

The match is another organizational challenge. You need to get the warmup going, talk with your players, and lay down the values. Chapter 8 looks at what really matters on match day.

If you organize effectively, your players are sure to improve. The activities will do most of the teaching, as your players learn through trial-and-error.

INTRODUCTION: GREAT NEWS FOR NEW COACHES

But to speed up the improvements, you'll have to be a teacher as well. Chapter 9 explains a great way to teach soccer ideas.

Once you can organize practices and teach, you're ready for Part II: *Coaching Soccer's Parts*. There isn't one *right* way to break soccer into parts, but you'll need *some* way. Part II is about Thoughtful Soccer's approach to parts.

Chapter 10 provides a detailed introduction to Part II. Soccer's parts are depicted with scenes from a match. The remaining chapters cover the off-side rule, preventing goals, winning the ball back, defending with a system, playing Keeper, scoring goals, and taking free kicks and corner kicks.

Tips for Reading the Book

Each chapter begins with a fable, to capture the chapter's purpose and stir your curiosity. You can also tell such fables to your players. And if you make it through the chapter, another metaphorical morsel awaits.

Accompanying each soccer idea is a related practice activity. The rules are set apart from the main text, creating several options. You can jump into the ideas, the activities, or both.

The rules might seem nit-picky. That's because each activity is like a sport, with winners and losers. The activities are easy to understand, though, if you skim over the rules and glance at the pictures. And feel free to tailor the rules to your own needs.

 Thirty different games and fourteen different shots are a lot. To help you prioritize, some activities have been given the TSF—Thoughtful Soccer Favorite—seal of approval. If you can't try all the activities, be sure to try these.

You won't need all the chapters right away, but check them out anyway. You'll get a clearer picture of *all* of soccer's parts. You'll be able to sculpt a beautiful team!

PART ONE: ORGANIZING

1
PRACTICING THE THOUGHTFUL SOCCER WAY

Tough Times on the Hill

The red ants surrounded the black ants. "You are all weaklings," they laughed. "Slaughtering you now would bring us no pleasure. We'll give you a year to get stronger, and then we'll slaughter you."

PART I: ORGANIZING

The black ants accepted the challenge, and began working out. They exercised their major muscles every day, with the bench press, biceps curl, abdominal crunch, and leg press. Each workout ended with a little fighting practice.

A spy for the red ants watched these workouts for a few days. He noticed very few improvements in the black ants. "We have nothing to worry about," he told his comrades.

Day after day, the workout was repeated: bench press, biceps curl, fighting practice. The weights gradually became heavier, and the workouts more demanding. The year went by, and the red ants returned—to be slaughtered by the muscular black ants.

The black ants figured out what to strengthen, and they strengthened it in every workout. Their progress was barely noticeable after each workout. But over the long haul, their plan made sense.

What's obvious with weightlifting applies to soccer as well. You can figure out what needs strengthening—the key skills and ideas required in a match. Then, you can strengthen these skills and ideas in every practice. The progress after a season or two will amaze you.

What are those key skills and ideas? And how can you strengthen them in practice?

Check Out This Practice

A typical Thoughtful Soccer practice is shown below. The activities are covered in later chapters. For now, get a feel for the organization.

> **Skill-Building Half (45-60 minutes)**
> Soccer Volley, for ball control
> Headmaster, for heading
> Air Control, for chipping
> Shooting competitions (three different shots)
> Run the Gauntlet, for dribbling
> **Scrimmaging Half (45-60 minutes)**
> One-Time
> Three-and-a-Drop
> Reset
> Side-to-Side

CHAPTER 1: PRACTICING THE THOUGHTFUL SOCCER WAY

This little practice packs a wallop. It takes eight organizational tips seriously. Here they are.

Cover All the Options

When organizing practice, remember that soccer is a sport of options. If you could read the mind of a smart player, options would figure prominently:

"Keep your options open! Don't commit too soon to one option! Decide on an option at the last possible moment! Fake one option, and choose another!"

Scene 1-1 shows a typical option situation. Should the player with the ball shoot, dribble, or pass?

Scene 1-1
A typical option situation: shoot, dribble, or pass?

Some coaches would yell for a shot, and question the player for passing. But the Keeper and defender have an easier job if they know a shot is coming. A smart player would keep all three options open, and choose one at the last moment.

Options are closely related to skills. A skill is the physical ability to do something, like shoot, dribble, or pass. Options imply an ability to *choose* between different skills. To have options, players must first have skills.

To have options, players must first have skills.

Practice should include five basic skills: passing, receiving, dribbling, shooting, and heading. That sounds easy enough. What complicates practice are the many *variations* of each skill. Passes can be short or

PART I: ORGANIZING

long, through the air or on the ground. Dribbling can be through open space or past defenders. And there are many different shots.

How can your practices cover all these skills and variations? You must break a practice into smaller chunks of time. Since there are five skill areas, you'll need ten or fifteen minutes for each one. For skills with variations, you can address a few variations in one practice and a few in the next.

Spend a Little Time on All the Skills

Why not spend an entire practice on one skill, like heading or shooting? That goes against how players improve. In one practice, they'll improve just a little at each item they work on. The amount of time spent on a skill, fifteen minutes or two hours, won't matter a great deal.

What matters more is how *often* the skill is worked on. A skill that's included in every practice will get a little stronger each time. And a skill that's ignored for a week or two will begin fading.

To include the key skills in every practice, you must limit the time spent on each one. Twelve minutes for receiving, twelve for shooting, and so on. Bottom line: spend a little time on several skills, not a lot of time on one!

> **Bottom line: spend a little time on several skills, not a lot of time on one!**

Include Skill Work and Scrimmaging

A practice should address all the skills, but that's not all. In a match, players will have to organize, communicate, and think together. They should do these things in every practice, by scrimmaging.

Scrimmaging has a major advantage over all other activities. It closely resembles playing a match. It can even be *more* difficult than playing a match. Whatever players can do in a scrimmage, they'll be able to do in a match.

You wouldn't want to scrimmage the entire practice, though. Scrimmaging might provide very few tries at shooting, heading, or chipping. And when scrimmaging, players usually avoid their weaker skills, like passing with the left foot. Every practice should include scrimmaging *and* skill work.

CHAPTER 1: PRACTICING THE THOUGHTFUL SOCCER WAY

As a rule of thumb, skill work comes before scrimmaging. Skill work can begin as players arrive, and it's less strenuous. Also, skills polished in the first half of practice can shine during the second half.

Use Competitions, Not Drills

What kind of practice activities should you use?

For skill work, *drills* are one possibility. A drill is distinguished by the absence of competition. For example, one player tosses a ball and the other heads it back, or players dribble through cones. Drills have two problems, though: they don't resemble the match, and they're not particularly fun.

Fun, competitive games work better. They're more like the match, which is also competitive. They keep players active and focused. And they provide many tries in a short period of time. In Thoughtful Soccer, such games are called *High-Impact Skill Activities*, or *HISAs*.

A HISA is like a separate sport. It has boundaries, rules, and a way to score. It allows strategies and innovations. It produces winners and losers. No wonder players can't outgrow a HISA!

A HISA is like a separate sport.

When scrimmaging, you *could* use the regular rules of soccer. But with *special* rules, you can emphasize one idea at a time and influence players more quickly. In Thoughtful Soccer, scrimmages with special rules are called Thoughtful Scrimmages, or *Thoughtscrims*. A Thoughtscrim is also like a separate sport, with rules and a scoring system, winners and losers.

Stick With a Good Thing

Many coaches continually change their practices. Experienced coaches change their practices to address the most pressing problem, or to cover more topics. New coaches change their practices to find something that works, or to entertain their players.

Here are three good reasons to make each practice similar. First, players improve noticeably at activities that are repeated from practice to practice. Second, practices are easier to organize when they're all similar. And third, practices *have* to be similar if they're to include all the skills and scrimmages.

PART I: ORGANIZING

Won't players get bored if each practice is similar? Not if the activities are fun, competitive sports! Competition brings players back for more. So find a great way to organize practice, and stick with it.

Make a Few Adjustments

Although the basic Thoughtful Soccer practice works for everyone, consider these two adjustments for experience level.

First, new players can begin with a simpler version of an activity. They'll have trouble juggling a ball over a net, for example, and spend all their time retrieving wild kicks. They need a simpler activity as a stepping stone.

Second, experienced players can benefit from a *three*-part practice. The idea is to get through the HISAs and Thoughtscrims more quickly. That leaves a chunk of time at the end of practice, to work on defense, offense, or a problem from the last match.

Keep the Practice Moving

Many coaches would *like* to address everything in one practice. Their downfall is time management. You'll have to watch your watch and keep the practice moving. You can save time by:

- Setting up several activities before players arrive
- Starting practice as players arrive, rather than after all have arrived
- Setting up one activity while another is still in progress
- Starting activities quickly, with little talk
- Using the same activities from practice to practice, so that no rule explanations are required.

Time management is more important than you might think. And it requires no soccer expertise.

Organize for the Long Term

If you squeeze so much into one practice, will your players be overwhelmed and confused? No more than weightlifters who strengthen all the muscles, or tennis players who practice all the shots.

The practice that includes too *little* is the one to worry about. Suppose your players spend a half hour stretching, a half hour dribbling, and a half

CHAPTER 1: PRACTICING THE THOUGHTFUL SOCCER WAY

hour scrimmaging. The other half hour is spent standing in lines, watching you lay down cones, and listening to you talk. You've left out heading, shooting, and chipping altogether. In the long term, that can be disastrous. Player options will dwindle.

Look closely at your practice organization. Are all the skills covered, and are players getting enough tries at each one? Are the skills applied in scrimmages? Are activities repeated from one practice to the next? If you can answer yes to each question, you'll have the strongest ants in town.

2
SKILLS GENTLE TO STRENUOUS

Arnold the Landlocked Alligator

Arnold was an alligator who couldn't swim. He watched sadly as his friends dove, frolicked, and raced in the river. His father, himself a poor swimmer, decided some instruction was in order.

PART I: ORGANIZING

Dad did a pretty decent job of teaching. He showed Arnold how to extend the legs, paddle, and stare menacingly out of the water. He had Arnold practice in a wading pool. And he pointed out Arnold's mistakes.

Arnold then slid into the river to give swimming a try. After a few seconds of thrashing about, he proclaimed, "I can't do this!" He returned to shore, and resumed his lonely vigil.

Suddenly, Arnold's father grabbed him by the tail and slung him far into the water. Arnold splashed down near his racing friends, and floundered for a moment. But not wanting to finish last, he tried every possible combination of leg extensions, paddles, and menacing looks. Within moments, he was winning the race!

Arnold's dad wasn't a great swimmer, and his swimming instructions could only take Arnold so far. The sink-or-swim approach worked better. Arnold now swims better than his father ever could.

High-Impact Skill Activities are the sink-or-swim approach to soccer skills. A HISA is a competitive game that requires using a skill over and over. Since players improve through trial-and-error, little instruction is needed. End result—your players perform the skill better than you ever could!

> **End result—your players perform the skill better than you ever could!**

In what order should you practice the different skills? Start with gentle and move to strenuous. Here's a logical sequence:

- Begin practice with a HISA for receiving balls in the air. This often-neglected skill is low on the strain meter, and helps with later skills.

- Chipping, crossing, and heading HISAs are a little more strenuous, and can come next. If you don't include these early, you might leave them out altogether.

- Shooting activities come later. Though not exhausting, they're very strenuous. If players shoot too soon, they might pull muscles.

- Dribbling HISAs come last. Dribbling is strenuous *and* exhausting, and players need a break afterwards.

CHAPTER 2: SKILLS GENTLE TO STRENUOUS

The basic Thoughtful Soccer practice doesn't include a passing HISA. Create one if you like, but the scrimmages provide plenty of passing.

Controlling Balls in the Air

As your players arrive at practice, get them working right away with soccer balls. You'll reward players who arrive early, give them more touches, and save time. Rather than a juggling drill, discover the HISA advantage with *Soccer Volley*.

This soccer version of volleyball gets the ball moving through the air. Players must use different body surfaces, like the chest, thigh, and head. And special bounce and touch rules allow newer players to play.

Special bounce and touch rules allow newer players to play.

Set up a Soccer Volley court on any grassy or smooth surface. The ideal court looks like a miniature volleyball court, with boundary lines and a waist-high net (Scene 2-1).

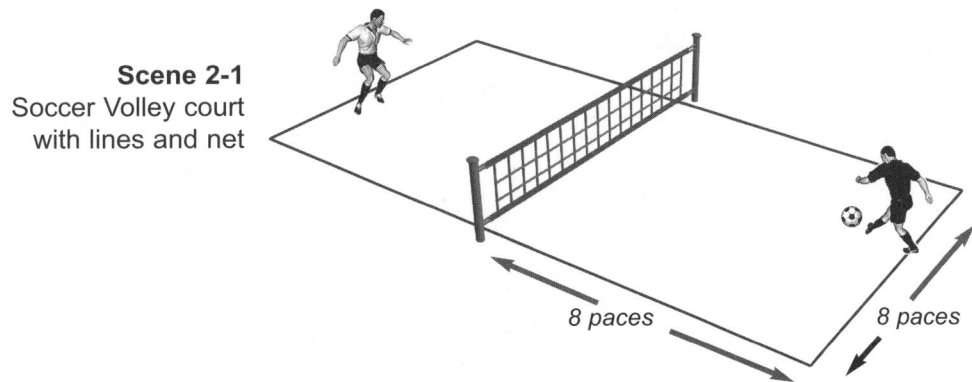

Scene 2-1
Soccer Volley court with lines and net

8 paces   8 paces

21

PART I: ORGANIZING

When lines and a net aren't available, create the boundaries with cones. The dividing line down the middle takes the place of a net (Scene 2-2).

Scene 2-2
Soccer Volley court made of cones

Without the bounce and touch rules, the no-net approach would be impossible. Here are the official rules.

Rules for Soccer Volley Singles

Court and Starting Positions The court is divided by a net or line into two halves. Each half is eight paces long in all four directions. A player is on each side, near the back line. One player holds a ball and will serve, as the other receives.

How a Point Proceeds The server drops the ball, lets it bounce once, and kicks it over to the other side. The returner must let the serve bounce at least once, and is allowed up to three bounces and three touches before sending the ball back. Players continue sending the ball back and forth, using up to three bounces and three touches each time. The point ends when a shot goes out, when too many bounces or touches are used, or when the ball begins rolling

Scoring Only the server may register a score, as in volleyball. After winning a point, the returner takes over the serve but does not register a score. Games are played to ten, or until the time runs out.

Leaving the Court to Retrieve the Ball While the kick over the net must land in bounds, the ball may leave the court at other times. Players may run far off the court, and even to the other side of the net, to retrieve the ball. However, the kick over the net must be made from one's own side of the dividing line.

Receiving the Ball in the Air After the serve, players may make the first touch in the air, enabling players to charge the net.

Since Soccer Volley can be played by three or four players, new games can begin as players arrive at practice. Four play doubles (Scene 2-3),

CHAPTER 2: SKILLS GENTLE TO STRENUOUS

while three play a hybrid version. Larger teams, like 3 v 3, are also possible.

Scene 2-3
Soccer Volley
Doubles

Rules for Soccer Volley Doubles, Other Sizes

Basic Rules The rules are the same as for singles unless otherwise noted.

How a Point Works One team serves while the other team returns. A team of two may use up to four bounces and four touches before sending the ball over the net. The players may divide up these touches and bounces in any way they like. However, each player must touch the ball at least once.

The Heading Exception There is one exception to the rule that each player must touch the ball at least once. As the ball comes over the net, a player may head it directly back, without passing to a teammate.

2 v 1 Game The team of two is allowed four bounces and four touches. The lone player is allowed three bounces and three touches.

3 v 3 Game Each team is allowed four bounces and four touches, as in doubles. At least two of the three players must touch the ball before it is sent over.

As your players improve at Soccer Volley, add these challenging rules now and then:

Rule Variations for Soccer Volley

Weak Foot Only Players must send the ball across the net with the weaker foot or the head. Other touches may be made with either foot.

Headers Only This variation may be used during doubles. The touch sending the ball over the net must be made with the head. Typically, one player gets the ball up in the air and the other heads it over.

PART I: ORGANIZING

First Touch in Air As the ball comes over the net, it must be touched once before it bounces. Afterward, the usual number of bounces and touches are allowed. If a dividing line is used rather than a net, the players on both sides work together to sustain a long rally.

A Soccer Volley Stepping Stone

For players who aren't quite ready for Soccer Volley, *Settlers* provides a stepping stone. Players pair off and work together on different Soccer Volley skills. No boundaries are required.

A serve-like maneuver is practiced first. One player drops the ball, lets it bounce, and kicks it through the air with the inside of the foot. The partner catches the ball, and serves it back. Each successful catch earns a point, and someone on the team must call out the point total. When the coach yells "Time!" the team with the most points wins.

More challenging maneuvers come next. One player tosses the ball through the air. The other lets the ball bounce once, cushions it with the chest, lets it bounce again, and passes it back through the air (Scene 2-4). A catch in the air again earns a point. Players who can perform this maneuver are soon ready for big-time Soccer Volley!

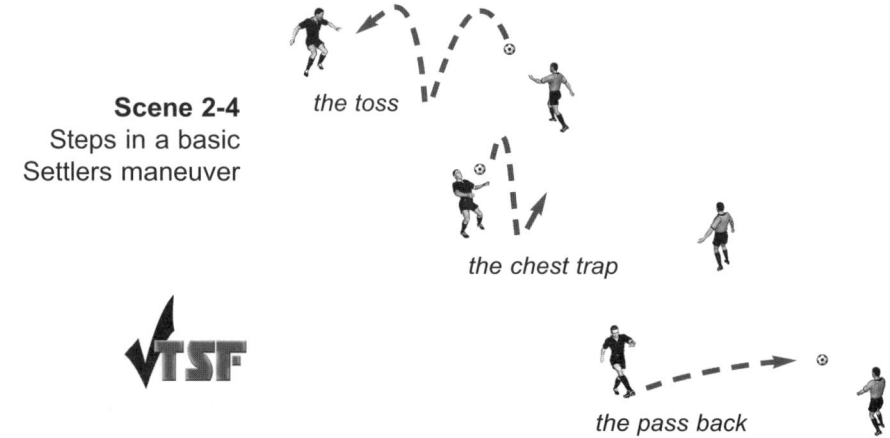

Scene 2-4
Steps in a basic Settlers maneuver

the toss

the chest trap

the pass back

A similar maneuver can be practiced using the thigh or foot for the first touch. Next, players can pass the ball back and forth, rather than catching it; the team with the most successive passes wins. Be sure to make each maneuver a competition!

CHAPTER 2: SKILLS GENTLE TO STRENUOUS

Heading Practice

Heading practice is next, with a HISA called *Headmaster*. The game requires no setup time, because it's played on a Soccer Volley court. The balls to be headed are tossed from close range, so your players won't get headaches (Scene 2-5). As two players try to score, the other two become Keepers.

Scene 2-5
Headmaster

Keepers

goal

Rules for Headmaster

Court and Teams The two cones at each end of a Soccer Volley court represent a large goal. The court may be widened several paces to allow more scoring. Teams of two or three players are on each side of the dividing line. Players may not cross the dividing line.

Object of the Game One team tries to score by heading the ball through the goal, as the other team tries to prevent a score. The ball must go through the goal at head height or lower.

How the Game Proceeds One player tosses the ball to a teammate, who tries to head it through the goal. The players on the other team may catch, punch, or kick the ball to prevent a score. Those players then make a scoring try, by tossing and heading. Teams alternate between heading and defending until the time runs out.

Two-Point Attempts Two-pointers may be scored in two ways. The player receiving a toss may head the ball back to the tosser, who in turn heads the ball through. And instead of catching the ball, a Keeper may head it directly through the other team's goal.

Below are the variations of Headmaster. Each one zeros in on a different type of header.

PART I: ORGANIZING

Rule Variations for Headmaster

Jumping Headers Only When head meets ball, a player's feet must be off the ground. Otherwise, the header doesn't count. A higher toss is usually required.

Bouncing Headers Only After being headed, the ball must bounce before going through the goal. Players learn to head down into the ground, at the Keeper's feet.

Diving Headers Only Only diving headers may register a score. The toss must be placed further in front of the heading player, who dives forward and contacts the ball close to the ground. For this variation, soft or muddy ground is recommended.

Roam and Head This variation works best with wide goals and three players per team. To score or prevent goals, players may run wherever they please. Players on the defending team may either protect the goal, or come out to snare a toss. The attacking team may catch the ball one time, but otherwise may only head the ball. An attempt ends once the ball hits the ground or is stolen.

In just fifteen minutes, your practice has accomplished a great deal. Your players have warmed up gradually. They've touched the ball many times, in ways that are often neglected. They've even competed. What's next?

Chipping Practice

Never leave out chipping! This skill makes distant teammates accessible, and creates scoring opportunities. For players who can get the ball in the air, *Air Control* is the HISA of choice.

One court can accommodate four players, in teams of two. To accommodate more players, set up as many adjacent courts as necessary. A player must chip over an opponent's box to the box of a teammate. Both teams chip at the same time (Scene 2-6).

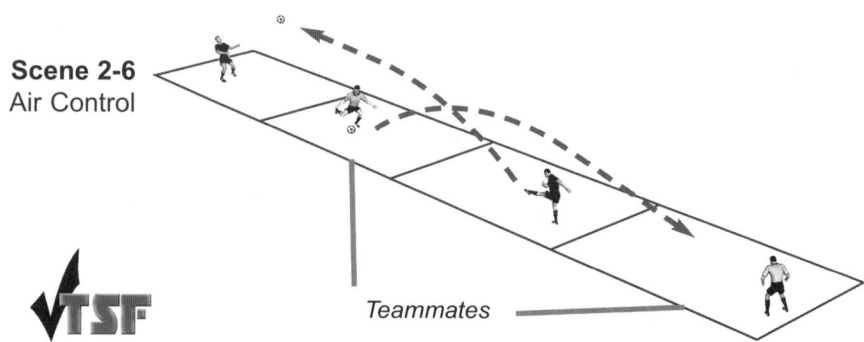

Scene 2-6
Air Control

Teammates

CHAPTER 2: SKILLS GENTLE TO STRENUOUS

Rules for Air Control

Court Four large boxes are arranged in a row. Each box is fifteen to twenty-five paces long. Larger boxes force players to try longer chips.

Teams and Starting Position Players pair off into teams. Each player occupies a box two boxes away from a teammate, with an opponent's box in between. Each team has a ball.

Object of the Game Players try to score points by chipping over an opponent's box to the box of a teammate. The first team to perform ten successful chips wins.

How the Game Proceeds Both teams begin chipping at the same time. The ball must be moving when it's chipped, and reach the teammate's box in the air. The teammate must then touch the ball at least twice inside the box, and the team must announce its point total. Players in the middle boxes may pause at any time to catch or deflect an opposing chip, but must give the ball back immediately. Each player must alternate between a right-footed and left-footed chip.

Air Control proves the value of a good challenge. Players don't want to fall behind . . . or nail opponents *in* the behind. They find a way to get the ball up.

A Stepping Stone for Chipping

New players usually aren't ready for Bombs Away. Their chips *will* nail opponents. They need *Alligator River* as a stepping stone. Players chip over an imaginary river instead of over opponents (Figure 2-7). For a giggle, tell players that an alligator will eat balls that land short.

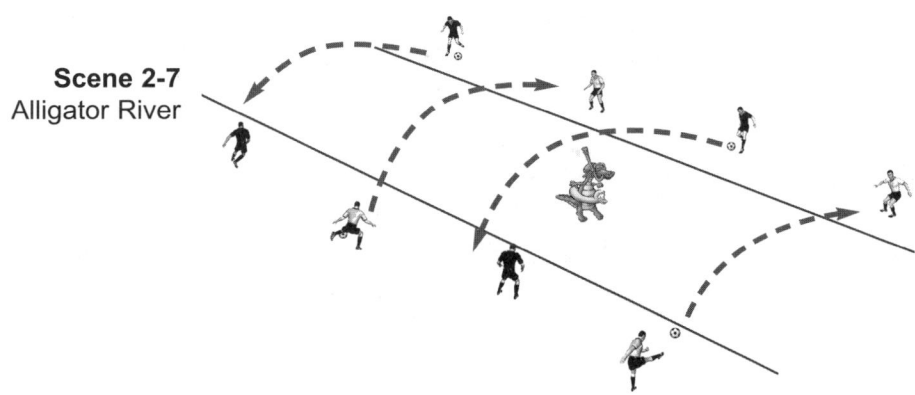

Scene 2-7
Alligator River

PART I: ORGANIZING

Rules for Alligator River

Playing Area Two parallel lines of cones, at least fifteen paces apart, represent a river. The river should be wide enough that players can't chip over it too easily. If the players are of vastly different skill levels, the river may be wider at one end than the other.

Teams and Starting Positions Players pair off into teams, and each team has a ball. One teammate begins on each side of the river, about three paces from the river bank.

Object of the Game Teams try to score as many goals as possible by chipping over the river. The ball must be moving when it's chipped, reach the other side in the air, and be touched twice on the other side before it stops rolling.

How the Game Proceeds All the teams begin chipping at the same time. Players must alternate between right-footed and left-footed chips. After scoring a point, a team must announce its total score. The coach keeps time, and proclaims when the game is over. The team with the most points wins.

Once again, a drill-like activity is transformed into a competition.

Chipping to the Head

As your players improve at heading and chipping, include this HISA which combines the two. In *Bombs Away*, players chip into the goal area, where teammates head or shoot on goal (Figure 2-8). If the chips are too short, opponents may head them in.

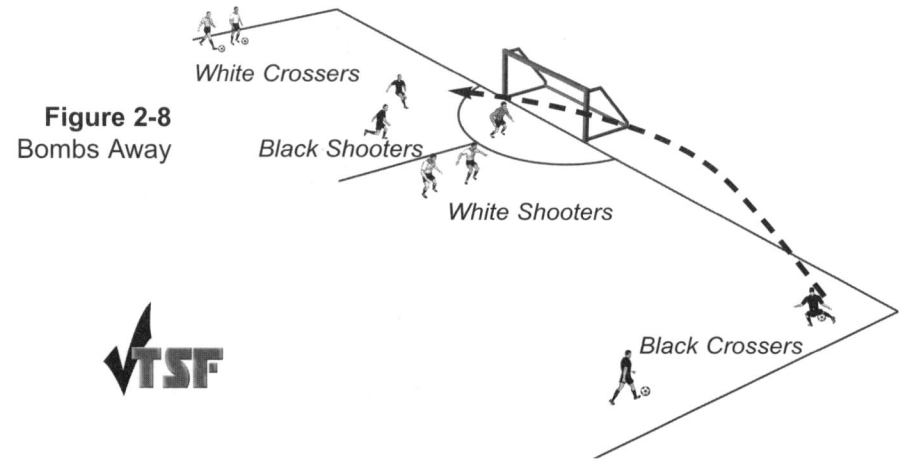

Figure 2-8
Bombs Away

CHAPTER 2: SKILLS GENTLE TO STRENUOUS

Rules For Bombs Away

Field Setup The field is set up around a regulation-size goal. Corners and touch lines are located thirty to forty paces from the goal. An arc-shaped Keeper area surrounds the goal, and a dividing line extends from that arc.

Teams and Starting Positions Each team has two to six players, divided evenly between Crossers and Shooters. Crossers line up along a touch line with several soccer balls. Shooters begin near the opposite post, behind the dividing line. Shooters may not cross the dividing line, or enter the Keeper area. The Keeper may not leave the Keeper area.

Object of the Game Teams score as many points as possible by crossing balls and shooting on goal. A headed shot counts two points, while other shots count one point.

How a Try Works A Crosser gets the ball moving and crosses it to teammates, one of whom may shoot. The shot must be made with one touch. If the cross is short, a Shooter from the opposing team may shoot for points or clear the ball away.

How a Round Proceeds After crossing the ball, the crosser gets back in line as the other team crosses from the opposite side. The round continues for two minutes, with one team crossing and then the other. Each Crosser must cross with the right foot and then the left foot. To use the required foot, a Crosser may dribble into the corner, and pull the ball back in the opposite direction. After each score, a team must announce its point total.

Rotating to Other Stations A new round begins every two minutes, as players rotate to new stations. For the second round, players switch places with their teammates. Then, they rotate to the other two stations. After four rounds, the team with the most points wins.

Bombs Away has several advantages. In ten minutes of practice time, players get many tries at crossing and heading. The game is competitive and fun but not too strenuous, making it great for hot days. And as players develop crossing skill, they begin applying it in matches.

The Same Exciting Routine

The first half hour of practice follows a routine. Control balls in the air, head balls on goal, chip through the air, and cross balls into the goal area. Your players warm up gradually while developing these important options.

The routine is exciting, though, because each activity is like a sport. No two Soccer Volley games or Bombs Away games are the same. Your players will socialize, laugh, and accuse each other of cheating, but don't be alarmed. If your players compete and have fun, they'll improve faster than Arnold the Alligator.

3
SMART SHOOTING

Jumbo Yumbo Picking Practice

The only food on the small island was the yumbo fruit, high atop the jumbo yumbo tree. The fruit hung in many different ways. Some pieces bobbed up and down, while others spun in a circle or pointed toward the sky.

One day, a ship wrecked on the island. Having heard of the challenging jumbo yumbo tree, the survivors tried some picking practice. They created yumbo fruit from clay, hung it motionless from a scaffold, and picked it. But when they climbed a real tree, they were baffled by the spinning, twirling fruit. They tumbled down empty-handed.

The survivors decided to practice differently. They hung clay fruit in every possible way: bobbing up and down, spinning in a circle, and pointing toward the sky. Soon, they could pick fruit no matter how it might hang. The jumbo yumbo tree was at their mercy.

At first, the picking practice wasn't like the real thing. The practice fruit hung motionless, while the real fruit hung in many different ways. Once practice resembled the real thing, the problem was solved.

In soccer, a great deal of shooting practice isn't like the real thing. The players stand directly in front of the goal, and shoot motionless balls with the stronger foot. That won't help in the match, when a ball comes flying through the air to the weaker foot. Many different shots can arise in a match, and they all require practice.

The Shot Food Groups

There could be hundreds of shots, considering the flight of the ball, the shooting location, and the shooting foot. Fortunately, you can develop great shooters by practicing fourteen shots. The shots fall into three categories:

- Shots taken while dribbling
- Two-touch shots
- One-touch shots

Choosing the shots to practice is like choosing from the food groups. You can't cover all the shots in one practice, so pick one or two from each category. In the next practice, pick three or four of the remaining shots. Then, return to the same shots every third or fourth practice.

Shots While Dribbling

The first six shots are taken while players are dribbling. For these shots, players must get the ball moving before shooting—so that practice is like the real thing.

CHAPTER 3: SMART SHOOTING

The Gate Shot

Shots won't always be taken from directly in front of the goal. The *gate shot* lets players shoot from difficult angles (Scene 3-1). Six gates are marked off with cones, forming a semi-circle around the goal. A short line of shooters begins at the first gate, to the far right of the goal.

Scene 3-1
Gate shot

One by one, the shooters take a right-footed shot through the first gate and get back in line. Then, they take a left-footed shot through the same gate. The line moves on from gate to gate, with players taking two shots through each one.

The L-Shot

Players won't always be facing the goal when shooting. Sometimes, they'll be dribbling away from the goal to get away from defenders. With the *L-shot*, a player must dribble in an L shape before shooting—as if moving away from a defender (Scene 3-2).

Scene 3-2
L-shot with right foot

shot must come from behind cones

33

PART I: ORGANIZING

Three cones represent the defender, about fourteen paces from the goal. A short line of shooters, each with a ball, begins five paces beyond the cones. The first shooter dribbles to within a step of the middle cone, then turns sharply to the right in an L-shaped path. Once outside the cones, the shooter takes a right-footed shot.

The other shooters take the same shot, and get back in line. The next time through, players turn left for a left-footed shot. The shooting continues until players have had four tries with each foot.

The Dribble-By Shot

A shooter might be dribbling parallel to the goal, and the *dribble-by shot* provides this experience (Scene 3-3). Since the cone setup is the same as for the L-shot, both shots can be practiced at the same time. The line of shooters is to one side of the cones, stretching parallel to the goal line. Each shooter has a ball.

Scene 3-3
Dribble-by shot

The first shooter dribbles quickly past the cones, and then shoots with the right foot. The shot must come from beyond the last cone. The other shooters quickly follow. Rather than getting back in line, the shooters form a new line on the other side—and dribble back for the left-footed version.

The Chipperoo Shot

The *chipperoo shot* provides practice at chipping over the Keeper's head (Scene 3-4). Up to six shooters begin outside an arc of cones. The Keeper must stay outside a second arc of cones, so that the chips have a chance. With larger numbers of shooters, two Keepers may guard the goal together.

Rather than taking turns, the shooters begin chipping at the same time. The ball must be moving when it's chipped, and float over the Keeper's head. Each shooter must alternate between a right-footed chip and a left-footed chip. Players score as many goals as possible in three minutes.

Scene 3-4
Chipperoo shot

two Keepers may be used

The Mighty Moe Shot

A shot powered on goal from further out is called a *mighty moe* (Scene 3-5). Two cones are placed beyond the penalty area. A short line of shooters begins behind the cones, and each shooter has a ball. The Keeper must remain on the goal line, inviting a powered shot rather than a chip.

Each player pushes a ball forward, shoots from behind the cones, and gets back in line. Newer players can take all the shots with the stronger foot. Experienced players should alternate feet.

Scene 3-5
Mighty moe shot

PART I: ORGANIZING

The Breakaway Shot
The *breakaway shot* recreates those situations where a player dribbles in on the Keeper. The Keeper will usually be charging out to cut off the angle. But the shooter has the advantage of three options.

The shooters line up about thirty paces from the goal (Scene 3-6). One Keeper begins in the goal, and alternates tries with a second Keeper. The coach stands to the side, keeping time. The first shooter breaks in on the Keeper, who charges out of the goal. The ball must be in the net within eight seconds.

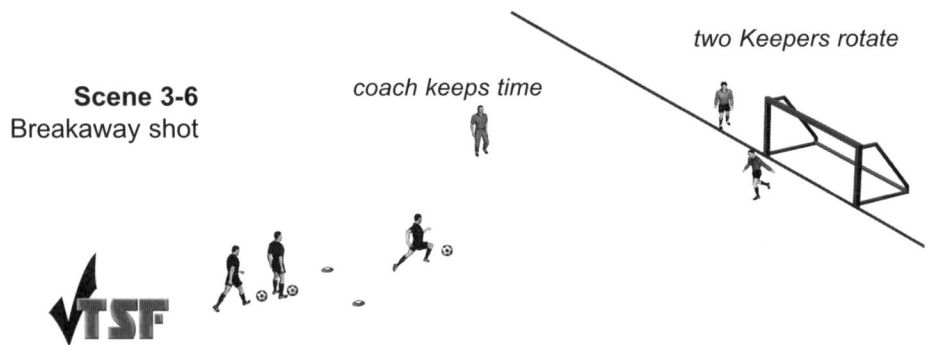

Scene 3-6
Breakaway shot

coach keeps time

two Keepers rotate

Immediately after the first attempt, the second shooter goes against the second Keeper. The competition continues until each player has had at least three tries.

How do options figure in? A shooter has three: shoot around the Keeper, chip over the Keeper, or dribble past the Keeper. One option can be practiced at a time. Then, players can choose unpredictably between the three.

Two-Touch Shots

The next three shots are two-touch shots—one touch to control the ball and one touch to shoot. The better the first touch, the easier the shot. These shots are trickier to organize. You've got to *serve* balls to the shooters.

The Box Shot
The *box shot* is a simple way to create a two-touch situation (Figure 3-7). The shooters line up outside a box, facing the server. One by one, they receive a pass, push the ball into the box, and shoot right-footed. After

each shooter has had three tries, the shooters and servers change their locations to practice the left-footed version.

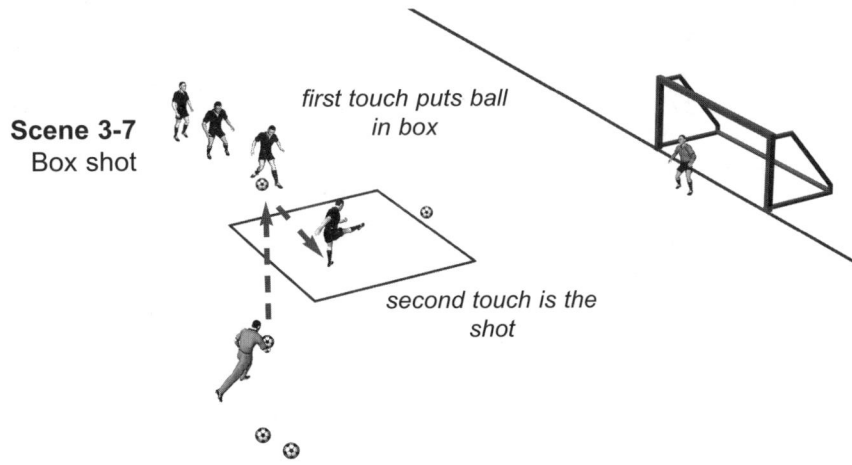

Scene 3-7
Box shot

first touch puts ball in box

second touch is the shot

The Wide Receiver Shot

A sprinting player must sometimes pull a long pass from the air and shoot. The *wide receiver shot* provides the necessary practice (Scene 3-8). The first touch pulls the ball from the air, and the second touch is the shot.

Scene 3-8
Wide receiver shot

The shooters begin about thirty paces from the goal, while the server is twenty yards away on the other side. The first shooter sprints forward and the server heaves a long pass—like a quarterback throwing to a wide receiver. The shooter pulls the ball from the air with the chest, thigh, foot, or head, and then shoots. The ball may touch the ground between the first and second touches. Shooters should take at least three shots with each foot.

PART I: ORGANIZING

The Chest Trap Shot
With the *chest trap shot*, the server tosses the ball through the air. The shooter receives the ball with the chest, pops it up into the air, and shoots with the right foot—all without letting the ball bounce (Scene 3-9). To save time, each shooter takes three shots in a row. Shooters and server then change sides, to practice the left-footed version. Once players can make this shot, their shooting confidence soars.

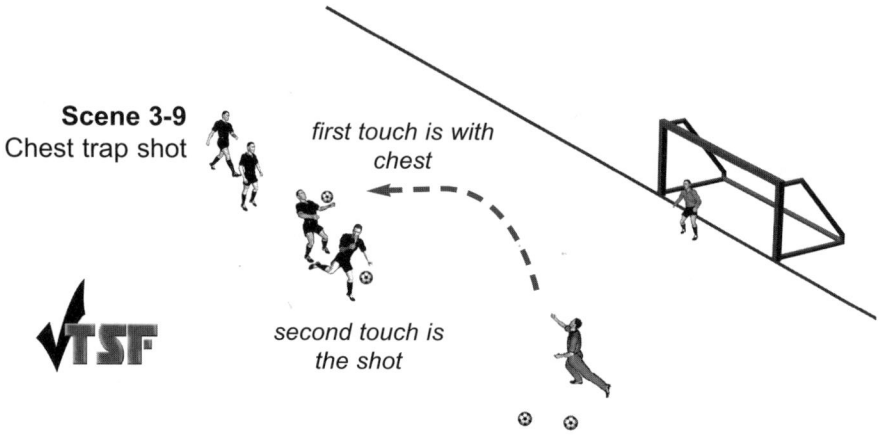

One-Touch Shots

In the match, a shot must often be taken with the first touch, before defenders close in and the Keeper is in position. The ball to be shot might be rolling, bouncing, or flying through the air. The last five shots recreate these different flight patterns. Balls must again be served to the shooters.

The Golden Roller Shot
A *golden roller* is the one-touch shot of a rolling ball. The server rolls or kicks the ball across, and the shooter moves forward and shoots (Scene 3-10). The serves can be slow or fast, and they can roll smoothly or bounce. As always, the shooters alternate feet. Serves can also come from the other side, time permitting.

CHAPTER 3: SMART SHOOTING

Scene 3-10
Golden roller shot

The Give-and-Go Shot
The *give-and-go shot* uses a simple combination before the shot. The server stands about fifteen paces from the goal, facing a short line of shooters (Scene 3-11). The first shooter passes to the server, who sends a one-touch pass to the shooter's right. The shooter breaks forward, and shoots with the first touch. The next time through, players break to the left for the left-footed version.

Scene 3-11
Give-and-go shot

The One-Hopper Shot
With the *one-hopper shot*, the server tosses the ball about ten feet into the air, so that it takes a high bounce (Scene 3-12). The shooter then takes a right-footed shot before the ball bounces again. The second time around, players take a left-footed shot, the throws coming from the same location. The server can also toss balls from the other side.

PART I: ORGANIZING

Scene 3-12
One-hopper shot

One-hopper shots tend to sail high over the goal at first. Encourage your players to contact the upper half of the ball, or to delay contact until the ball is close to the ground—two ways to keep the shots down.

The Volley

A *volley* is the one-touch shot of a ball in flight. The shooters face the server, who tosses balls from a few steps away (Scene 3-13). The first shooter shoots with the right foot, without letting the ball bounce. Each shooter takes three shots in a row to save time. Server and shooters then switch sides for the left-footed version.

Scene 3-13
Volley shot

Volleys can take different trajectories as they leave the shooter's foot. They can be driven on a line, bounced down into the ground, or lofted over the Keeper's head. When time permits, cover all these variations.

The Penalty Kick Game

A penalty kick is a one-touch shot of a stationary ball. The *Penalty Kick Game* is a competitive way to practice this shot (Scene 3-14).

Scene 3-14
Penalty Kick Game

shooter who misses becomes the Keeper

Up to six players compete on the same goal, with one beginning as the Keeper. The penalty kick spot can be marked with two cones, twelve yards from the goal. The first shooter shoots, as the others wait their turn. If the shot is made, the shooter announces the total. If the shot is missed, the shooter changes places with the Keeper. The first player to six is the winner.

Shooting HISAs

Shooting practice is fun, particularly when you transform it from drill to HISA. Set up teams, let them compete, and provide as many tries as possible. Here are three ways.

Shooting and Retrieving Teams
If only one goal is available, divide your players into two teams. While one team shoots, the other retrieves the shots that miss (Figure 3-15). One retrieving player stays over with the coach and shooters, to help circulate soccer balls.

The players on one team take three or four shots with each foot. After a successful shot, the team must announce its total. The teams then switch places, and the team with the most goals wins.

PART I: ORGANIZING

Scene 3-15
Shooting and retrieving teams

Shooting From Both Sides of the Goal

You don't need nets to practice shooting. In fact, a goal with no net is ideal if there is open space behind it (Scene 3-16). A goal created with cones or corner flags has the same effect.

Scene 3-16
Shooting from both sides

One team begins in front of the goal, the other behind. The players on one team take a shot, and then the players on the other team. The Keeper simply faces whichever team is shooting. When players have taken three or four shots with each foot, the team with the most goals wins—as you move on to the next shot.

Shooting on Back-to-Back Goals

Here's an even better time saver. Place two goals with nets and Keepers back-to-back (Scene 3-17). Two teams can then shoot at the same time, giving players twice as many tries. Ball retrieval is easy, because the shots that miss sail over to the other team. After three minutes, the team with the most goals wins.

CHAPTER 3: SMART SHOOTING

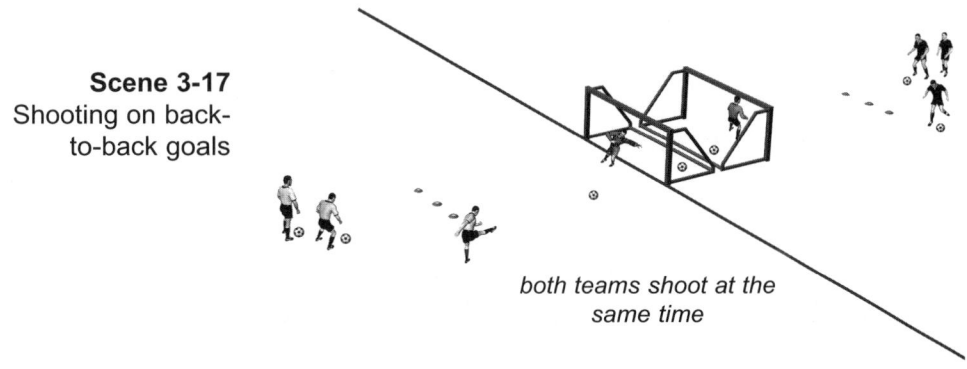

Scene 3-17
Shooting on back-to-back goals

both teams shoot at the same time

Worth the Hassle

Hopefully, you see the wisdom of shooting in every practice. There are fourteen different shots, and some of them branch into different variations. You won't get to all these shots unless you include a few in each practice.

> **You won't get to all these shots unless you include a few in each practice.**

To be honest, shooting practice can be a hassle. You need to set up the goals, rotate the shots, and serve hundreds of balls. And although the lines can be very short, they are lines nonetheless.

Shooting practice is worth the hassle, though. Players who can score in many different ways have an advantage over players who can't. They won't fall from their tree when balls come spinning and bouncing into the penalty area!

4
DRIBBLING WITH VARIETY

Frogs in the Fog

Though highly regarded as athletes, the frogs had never competed in the Animal Olympics. They decided to participate in the upcoming contest. But when it came to understanding the actual events, the frogs were "in the fog."

PART I: ORGANIZING

Since the other animals were holding their Olympic Trials, the frogs sent committees to learn the different sports. One committee watched gymnastics, another followed water polo, and another took in the triathlon.

The triathlon committee arrived just as the turtles, raccoons, and ground hogs began to swim. "No problem," chuckled the frogs. "We've been *triathloning* all our lives!" They returned home without watching the bike ride and the run.

The Olympics finally arrived. The frogs excelled at gymnastics and water polo. But without bikes, they finished last in the triathlon.

The frogs assumed the triathlon was one activity instead of three. New soccer coaches make the same mistake with dribbling. They assume it's just one skill, when it actually comes in three varieties:

- Dribbling past defenders
- Dribbling for possession
- Dribbling through open space

Your practice has now covered ball control, heading, chipping, and shooting. Scrimmaging is fifteen minutes away. How will you cover three varieties of dribbling? By rotating the varieties from practice to practice.

Dribbling Warmup

If you have time, start the dribbling with a three-minute warmup. Each player has a ball inside the circle, oval, or square (Scene 4-1).

Scene 4-1
Dribbling Warmup

All the players dribble at the same time, using different foot surfaces, changing directions, and glancing about. For the first minute, either foot may be used. For the second, only the weaker foot may be used. And during the last minute, both feet should be used at a faster pace.

Warmup dribbling becomes a great fitness activity if a few minutes are added. Why have players jog when they could be jogging with soccer balls through an enclosed space?

Dribbling Past Defenders

For this variety of dribbling, *Run the Gauntlet* is a top-notch HISA. Players attempt to dribble from one end of the course to the other, past two defenders (Scene 4-2). Each defender is confined to a defensive zone.

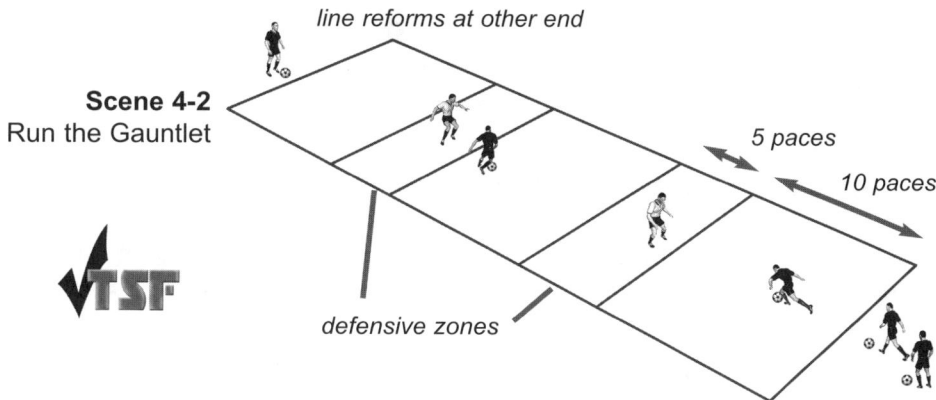

Scene 4-2
Run the Gauntlet

line reforms at other end

5 paces

10 paces

defensive zones

Rules for Run the Gauntlet

Course Setup The course is forty paces long and fifteen paces wide. Walking from the corner at one end of the course, place cones after ten paces, five paces, ten paces again, five paces again, and ten paces (see scene). The cones placed five paces apart create defensive zones.

Starting Positions Two players start out as defenders, one inside each defensive zone. The other players have soccer balls, and begin as dribblers at one end of the course. There should be at least two and no more than five dribblers in a line. To accommodate more players, an adjacent course should be set up.

Object of the Game Dribblers try to score points by dribbling past one defender and then the other, while keeping their soccer balls inside the course. The defenders attempt to prevent points, by stealing balls or knocking them off the course. Defenders may not touch the ball outside their zones.

PART I: ORGANIZING

How a Try Works The first dribbler enters the course, makes a move on the first defender, gathers the ball in, and makes a move on the second defender. The attempt must be continuous; the dribbler may not shield the ball or pause.

How the Game Proceeds As soon as a dribbler is past the first defender, the next dribbler begins. After all the dribblers have had a try, they form a new line at the other end of the course, and dribble back from that direction. After all the dribblers have had three tries, two of them become the new defenders. When players have all had the same number of dribbling tries, the player with the most points wins.

Run the Gauntlet works because it restricts defender backpedaling. That might seem unsoccerlike. But dribblers get many tries at pushing the ball past defenders. If the defender could backpedal through the whole course, most tries would be stalemates.

The HISA's time-saving features are critical. When one dribbler is halfway through, the next one begins. And rather than walking back to their starting point, dribblers form a new line at the other end. The game moves so quickly you'll think there *are* no lines!

Teamwork on a Gauntlet Course

Before you take down the Gauntlet course, try a game of *Team Gauntlet*. Two players must get through the course together, by passing and dribbling (Scene 4-3).

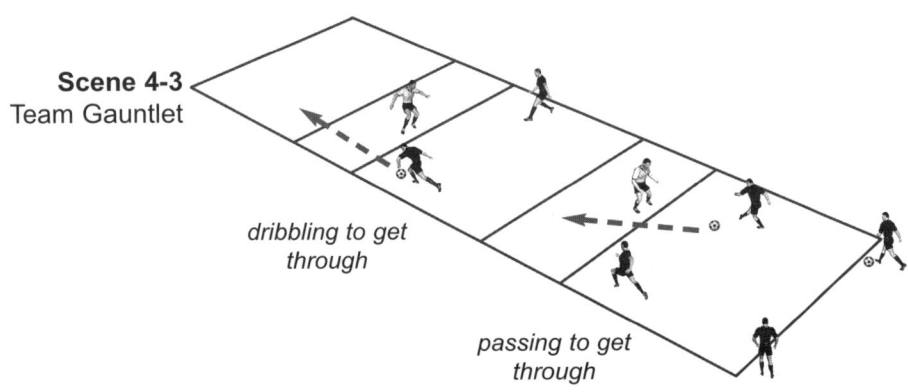

Scene 4-3
Team Gauntlet

dribbling to get through

passing to get through

Rules for Team Gauntlet

Course Setup The course is the same as for Run the Gauntlet, but may be widened a few paces.

Starting Positions Players pair off into teams. One team begins on defense, with a player in each defensive zone. The other teams begin on offense, at one end of the course. As a team steps up to the course, the two players spread out. One player has a ball.

Object of the Game Teams try to score points by escorting balls through the course.

How a Try Works One offensive player dribbles forward as the teammate runs forward for a pass. The player with the ball may pass or dribble. The defender in the first zone attempts to end the try by stealing the ball or knocking it off the course. The attempt must be continuous, and the offensive players may not shield the ball or pause. They take on the second defender in the same fashion.

How the Game Proceeds When an attacking team is past the first defender, the next attacking team enters the course. The teams then dribble back from the other end of the course. When the teams have had three tries each, a new team moves to defense. After the teams have had the same number of dribbling tries, the team with the most points wins.

During the game, ask your players a trick question. What's the best way to get through the course together—passing or dribbling? The correct answer is *neither*. Players will lose the ball if they telegraph their intentions. If they choose unpredictably between dribbling and passing, they'll usually get through. Team Gauntlet teaches unpredictability.

Dribbling for Possession

When a player has nobody to pass to, dribbling for possession is the variety of choice. The dribbler *shields* the ball, by turning away from the defender and placing a body in the way. Darting in different directions is another way to dribble for possession.

For this variety, *Ride the Bronco* can't be beat. In a circular playing area, one player shields the ball and darts about while another tries to tackle the ball away (Scene 4-4). For extra incentive, players may divide into teams.

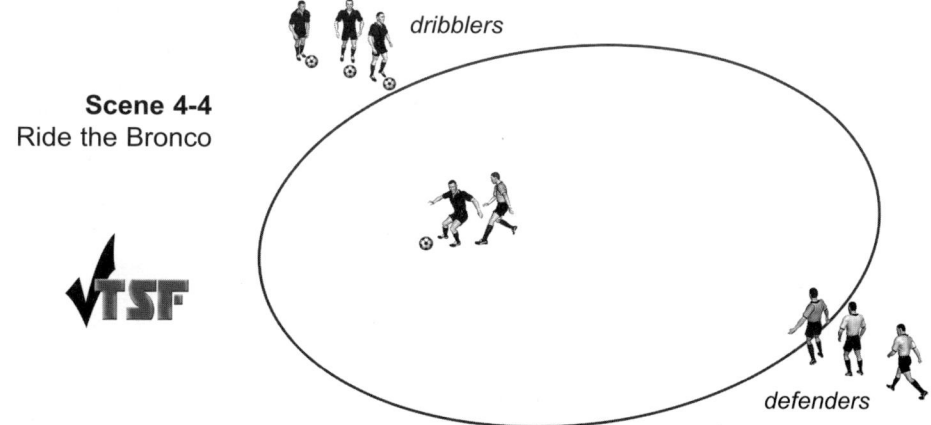

Scene 4-4
Ride the Bronco

PART I: ORGANIZING

Rules for Ride the Bronco

Playing Area The playing area is a circle about twenty paces in diameter. A square, rectangle, or semicircle may also be used.

Teams and Starting Positions At least two and no more than ten players compete in a playing area. The players are divided into two even teams. The players on one team each have a ball, and begin as dribblers. They line up outside the circle. The other team's players begin as defenders on the opposite side. The coach keeps time.

Object of the Game A dribbler tries to keep the ball in the circle for as long as possible, by darting about and shielding. The team with the longest cumulative dribbling time wins.

How a Try Proceeds When the first dribbler enters the playing area, the first defender gives chase as the coach starts the clock. The dribbler may put moves on the defender, dart about the playing area, or turn to shield the ball. The defender tries to end the attempt by getting two consecutive touches on the ball or kicking it out. Players may lean against each other, but may not push or foul. The coach calls fouls, and a foul by the dribbler ends the try. A foul by the defender adds ten seconds to the total time.

How the Game Proceeds After the first try, the dribbler and defender return to their original lines. The next dribbler and defender then jump in quickly, as the clock continues to run. When each dribbler has had two tries, the coach stops the clock and announces the cumulative time. The teams then switch roles.

Double Bronco Provision If a defender chases the ball for twenty seconds without success, the coach may call out "Double Bronco!" A second defender then joins the first to pursue the ball.

The defender who can't get the ball away will be tempted to foul. The Double Bronco rule offers relief. And before every game, remind your players—safety first!

Double Bronco can also be the feature HISA now and then. As a dribbler enters the playing area, two defenders give chase (Scene 4-5). Dribblers who survive for twenty seconds earn the coveted Double Bronco Certification. They can divide and conquer multiple defenders.

Dribblers who survive for twenty seconds earn the coveted Double Bronco Certification.

CHAPTER 4: DRIBBLING WITH VARIETY

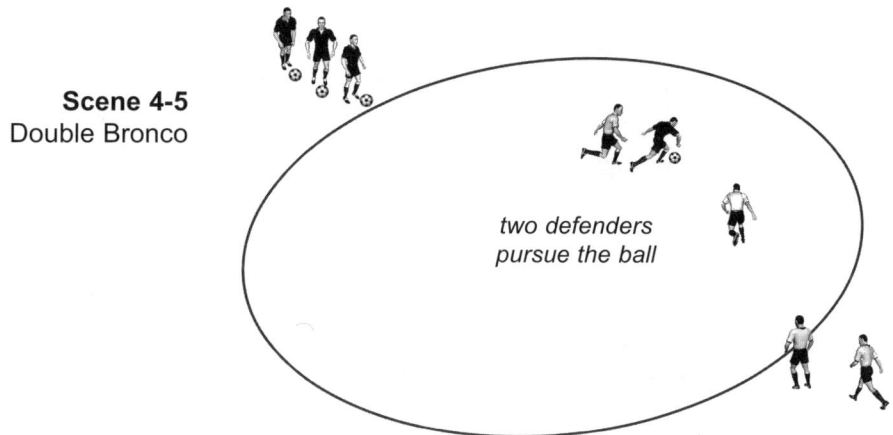

Scene 4-5
Double Bronco

two defenders pursue the ball

Dribbling Through Open Space

Dribbling through open space requires precise control over each touch. Unwanted deviations in the distance or direction of a touch will slow the dribbler down, and turn scoring chances into turnovers.

The HISA called *Giant Slalom* develops this precise control. Players weave their way through gates, like skiers on a mountainside. While the four-player version works best (Scene 4-6), other player numbers are also possible.

Use your imagination when setting up the course. The gates should create a circle or oval. Some gates should be close together, so players must weave their way through rapids. Other gates should be further apart, so players must sprint through straightaways.

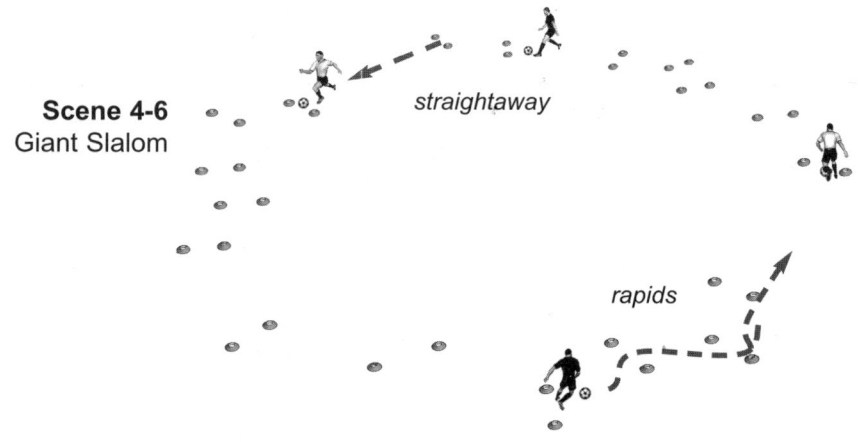

Scene 4-6
Giant Slalom

straightaway

rapids

51

PART I: ORGANIZING

Rules for Slalom Course, Four Players

Course Setup For the first gate, two cones are placed two paces apart. The next gate is placed at least four paces away, and slightly to either side. A circular or oval course, about forty paces in diameter, is created in the same fashion. Some of the gates are close together, and zigzag from side to side. Other gates are at least twenty paces apart, creating straightaways.

Teams and Starting Positions Four players compete, in teams of two. Each player has a ball. The four players spread evenly around the course, so that each player is in between two opponents.

Object of the Game Players earn points for their teams by catching opponents from behind. The first team to three wins.

How a Round Proceeds At the coach's signal, players begin dribbling in a clockwise direction. A player who knocks over a cone must stop to fix it. A player who misses a gate must return and dribble through it. The round continues until a player overtakes and dribbles past an opponent. The round also ends if a player is unable to return to a missed gate. Rounds that last one minute are declared draws.

How the Game Proceeds After the first round, players spread evenly around the course for the second round. This time, they dribble counterclockwise. The dribbling direction keeps changing from round to round until a winner is decided.

Here's how to accommodate other player numbers. With fewer than four players, hold time trials. One by one, the players dribble twice around the course. Players must return to any missed gates. The best time wins.

With exactly eight players, create four teams. Two teams compete for a round, and then catch their breath as the other two teams compete. The rotating continues until each match is decided. Championship and third-place matches can then take place.

With other player numbers, the drill version works fine. All the players dribble at the same time. To prevent collisions, players dribble at three quarters speed. The round ends when a player misses a gate or knocks over a cone, and that player sits out. Once three players are out, all rejoin for the next round.

Giant Slalom beats weaving through a straight line of cones. Since every section of the course is unique, players must read the course and plan their touches accordingly. And players never have to return to the course's beginning, because the course has no beginning!

> **Since every section of the course is unique, players must read the course and plan their touches accordingly.**

CHAPTER 4: DRIBBLING WITH VARIETY

Dribbling Monsters

Your players change when they practice all three dribbling varieties. They easily keep the ball. They're uncatchable from behind. And their eyes light up when only one defender is in the way. Your frogs in the fog become dribbling monsters!

5

SECRETS OF POSSESSION

A Gremlin-Proof Plan

The knights and servants peered through the forest at the castle where their queen was imprisoned. Only a magic acorn could free her, and the knights were down to their last three. Meanwhile, evil gremlins patrolled the forest, watching the knights' every move.

PART I: ORGANIZING

Suddenly, a heroic knight grabbed an acorn and rode straight for the castle. The gremlins easily captured the knight, and stole his acorn. The other knights then rode forward, one holding an acorn as the others protected him. All the knights were soon in custody. The servants held the last acorn.

What could be done with it? The servants tossed the acorn back and forth among themselves, as if disinterested in reaching the castle! Whenever the gremlins got close to the acorn, it was tossed to the side, or back to its starting point. The gremlins grew tired and frustrated. As they quarreled, the acorn reached the castle and the queen was saved.

Eager to reach the castle, the knights went forward and lost their acorns. That's how new players play soccer. Eager to score, they move the ball forward and lose it.

The servants would have made great soccer players. They kept possession of their acorn by moving it quickly in different directions. This more thoughtful approach allowed them to reach their goal.

Possession is the most important part of soccer. It makes good things possible, like scoring goals. And it prevents bad things from happening, like being scored on. Here are six secrets to keeping possession. In the next chapter, you'll learn how to practice them.

Use All Four Directions

Understand this secret well. Without it, soccer is a chaotic scramble with no room for thought.

If your team always moves the ball north, toward the other team's goal, possession is impossible. North is usually the most heavily guarded direction (Scene 5-1). Within fifteen seconds, either a goal will be scored or the ball will be lost—usually the latter. And your players to the south, east, and west can only watch.

> **If your team always moves the ball north, toward the other team's goal, possession is impossible.**

CHAPTER 5: SECRETS OF POSSESSION

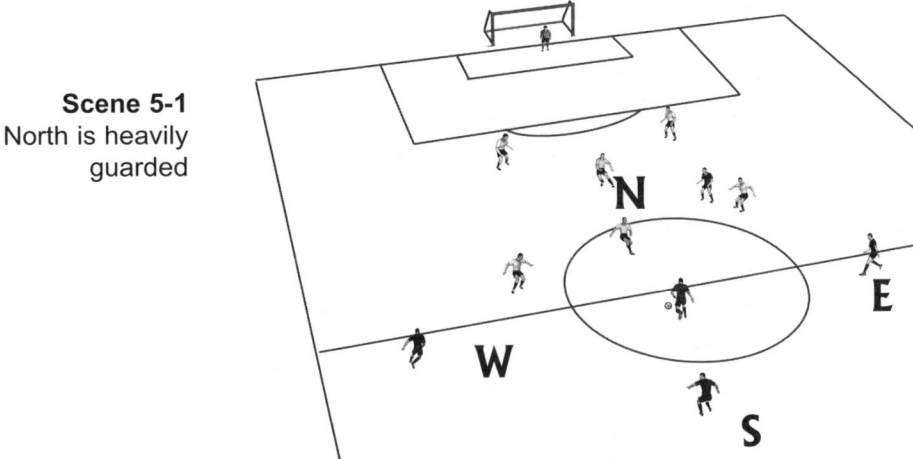

Scene 5-1
North is heavily guarded

To keep possession, your players must be aware of all four directions and choose the one that's best. If north is crowded, the ball can move south, east, and west—in other words, back and to the side. When your players use all four directions, opponents don't know which direction to guard.

Use Different Numbers of Touches

As you watch a match, notice how many touches each player uses. Did a player dribble, using many touches? Was the ball passed quickly, after only a few touches? Or was the ball sent on its way with only one touch?

New players use either too few or too many touches. The *too few* players use only one touch every time, a long boot forward. The *too many* players use three or four touches before looking up. In either case, the ball is usually lost.

> **New players use either too few or too many touches.**

To keep possession, players must look things over as the ball is arriving, and decide quickly how many touches to use. If a teammate is open, the first touch should usually be a pass. By the second touch, the teammate might be covered.

If a one-touch pass isn't possible, an open teammate can usually be found after two or three touches. But if no teammates are open, or the path forward is clear, more than three touches might be called for. In other words, the player may dribble.

PART I: ORGANIZING

Find the Open Space

This secret is closely related to the previous one. When new players have the ball in open space, they tend to dawdle. Since no opponents are near, why not get in a few extra touches? But the open space quickly vanishes, and teammates are soon covered as well.

> **When new players have the ball in open space, they tend to dawdle.**

Possession requires a preventive approach. The ball moves to open space *before* opponents come near. In Scene 5-2, the player with the ball has a little open space. Rather than dawdling, he passes quickly to a player with *more* space, who then does the same. By the time opponents arrive, the ball has moved on. (Note that the Keeper is also well supplied with space. More on this in Chapter 15.)

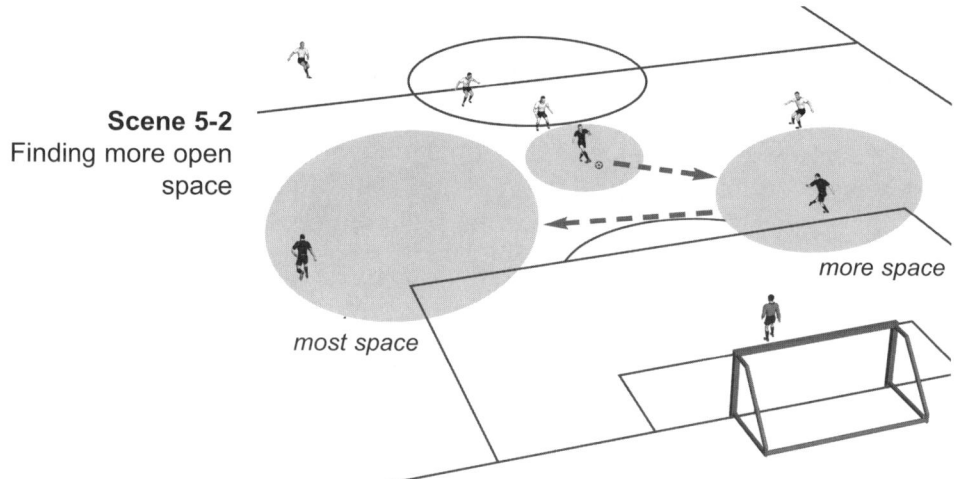

Scene 5-2
Finding more open space

Pass Long As Well As Short

Short passes on the ground are wonderful for keeping possession. They tend to be accurate and easy to receive. But possession suffers if players can *only* pass short.

In Scene 5-3, the player with the ball is being pressured. Teammates close to the ball are covered, and the ball is about to be lost. A long chip to the distant teammate saves the day.

CHAPTER 5: SECRETS OF POSSESSION

Scene 5-3
A long pass saves the day

Pass to Space, Not Just Teammates

New players usually pass directly to teammates. If those teammates are closely covered, the passes are stolen. Possession is easier when players can also pass to space.

In Scene 5-4, a pass directly to the teammate would be stolen. A pass to either space, as the teammate runs there, would have a great chance. Suddenly, the defender has three targets to worry about instead of one.

> **Suddenly, the defender has three targets to worry about instead of one.**

Scene 5-4
Passing to space rather than to a teammate

59

PART I: ORGANIZING

If the Attack Stalls, Retreat

Once they reach the goal area, new players refuse to retreat. Moving the ball that far was difficult, by golly, and they're going to shoot. The backward direction no longer exists. These forced scoring attempts almost always lose the ball.

For possession, your players must know when to retreat. If the attack stalls, and the ball is about to be lost, pass back to a Fullback. Pass back to the other half of the field. Pass back to the Keeper if necessary, but don't lose the ball (Scene 5-5)!

Scene 5-5
A retreat from the goal area

Such maneuvers, called *resets*, allow very long possessions. The entire field becomes available. Opponents tire. And a better scoring chance arises later.

Six Games in One

New players begin with only one game in mind—move the ball forward and score. Opponents know where the ball is going, and easily win it back.

The possession secrets let your players choose between *six* games: a direction game, a touches game, a move-the-ball game, a short/long game, a pass-to-space game, and an attack/retreat game. At every moment of a match, at least one of those games will usually work. No wonder the evil gremlins get frustrated!

Want your players to get better and better with all six secrets? The next chapter shows you how.

6
PRACTICING POSSESSION

Flash Sees the Light

Flash had a strange way of eluding predators. Other squirrels faked and darted in different directions. Flash tried to outrun whatever was chasing him. Concerned for Flash's safety, Wise Old Yazoo pulled him aside for a talk.

PART I: ORGANIZING

"Here's how to escape from cats, dogs, and the squashing-machines-on-wheels," said Yazoo. "Don't try to outrun the beast. Fake this way and that. Cut back and forth in different directions. Think!"

Impressed with the advice, Flash decided to try it out. But when chased by a cat, he sprinted straight for the woods.

Not called Wise Old for nothing, Yazoo built an elaborate maze. He placed Flash at its entrance, and called to a nearby dog. The dog charged, and Flash's only escape route was through the maze. He dodged through the corridors, this way and that, and even cut back between the dog's legs. Finally, he exited safely from the maze.

"That was easy and fun," thought Flash. "I'm one clever squirrel."

Flash wanted to use Yazoo's advice. But in the excitement of the chase, he resorted to old habits. The maze forced Flash to change. And since he liked the change, it probably lasted.

Thoughtscrims are the soccer equivalent of Yazoo's maze. These thought-intensive scrimmages force players to change. The changes last, because players like them.

There are Thoughtscrims for every part of soccer. The Thoughtscrims in this chapter are for working on possession. Later, you'll learn Thoughtscrims for defending, attacking, and taking free kicks.

Keep-away games are another way to work on possession. One team keeps the ball from the other, and there are no goals to score on. But goals give a field its north, south, east, and west. Goals also allow players to *score* goals. That's why Thoughtscrims have goals, and an advantage over keep-away games.

Getting Started

As your players grab a drink, get ready for scrimmaging. You'll need a field, goals, teams, and a plan.

There are several ways to create a scrimmage field, goals, and teams. The pictures in this chapter show Keepers protecting big goals, but some goals don't require Keepers. And although the pictures show three players per team, other team sizes are also possible. Chapter 7 looks at different setups. For now, rules are the focus.

62

CHAPTER 6: PRACTICING POSSESSION

Because of their rules, some Thoughtscrims require different field lines. To cover all the possibilities, set up your field like this (Scene 6-1). The cones create *side zones*, *final zones*, and a halfway line.

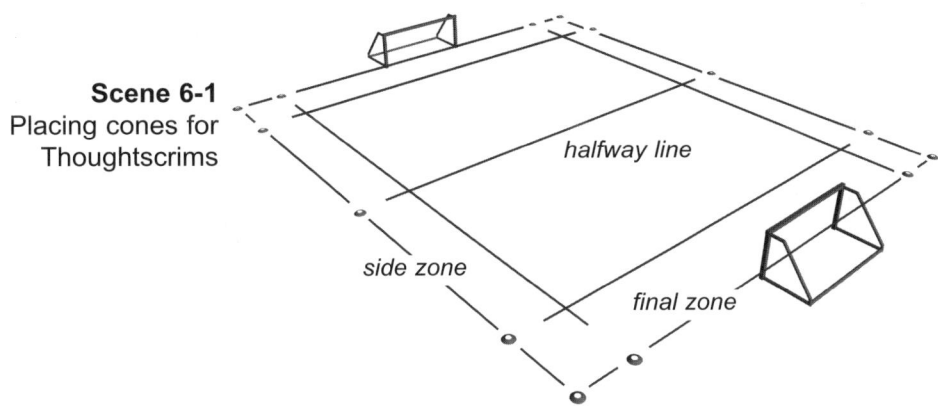

Scene 6-1
Placing cones for Thoughtscrims

halfway line

side zone

final zone

Your scrimmage plan will depend somewhat on your players. If you're working with experienced players, jump right into the Thoughtscrims. There are six in this chapter, and each requires only five or ten minutes. But in your first scrimmage session with new players, set the tone with the Quickstart Rules.

The Quick-Start Rules

Suppose you're working with brand new players. When your field and teams are ready, toss in a ball and yell, "Play!" For a few minutes, let the teams compete without any special rules. You'll soon see the *Three Deadly Habits*. Players will kick the ball aimlessly, without looking for a teammate. They'll fight with teammates for the ball. And their first touches will always send the ball forward.

These habits will kill your scrimmage session, but you can tame them with three *Quick-Start Rules*: *No Aimless Booting*, *One Player on the Ball*, and *Touch It Back*.

Enforce No Aimless Booting (NAB)

When a player boots the ball aimlessly, as in Scene 6-2, freeze the play and explain the rule:

"Billy just kicked the ball forward, but he has no teammates there. That's called a No Aimless Booting violation. You must look up, and pass to a teammate. Free kick for the other team!"

PART I: ORGANIZING

By pure luck, such aimless boots will sometimes reach a teammate. The culprit will then argue, "I was passing to Steve!" But did the player look up before kicking the ball? If not, stick with your NAB call.

Scene 6-2
No Aimless Booting (NAB) violation

Enforce One Player on the Ball (OPOB)

After a few minutes with the NAB rule, add the OPOB rule. Two players from the same team may not compete with each other for the ball. While one approaches the ball, the other must do something else. If two or more players from the same team hover over the ball, call an OPOB violation (Scene 6-3). The penalty is a free kick for the other team.

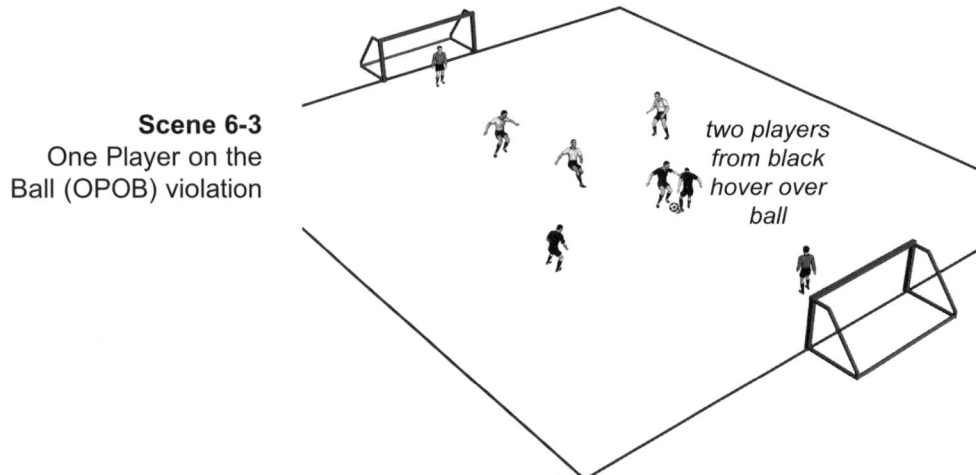

Scene 6-3
One Player on the Ball (OPOB) violation

two players from black hover over ball

Enforce Touch It Back (TIB)

When a player wins the ball or receives a pass, notice the direction of the first touch. Brand new players almost always send the first touch forward (Scene 6-4). The ball is then lost before other directions can be considered. Time to enforce the TIB rule.

CHAPTER 6: PRACTICING POSSESSION

When TIB is in effect, a player's first touch may not send the ball toward the other team's goal. The consequence is a free kick for the other team.

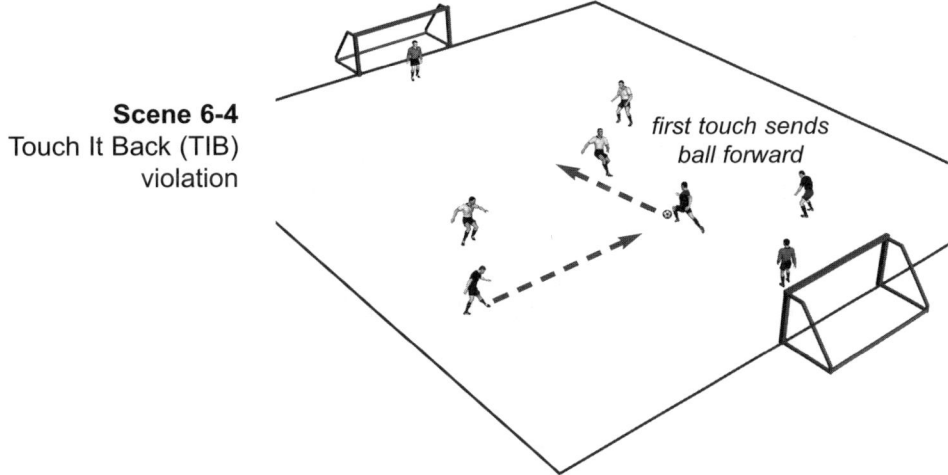

Scene 6-4
Touch It Back (TIB) violation

first touch sends ball forward

As Scene 6-5 shows, a violation is *not* called if a player:

    A. Touches the ball to the side or back, and then forward

    B. Sends the first touch forward on a diagonal

    C. Looks to the rear, or fakes a drop pass, before making the first touch forward

The most powerful rule in all of Thoughtful Soccer, TIB quickly changes the straight-to-goal habit.

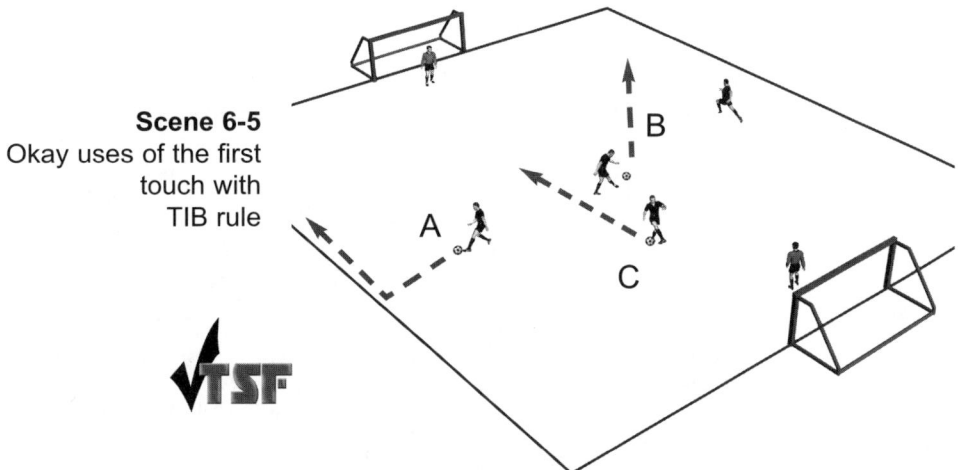

Scene 6-5
Okay uses of the first touch with TIB rule

Now You Need Them, Now You Don't

The quick-start rules aren't an exact science. Was that an aimless boot or a misguided pass? Did the ball go forward, or on a diagonal? Remind your players to play on if no call is made.

PART I: ORGANIZING

Sometimes, the Quick-Start Rules *should* be broken. An aimless boot can keep the other team from scoring, and a first touch forward can launch a counterattack. Your players must understand these exceptions at some point.

Initially, though, call as many violations as possible. The interruptions help players change. The only way to keep the coach quiet is to follow the rules! Toward the end of the first practice, you'll see fewer violations. And several practices later, you'll barely need the rules at all. They'll be stuck in everyone's mind.

The only way to keep the coach quiet is to follow the rules!

Three Bread and Butter Thoughtscrims

After ten minutes of the Quick-Start Rules, move on to three Thoughtscrims. Each of the three is a Thoughtful Soccer Favorite. The bread and butter of Thoughtful Soccer, make them a staple of every practice.

The object of every Thoughtscrim is to score goals and win. Keepers are optional, and the offside rule can be added if you like. Balls may be brought into play with either throw-ins or kick-ins.

Three-and-a-Drop
In Three-and-a-Drop, players are limited to three touches. Before scoring, a team must execute at least one drop pass.

Rules for Three-and-a-Drop

Field Lines The field requires touch lines, goal lines, and goals.

Three-Touch Rule Each player may use one, two, or three touches on the ball. If a fourth touch occurs, the other team gets a free kick at the spot of the violation. After using three touches, a player may not shield the ball from opponents. The consequence, again, is a free kick for the other team.

Drop Pass Rule Before scoring, a team must complete at least one drop pass, defined as a pass that goes backward at any angle. Once a team completes a drop pass, two consecutive touches by the other team erase the accomplishment. A single touch by the other team does not. A corner kick is considered a drop pass, and may result in a shot on goal.

The rules don't say *when* to make a drop pass, but players figure out the best times. The forward direction is often crowded when the ball is first won—a great time for a drop pass (Scene 6-6). Drop passes also help later on, whenever the ball is about to be lost.

CHAPTER 6: PRACTICING POSSESSION

Scene 6-6
Time for a drop pass

During the ten minutes of Three-and-a-Drop, you'll see several improvements. The three-touch rule makes the ball move quickly from player to player. And the drop pass rule keeps players behind the ball involved. They'll even yell "Drop!" when the ball is about to be lost.

Side-to-Side

This Thoughtscrim is a must, because it uses the field's width. There isn't a touch limit, so players may dribble. And before scoring, they must move the ball from one side of the field to the other (Scene 6-7).

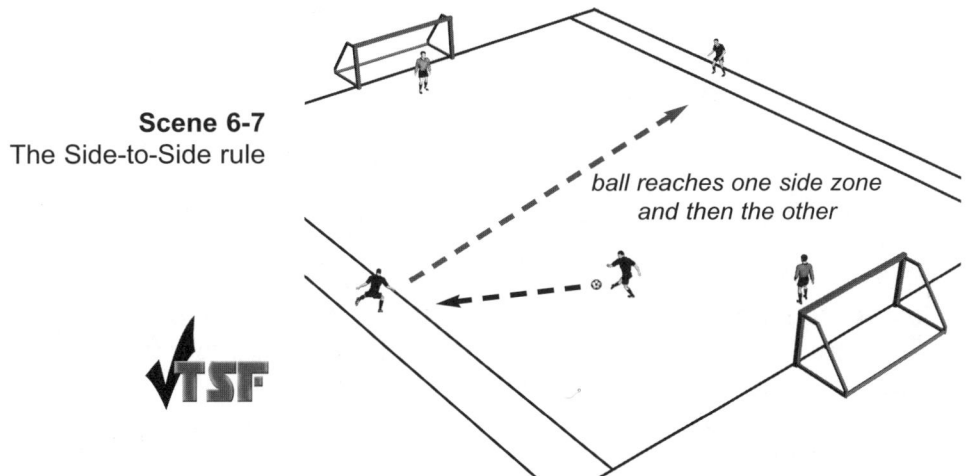

Scene 6-7
The Side-to-Side rule

ball reaches one side zone and then the other

Rules for Side-to-Side

Field Lines The field requires two side zones. A side zone extends the length of the field, three paces in from a touch line. It may be marked with cones along the goal lines, but this is usually unnecessary. Players may guess at the zone's location instead.

PART I: ORGANIZING

Touch Rule Players are allowed an unlimited number of touches. However, if a player dribbles excessively, or misses the chance for a quick pass, the coach may call a violation. The other team gets a free kick at the spot.

Side-to-Side Rule Before scoring, a team must escort the ball into each side zone. To reach these zones, any combination of passing and dribbling may be used. A player may dribble from one side zone to the other, although this is not recommended. Side zones may be reached more than once, and in any sequence. Once a team has reached both side zones, two consecutive touches by the other team erase the accomplishment. A single touch does not.

In this Thoughtscrim, two thought mistakes are typical. First, players go straight to the goal after reaching both side zones. Remind them that side zones can be reached more than once. Secondly, players try long passes across the crowded center of the field. Recommend the *drop-and-switch* maneuver instead. A player receives a drop pass, and switches the ball to the other side (Scene 6-8).

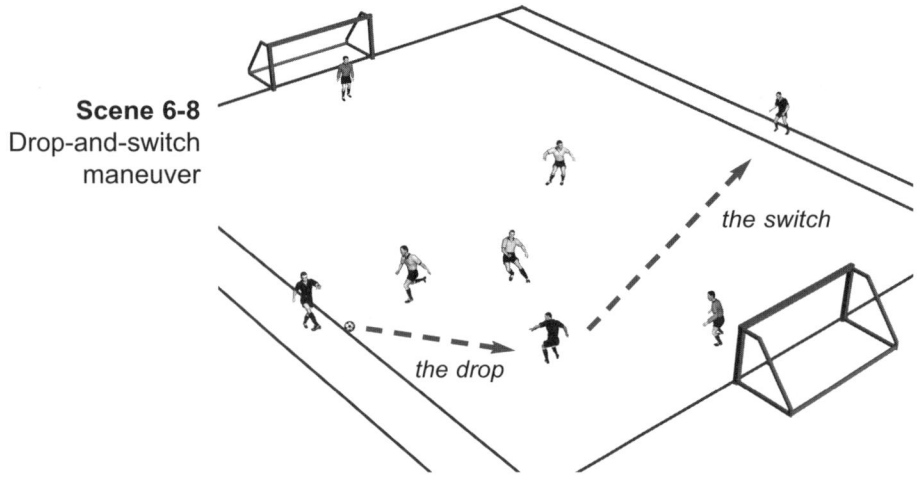

Scene 6-8
Drop-and-switch maneuver

Side-to-Side is great for keeping possession. Your players will use different numbers of touches, and move the ball in all four directions. They'll find open space on the other side of the field. And they'll spread out without being told to.

First-Time

In First-Time, each player gets only one touch. The touch must be a pass or a shot, since aimless boots are always forbidden. To make possession easier, neutral players may patrol the touch lines (Scene 6-9).

CHAPTER 6: PRACTICING POSSESSION

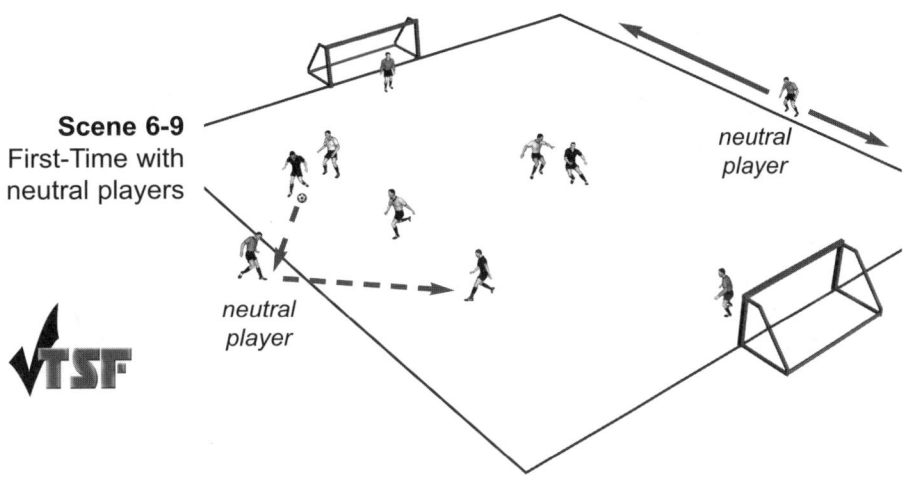

Scene 6-9
First-Time with neutral players

Rules for First-Time

Field Lines The field requires goal lines and touch lines

One-Touch Rule A player is allowed one touch on the ball at a time. That touch must be a pass or a shot. If a player touches the ball twice, or boots the ball without looking for a teammate, the other team receives a free kick. A player who has touched the ball may not shield it, and must immediately get out of the way.

Neutral Players One or two neutral players may be used, one along each touch line. A neutral player may move up and down the touch line, and come a few paces onto the field. Either team may pass to a neutral player, who must try to pass to the same team using only one touch.

Scoring Goals A team must complete at least one pass before scoring. A player may not steal the ball and shoot with the same touch.

Some coaches believe one-touch play with new players is harmful, if not impossible. Indeed, First-Time won't work if players flock to the ball and boot it forward. Fortunately, you've laid the groundwork with the NAB, OPOB, and TIB rules.

> **Some coaches believe one-touch play with new players is harmful, if not impossible.**

The one-touch play might be rocky at first, but it will improve toward the end of the game and in every later practice. Players will look up and plan while the ball is arriving. And players away from the ball will get open more quickly. With benefits like these, First-Time makes a great start to every future scrimmage session.

PART I: ORGANIZING

Three for Later

Here are three more Thoughtscrims. You might not have time for them in your first practice, but get to know them. Each Thoughtscrim strengthens a different possession secret.

Reset

Reset resembles Three-and-a-Drop, because only three touches are allowed. But before scoring, teams must work the ball forward to the final zone, and then back past the halfway line (Scene 6-10).

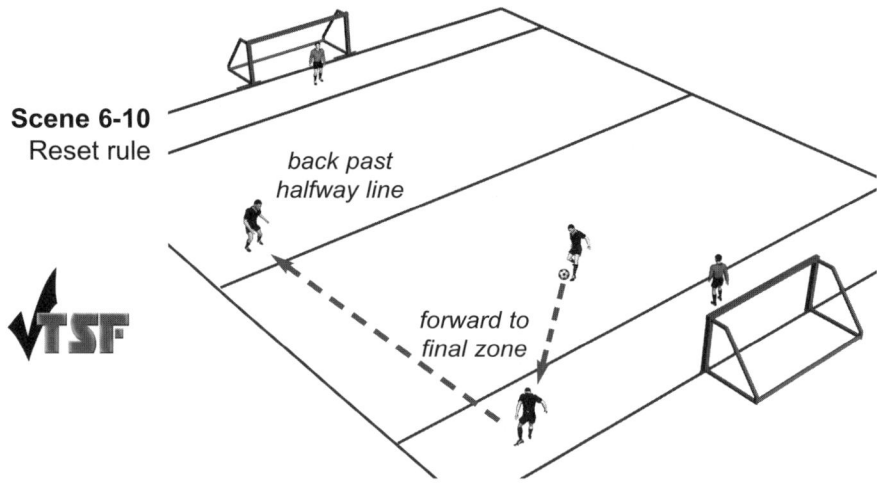

Scene 6-10
Reset rule

back past halfway line

forward to final zone

Rules for Reset

Field Lines The field requires a rectangular final zone at each end, plus a halfway line. A final zone extends five paces in from the goal line, and runs the width of the field.

Reset Requirement Before scoring, a team must move the ball forward into the final zone, and then back past the halfway line. This may be accomplished by passing, dribbling, or any combination of the two. Once the maneuver is completed, two consecutive touches by the other team erase the accomplishment. One touch by the other team does not.

Touch and Direction Rules Each player is allowed only three touches at a time. A drop pass will usually occur during a Reset maneuver, but isn't required.

The forward/backward requirement is challenging at first. Players will go straight to the final zone and lose the ball. A patient journey works better. Players will also wonder, "Why move the ball backward when moving it forward was so difficult?"

But Reset teaches three valuable lessons. All teammates are potential targets, no matter where they are on the field. A scoring try doesn't *have* to

CHAPTER 6: PRACTICING POSSESSION

happen just because the ball is close to the goal. And a retreat is sometimes the only way to keep possession.

A scoring try doesn't *have* to happen just because the ball is close to the goal.

Pass-and-Move

Players should pass to space *and* to teammates. *Pass-and-Move* gets at this secret. Players must be in motion—before receiving a pass, and after making a pass. Scene 6-11 shows a rule violation as well as an okay pass.

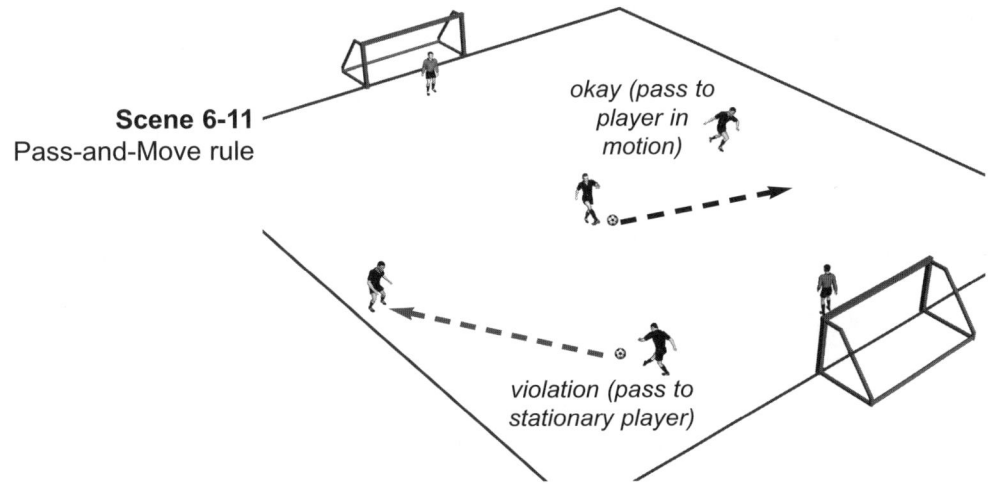

Scene 6-11
Pass-and-Move rule

okay (pass to player in motion)

violation (pass to stationary player)

Rules for Pass-and-Move

Field Lines The field requires goal lines and touch lines.

Touch Rule Players are limited to three touches at a time.

Receiving Rule The player receiving a pass must be running or jogging somewhere. If the player is stationary when receiving a pass, a violation has occurred, and the other team is given a free kick. The player may avoid a violation, however, by letting the ball run past. The player may then chase after the ball, or let it roll to a teammate.

Passing Rule After passing the ball, a player must immediately move at least three steps in any direction. A violation is called if the passing player remains in the same spot. After moving at least three steps, the passing player may return to the original spot.

Pass-and-Move encourages several positive habits. Players begin passing to space, and seeing new passing targets. After passing, players become targets themselves. And rather than standing in set positions, players swap positions on the fly. Habits with such great results will last!

Long Ball

Long Ball reminds players to pass long as well as short. Before scoring, a team must complete at least one long pass. The field lines are the key (Scene 6-12).

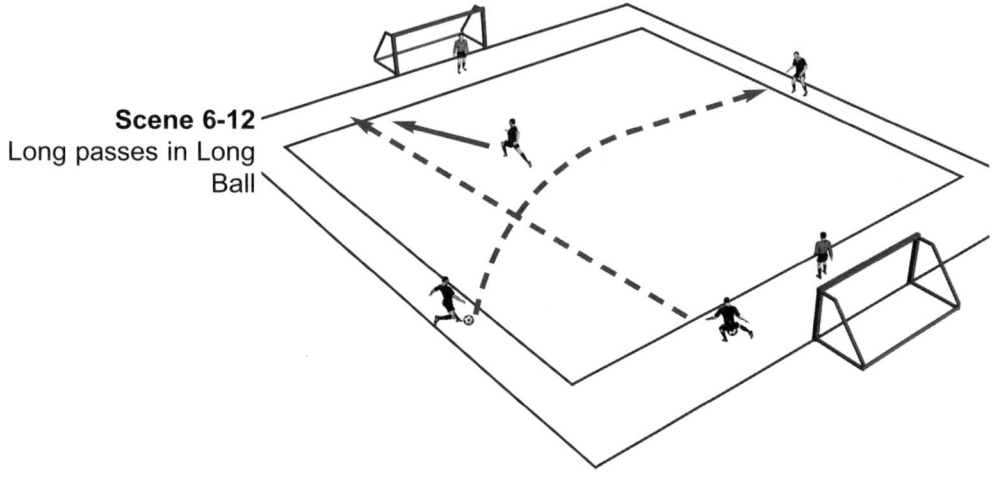

Scene 6-12
Long passes in Long Ball

Rules for Long Ball

Field Lines The field requires final zones at each end of the field, and side zones along each touch line. A final zone extends five paces onto the field, while a side zone extends three paces onto the field.

Long Pass Rule Before scoring, a team must complete at least one long pass. For the past to be considered long, the ball must travel from one final zone to the other, in either direction, or from one side zone to the other. The pass may bounce, or travel through the air. Once a team has completed a long pass, two consecutive touches by the other team erase the accomplishment. One touch by the other team does not.

Two-Point Goals Goals normally result in one point. However, if a team completes two or more long passes during the possession, the resulting goal counts as two points. When one long pass has been completed, the coach should call out, "One!" When a second long pass has been completed, the coach should call out, "Two!"

Long Ball's habits will also last. Players begin seeing near and far at the same time. Players away from the ball, knowing they'll be seen, make clever runs. And the long passes sometimes lead to goals.

Moved From Above

The ideal practice includes HISAs and Thoughtscrims. But if you only have time for one or the other, go with Thoughtscrims. They'll teach your players to think, and hook them on soccer.

CHAPTER 6: PRACTICING POSSESSION

Thoughtscrims nudge your players toward a particular style of play. Speed and aggressiveness aren't so critical, because the ball moves quickly to open spaces. It's as if Wise Old Yazoo was up above, moving the ball to the best spots. Once your players get this sensation, they'll leave selfish, thoughtless soccer behind.

7

ORGANIZING FLEXIBLY

The Wigglys Get Down

Tired of crawling through soil, the Wiggly family invented a new dance. The Wigglys even built a portable studio, for teaching the dance to other worms. Dancers could climb up on the studio, hook themselves to the special handles, and squirm to the beat.

PART I: ORGANIZING

There was a catch, though. The studio only worked when it was set in mud. And it required exactly twelve worms at a time.

The Wigglys hauled their studio down the road, and came upon a clearing. Twelve worms waited there, but no mud was available. The Wigglys moved on.

They paused alongside a muddy field, but only three worms showed up. Again, the Wigglys moved on.

Eager to learn the dance, a crowd of worms gathered around a bog. When the studio arrived, the worms pushed and shoved for a spot. Soon, there was a riot. The Wigglys dragged their studio home.

The dance studio lacked flexibility. Without mud and twelve worms, the whole operation fell apart.

Without flexibility, your soccer practices can fall apart as well. The field you were counting on might have no goals. And six players might show up when you were expecting sixteen.

Here are a few ways to organize flexibly.

Setting Up a Scrimmage Field

How large should a scrimmage field be? That depends on the number of players. Don't bother with a tape measure, though. Just guess at the paces from goal to corner, corner to halfway line, and so on. Throw down some cones, and yell, "Play!"

You'll know quickly whether your field is the right size. If the players look like bumper cars, and the ball keeps going out of bounds, your field is too small. If the players are running a marathon rather than playing soccer, your field is too large. Adjust the dimensions as play continues.

What types of goals should you use? Several types are possible—big or small, real or imitation. Some types require Keepers, and others don't. A different type can even be used at each end of the field.

Big Goals
You can't go wrong with big goals guarded by Keepers. After all, that's what your players face in matches. If real goals aren't available, place two cones or corner flags about ten paces apart. Players might argue whether a shot sailed high or wide, but they'll still get plenty of shooting practice.

Small Goals

If you want your Keepers out in the field, or if you *have* no Keepers, go with small goals. Such goals should be challenging to score on. They should leave no doubt about whether a shot was successful. And they should discourage those distant blasts that take five minutes to retrieve.

If you can't afford to buy small goals, the cheap alternatives in Scene 7-1 work fine. For one goal, two cones have been placed a few paces apart. The scoring rules eliminate controversy. After leaving the shooter's foot, the ball must bounce at least once or roll. Shots that go directly into the air are no good, even from point blank range. Shots that strike a cone are also disallowed.

For the other goal, five disc cones have been placed side by side. The cones are five paces inside the field of play. Players may dribble behind the cones, as in ice hockey, and shoot from any direction. The ball must strike one of the cones. Balls that bounce over the cones are no good.

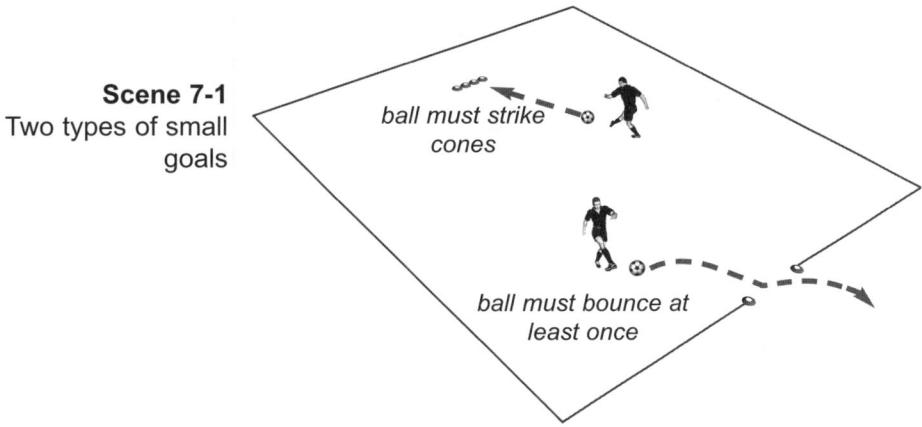

Scene 7-1
Two types of small goals

Two Goals to Score on

When scrimmaging without Keepers, the Big Goal/Small Goal setup is a great alternative. Each team has two goals to score on: a big goal at the end of the field, and a small goal inside the field (Scene 7-2). Big goals without Keepers—too good to be true? The scoring rules are the key.

> **Big goals without Keepers—too good to be true?**

PART I: ORGANIZING

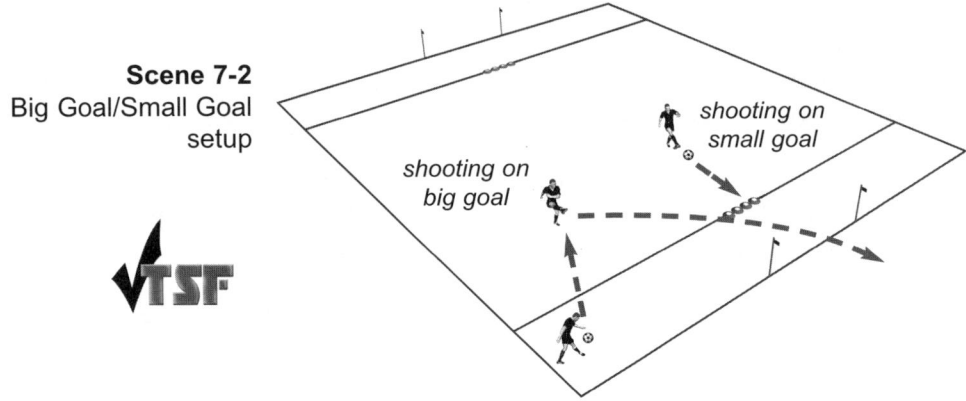

Scene 7-2
Big Goal/Small Goal setup

Rules for the Big Goal/Small Goal Setup

Field Lines The field must have rectangular final zones at each end. These zones run the width of the field, five paces in from the goal lines.

Goals At each end of the field, along the goal line, is a regulation-size goal. This goal may be represented by cones or corner flags, if necessary. At the edge of each final zone, five paces inside the field of play, is a small goal. This goal consists of five disc cones laid side by side.

Scoring on a Small Goal The shot must actually contact one of the disc cones. A player may shoot on a small goal from anywhere, and may dribble before shooting. A player may also dribble behind a small goal, as in ice hockey.

Scoring on a Big Goal To score on a big goal, two conditions must be met. The pass preceding the shot must come from the final zone. And although the shot itself may come from anywhere, it must be taken with the first touch. A shot on the big goal that accidentally contacts the small goal is also good.

Remember—to score on the big goal, the *pass* must come from the Final Zone, but the *shot* may come from anywhere. The idea is to move the ball into the final zone, and cross it or drop it back for the one-touch shot.

There are three good reasons to bother with the Big Goal/Small Goal setup. Players get real shots on big goals, even without Keepers. For a shot on the big goal, two players must combine their efforts. And players learn to take the indirect path to goal—an attacking idea from Chapter 16.

Creating Scrimmage Teams

What are the basics for creating scrimmage teams? The teams must be the right size. Usually, the more even the teams, the better. And the teams must wear different colors.

CHAPTER 7: ORGANIZING FLEXIBLY

Team Size

With eight players, a 4 v 4 scrimmage would be the obvious choice. But with twelve players, what's better—one 6 v 6, or two 3 v 3's? Team size is really up to you. The larger teams keep everyone together, and provide more complexity. The smaller teams provide everyone with more touches.

Five is a magic number, the fewest players possible for a Thoughtscrim. The match is 2 v 2, with a neutral player on the side (Scene 7-3). The neutral player helps the team with the ball, using only one touch. All the Thoughtscrims from the previous chapter can be played.

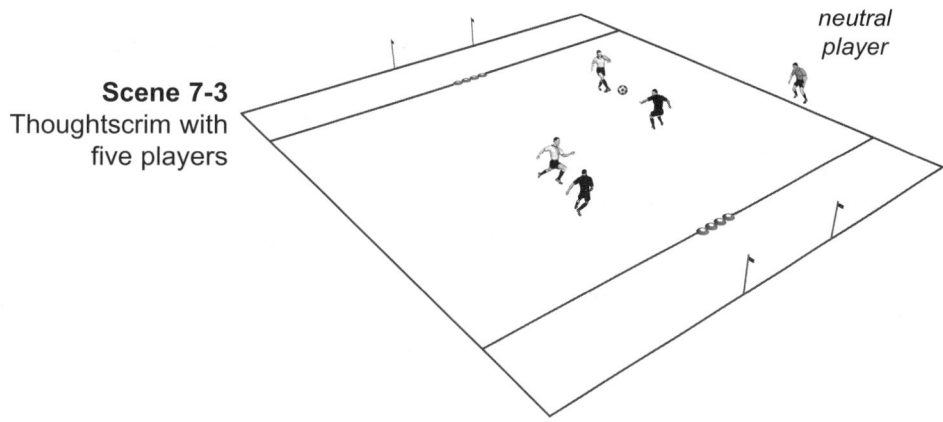

Scene 7-3
Thoughtscrim with five players

neutral player

Assigning Players

Traditional ways to assign players to teams can be ineffective or heartless. When players are assigned randomly, lopsided teams result. When captains pick teams, the players picked last feel inferior.

Here's a better way. Select two players of roughly equal ability, and assign one to each team. To avoid suspicion, don't select the two strongest or weakest players. Next, select two more players of equal ability, one for each team. Continue assigning players this way, bouncing from weaker players to stronger players, until everyone is on a team. The teams will probably be even, and everyone will be happy.

If your teams prove to be uneven, and one team has the ball the whole time, a trade is essential. Stop the play, and trade Amy for Catherine and a third-round draft pick. Amy might realize she's the weaker player, but life is unfair sometimes.

Team Colors

Scrimmage teams need different colors. Practice vests, the old standby, have three problems. Traded players won't appreciate sweat-soaked vests. The vests are often lost. And someone must wash them. The

PART I: ORGANIZING

color problem will be solved if players bring a white shirt and dark shirt to every practice.

Practice for the Dedicated Few

Suppose only four players show up to practice in the rain, or two players want to get an extra session in. Suppose your child hopes to play in college one day. You'll need a practice for the dedicated few.

The practice can still be fun, if you make a few adjustments. The skill part should last longer. More shots should be practiced. And the scrimmage part should consist of *Miniscrims* rather than Thoughtscrims.

Here's a fun, competitive practice for two players:

Skill Part (90 Minutes)
Soccer Volley
Juggling with the head
Chipping over soccer goals
Six different shots, alternating Keepers
Two dribbling HISAs (Ride the Bronco, Slalom Course)
Scrimmage Part (20 Minutes)
Miniscrims

Miniscrims are 1 v 1 or 2 v 2 scrimmages. *Cutthroat*, shown below, is a good example (Scene 7-4). Two players compete, and one or two others may rotate in. Goals are scored by striking the cones.

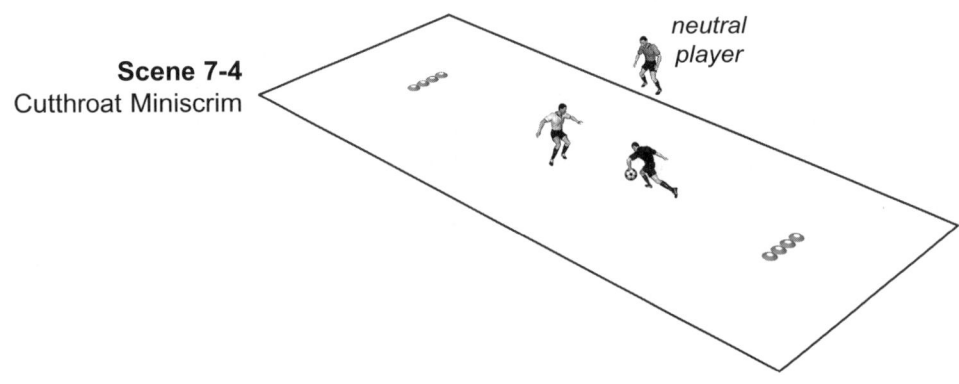

Scene 7-4
Cutthroat Miniscrim

neutral player

Rules for Cutthroat

Field Setup The field is approximately thirty paces long and ten paces wide, with touch lines and goal lines. Five paces inside each goal line is a small goal of five adjacent disc cones.

Players Two, three, or four players may participate on a field. Two players compete at a time, using one ball. With three players, one begins as a neutral player and rotates in. With four players, teams of two are formed. A player from one team competes against a player from the other team, as the other two serve as neutral players.

Object of the Game Each player attacks a different goal, and tries to strike it with the ball. The player with the most goals after three short periods wins.

How the Game Proceeds One player brings the ball into play as the other defends. The player with the ball attempts to score, by passing with neutral players (who are allowed only one touch), dribbling, and shooting. The other player attempts to prevent a score and win the ball back. After winning the ball, a player may shoot immediately. Shots may come from anywhere on the field. If one player puts the ball out of bounds, the other dribbles it in.

Rotating Into the Game With three players, the neutral player replaces a player who has been scored upon. If no goals have been scored within a minute, the neutral player replaces the player who has been in the longest. With four players, both neutral players rotate in at the same time—after a goal or a minute, whichever comes first.

The *Donut Scrimmage*, named after the field's appearance, is a 2 v 2 Miniscrim (Scene 7-5). The field is circular. It contains a smaller circle. And a ball in the smaller circle represents the goal. Players pass, dribble, and compete without a ridiculous amount of running.

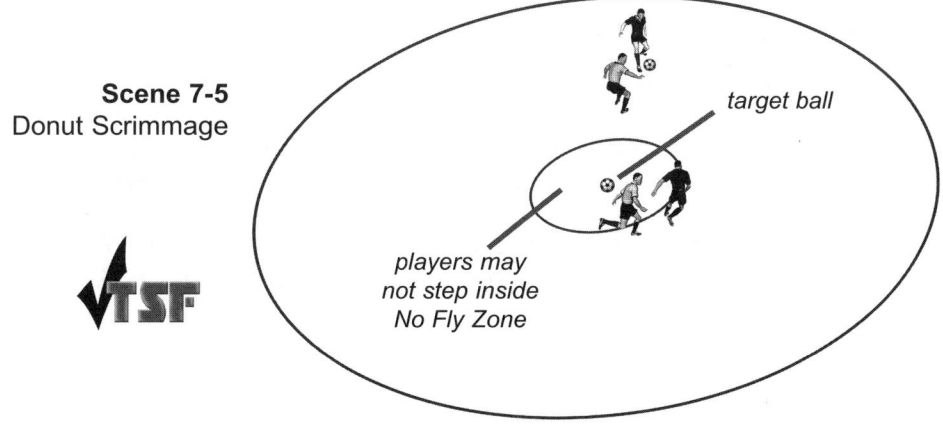

Scene 7-5
Donut Scrimmage

target ball

players may not step inside No Fly Zone

PART I: ORGANIZING

Rules for the Donut Scrimmage

Field Setup The field is a circle about thirty paces in diameter. A target ball sits in the middle of the circle. The target ball is surrounded by a circular No Fly Zone, four paces in diameter.

Teams Four players compete in teams of two.

Object of the Game Teams attempt to score by striking the target ball with a shot. Both teams attack the same goal. The team with the most goals after three short periods wins.

How the Game Proceeds One team begins with the ball, while the other defends. To strike the target ball, a team may use any combination of passing and dribbling. There are no touch or direction requirements. A team may steal the ball and shoot immediately. If one team puts the ball out of bounds, the other team passes or dribbles the ball in.

No Fly Zone Players may not step in the No Fly Zone while the game is in progress. All shots must come from outside that zone. Players running from one side of the field to the other must go around or leap over the zone. If a player sets foot in the zone, the other team receives a penalty kick—an unopposed shot from the field's perimeter. The penalty kick must strike the target ball.

Fun competitions like these are essential when working with smaller numbers. A few players will be glad to practice if the practice is fun. They might even practice on their own!

Tryouts and Larger Teams

What if you're working with twenty or thirty players during a practice or tryout? Scrimmaging will be the easy part. Set up two or more fields, and monitor them from a central location. Since you can mix and match goal setups, every team won't need a Keeper. Set up a tournament, if you like, with two teams advancing to the final.

The skill part of practice is trickier. A large number of players won't fit into an Air Control game. And setting up four Run the Gauntlet courses won't be your idea of a good time. Consider a *skill circuit* instead (Scene 7-6).

Several different HISA fields are set up before practice begins. Players divide into groups, and each group begins at a different HISA. Every twelve minutes, the groups rotate. You can have more HISAs than groups. For example, three groups can rotate between five HISAs.

> **Players divide into groups, and each group begins at a different HISA.**

CHAPTER 7: ORGANIZING FLEXIBLY

Scene 7-6
Skill circuit serving 32 players

Run the Gauntlet *Air Control*
L-Shot *Ride the Bronco*

The skill sequence won't be perfect. Some groups will begin with intense skills like shooting or dribbling. But the circuit approach is still a winner because it saves so much time.

Competing for a Spot

What if you must evaluate twenty or thirty players? Not all of them can make the team or start the match. Here's a bad way and a good way to decide which players are stronger.

> **Here's a bad way and a good way to decide which players are stronger.**

The *non-scoring* approach is the bad way. Players participate in drills, keep-away games, and scrimmages where the score doesn't matter. You look closely at a few player qualities, like speed, aggressiveness, and touch on the ball. From that, you decide who makes the team or starts the match.

This approach is ineffective and unfair. You're assuming Brad is better than Garrett because he's faster and stronger. Soccer is a sport of options, though. Garrett might be better at left-footed chips, or chest-trap shots. His greater mastery of options might help your team win. He might be a Thoughtful Soccer guy! But he'll have no chance to prove your evaluation wrong.

The *scoring* approach is the good way. Players compete at HISAs, Miniscrims, and Thoughtscrims as you note the scores. During the Thoughtscrims, you trade players from team to team, and note the impact. The players who usually win these contests are probably the strongest

PART I: ORGANIZING

players—even if they get results by *thinking*. They deserve to make the team or start the match.

Ready for Anything

With one or two players, you can still have a great practice. If only five players show up, or the soccer goals are missing, no problem. If twenty players arrive late, you can shift to a new plan. Who needs mud and twelve worms? The flexible organizer is ready for anything!

8
THE MATCH, WITH VALUES

Cleo the Misguided Sparrow

Cleo lived for the approval of other sparrows. She couldn't wait for the air show, where she'd soar through the air, swoop down in amazing loops and spins, and listen to the cheers.

PART I: ORGANIZING

On the day of the air show, sparrows assembled from all around. Cleo stepped up to the runway, paused a moment, and shot up into the sky. She performed several amazing stunts, and hovered to take in the cheers.

Not a sound! Cleo's fellow sparrows were too amazed to cheer. Cleo assumed from their silence that they disapproved. She climbed into the air for another try, but tried too hard. After crashing through some branches, she heard laughter and even a boo or two. Now angry, she began diving into the crowd. Finally, the sparrow police took Cleo away.

Cleo had a values problem. Approval, her most important value, was outside her control. Her splendid dives couldn't force sparrows to cheer. Rather than gaining approval, she's doing time.

Winning is a value your team can't entirely control. No matter how impressive the effort, something might interfere: an unlucky bounce, a bad call, the other team.

Suppose your team's values, in this order, are: 1) winning, 2) playing aggressively, and 3) scoring goals. Watch out! Your players will charge around the field recklessly. They won't care a great deal about keeping possession. And they'll become even more thoughtless if the match goes poorly. Winning is more difficult when it's too high on your list.

> **Winning is more difficult when it's too high on your list.**

A Winning Values List

As a soccer coach, you've entered a world of values. Players and parents are watching you. They'll either question your values, or follow your lead. You can't *not* have values, but you can be aware or unaware of them.

Values get prioritized.[1] When push comes to shove, a higher value will override a lower one. For example, if winning is a higher value than safety, players will risk injury to win. Rather than putting winning at the top, consider values that contribute to winning.

Here's a useful list: 1) playing safely, 2) respecting the referee, 3) improving, 4) playing intelligently, and 5) doing everything possible to win.

CHAPTER 8: THE MATCH, WITH VALUES

Why this list? A win won't matter if someone wrecks a knee or decks the referee, so safety and respect come first. These two values also prevent sportsmanship problems, penalty kicks, and red cards.

The next value, improving, provides perspective. Mistakes and losses aren't tragic, because they help your team improve. Your players can improvise and take risks without fear of criticism.

Playing intelligently is a style-of-play value. It doesn't guarantee a win, but it makes winning possible. If your team plays intelligently, consider the match a success.

Doing everything possible to win, giving 100 percent, fighting to the bitter end—such values are more useful than winning. They are within your team's control. They encourage a consistent effort, regardless of the score.

What values guide your coaching? Make a list and evaluate it. See a few problems? Then change your list—add a value, delete a value, or reorder them all. Values are always subject to change.

The Value of a Warmup

If your players arrive at the match whenever they like and then kick a few balls around, your warmup needs work. An effective warmup can reduce the chance of injuries, get your players thinking together, and help your players improve.

Make the warmup a miniature practice. Cover the skills from gentle to strenuous, and include a few Thoughtscrims. For a 1:00 PM match, the warmup could look like this:

12:15	Latest time for arriving at field
12:20	Soccer volley on imaginary courts
12:25	Passing and chipping in pairs
12:30	Stretching
12:35	Shooting (L-Shots, Wall Pass Shots, Rock and Rollers)
12:45	Scrimmaging (One-Time, Three-and-a-Drop, and Side-to-Side)
12:55	Pre-match chat

Most teams use keep-away games in the warmup. But don't forget the Thoughtscrim advantage. Players think about all four directions. That will come in handy once the match starts.

87

PART I: ORGANIZING

The best-planned warmup will fail if players don't arrive on time. Here's a team rule to consider. Players arriving late must complete the missed parts of the warmup after the match has started. Follow through with the consequence, even if your team must begin the match short-handed. You'll only have to follow through once.

Values in the Pre-Match Chat

There are three times to gather your players for a chat: before the match, during halftime, and after the match.

Your pre-match chat should answer three questions. Who will play where? What's the plan? What are the important values? Here's a chat that gives the wrong values message.

"This is our last home match, and we've got to win. Nobody comes into our backyard and beats us. I want you to be aggressive, and go shoulder-to-shoulder. That's why we have an ambulance here. Move the ball forward, and take as many shots as possible. And let's finish those scoring chances!"

Your first words in this cliché-ridden talk are about winning. Yet there aren't any ideas about how to win. A predictable, aggressive, thoughtless style of play is encouraged. Players who listen might soon need legal counsel.

Here's a can't-miss alternative to tape to your wrist:

"First, we want to play safely. There shouldn't be any fouls from behind, or reckless challenges. Second, we want to respect the referee. We know he's going to make mistakes, but we're not going to argue. Third, we want to have some long possessions early in the match. Look for those passes back and to the side."

The first words from your mouth are about safety and respect. These are clearly your most important values. The soccer items are brief, and come last. Your players will be ready for a composed, thoughtful effort.

> **The first words from your mouth are about safety and respect.**

Evaluating For the Halftime Chat

Once the match begins, avoid shouting instructions to everyone—particularly to the player with the ball. You want creativity and unpredictability, not obedience. If you can't resist shouting, focus on the players away from the ball. And shout encouragement when something smart happens:

"Way to look up while the ball is still arriving! Great choice, that drop pass! What hustle to get back on defense!"

During the match, your main task is to evaluate. Remember your picture of what soccer should look like? Pretend it's a pair of glasses through which you're watching the match. You'll discover what's going well and what's going poorly.

> **While the clock is running, your main task is to evaluate.**

The halftime chat is for sharing your insights. Limit yourself to three or four items, because players can't absorb much more. And include ways to improve, even if your team is winning. Here's an example.

"I've got three ideas for the second half. First, those drop passes are working well so let's keep using them. Second, when we've got the ball on one side of the field, we're forcing it forward. Let's switch it to the other side now and then. Third, they've had two nice headers off corner kicks. Brian, I'd like you to protect the back post on those corner kicks.

What makes this chat a winner? Thought-focused. Specific, not global. No phony emotional appeals.

Encouragement in the Post-Match Chat

Once the match is over, resist the temptation to criticize or blame. Your players probably know what lost the match. Make a mental note, but save it for the next practice. In the post-match chat, encourage your players with positives:

"We lost today, but what a great effort you gave. That time we moved the ball from one side to the other was right on target. We even had a few one-touch passes in the second half. And not one foul!"

Stay on an even keel, win or lose. If you're depressed after a loss and jolly after a win, you'll convey that winning is number one. Your chat should put the match in the past and look to the future. When is the next practice? Who can help with the team picnic? Your players are reminded again that improving is more important than winning.

PART I: ORGANIZING

The Power of Values

A sensible list of values—when shared by coach, players, and parents—makes match day go well. With sportsmanship issues out of the picture, everyone can relax and have fun. Positives will abound, win or lose. And nobody will end up in the sparrow clink!

---

[1] Robbins, Anthony, *Awaken the Giant Within* (New York: Summit Books, 1991). Robbins' work on values and value hierarchies is of great value to soccer coaches.

9

STEPPING IN TO TEACH

Grandpa Makes His Point

The sea gull was teaching his grandchildren to catch fish. He carefully explained and demonstrated the secrets. But the youngsters paid no attention. They were having too much fun prancing around the rocks.

PART I: ORGANIZING

Grandpa had an idea. He made up a game called Go Fish, in which real fish must be caught. The youngsters played enthusiastically, but kept making mistakes. Some belly-flopped into the water. Others tried to fish beak-first.

After one of these mistakes, Grandpa stopped the game for a moment. "Glide with your wings like so," he demonstrated, "and grab the fish with your claws."

As Grandpa talked, the young sea gulls watched and listened. They could hardly wait to try out the suggestions. That night, they pranced around the rocks again—at their first fish fry!

Grandpa had no luck at all lecturing. The young gulls didn't pay attention until he changed his teaching style. His new style allowed the young gulls to experience problems. Only then were they hungry for solutions.

Grandpa's new teaching style also works for soccer coaches. Start a game, spot a problem, and step in with a solution. Your players will pay attention, and try out your suggestions. This teaching style is included in most coaching courses. In Thoughtful Soccer, it's called the Coachable Moment or COMO style.

How to Teach Poorly

If you want to waste practice time and prevent players from learning, try one of these teaching styles.

All Talk and No Action
For this style, give lengthy talks laced with tips and theories. Your players will listen to a few sentences, and tune out the rest. They can't apply ideas they've never experienced. Players change by seeing and doing, not by listening.

Dwelling on What Went Wrong
For this style, point out what went wrong without offering a solution. Get a little angry, use a blaming tone, and focus on the past. Your players will feel bad without knowing how to change. Solutions, not problems, are what help players change.

Teaching at the Wrong Times
For this style, you have three choices. Teach before a practice activity, while a practice activity is in progress, or before a match.

The moments before a practice activity are too early. Your players haven't experienced a soccer problem yet. They're not ready for a soccer solution.

The moments while an activity is in progress are too confusing. If you're talking while players are playing, they won't know what to focus on—you or the activity.

The moments before a match are too late. If your players haven't learned something in practice, save your breath. Once in the match, they'll play as they have in the past.

A Close Look at Coachable Moments

If those teaching styles are wrong, what style is right? The coach who teaches *during* an activity is on the right track. But *freeze* the activity before opening your big mouth—the key to the Coachable Moment style.

> **But *freeze* the activity before opening your big mouth. . .**

Coachable Moments are moments during a scrimmage or HISA that invite coaching points. They come in two varieties:

- *Corrective* COMOs arise when players do something wrong. You point out the problem, and walk through a solution.
- *Encouragement* COMOs arise when players do something right. You walk through the moment of brilliance for all to see.

Here's a detailed example. You're watching a game of Three-and-a-Drop, when the situation in Scene 9-1 arises. Mike has just won the ball, but has no teammates to the rear. Nate is poorly positioned to help. Mike forces the ball forward, even though two opponents stand in the way.

You shout, "Freeze!," and step onto the field for a Corrective COMO. You return players to wherever they were at the moment of truth, and give this spiel:

"Mike has the ball, but if he goes forward he's going to lose it. We'd like him to turn with the ball like this, and look to the rear for a teammate. Now we'll move Nate over here for a drop pass. A little further back, Nate."

PART I: ORGANIZING

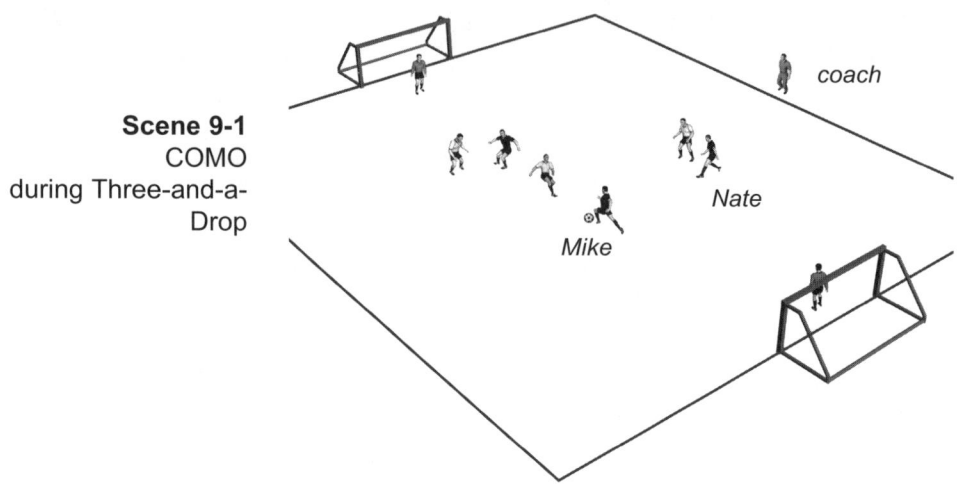

Scene 9-1
COMO
during Three-and-a-Drop

While talking, you're also directing traffic and demonstrating. Mike is now facing to the rear, and Nate is in position to receive the pass (Scene 9-2). Mike makes the pass, you shout "Play on!", and the scrimmage resumes.

Scene 9-2
Better positioning after the COMO

As the teams go at it, you watch closely for an Encouragement COMO. There it is! Mike wins the ball again, Nate moves behind him for a drop pass, and the pass is made. Again, you shout, "Freeze!" You return the ball to Mike, and move Nate back to his pre-run location. Talking and orchestrating, you give your spiel:

"Let's look at this again. Mike's facing forward with the ball, and three opponents are in the way. So he turns to the rear, where Nate has made this great run—do it again for us, Nate. Make that pass again, Mike. Brilliant! Play on!"

The other players now get the idea, and can't wait to try it out. And Mike and Garth are thinking, "What a cool coach!"

Steps in the COMO Teaching Style

The example shows the five steps in a Corrective COMO:

- Start an activity quickly, with little talk
- Watch for a thinking mistake of some kind
- Freeze the action at the point of the mistake
- Walk through a solution
- As the walk through is completed, start the activity again

A Corrective COMO works for several reasons. You let players experience a problem before offering a solution. You stop the action before talking. You walk through the solution instead of just talking about it. And you talk to the whole team without embarrassing one player. Not bad for a minute of coaching!

An Encouragement COMO follows the same steps, but after a success has occurred. Why fuss over a success? So that it will happen again!

> **Why fuss over a success? So that it will happen again!**

The COMO teaching style meets the two requirements for changing soccer players. Players try something different in practice, like a drop pass. And their efforts have positive results, like keeping the ball and being praised by the coach.

The Number One COMO Mistake

Avoid this common COMO mistake. You spot the problem, and freeze the action. All is well until you launch into a lecture:

"Mike has the ball, but nobody is providing support. Nate should have moved in behind him, to provide support. Support is very important for keeping possession. If we always force the ball forward, we'll lose it. That was our problem on Saturday. We've got to do a better job with support. Pay attention! Wake up!"

You've disguised your lecture as a COMO! It can't be a COMO if you're just talking. You've got to be showing players something, moving them about. And later, they've got to try that something on their own. Otherwise, your interruption was a waste of time.

PART I: ORGANIZING

Other COMO Examples

Whenever you have something to teach, find a COMO to teach it with. A COMO can arise during any scrimmage or skill game. Here are a few examples.

Three-and-a-Drop Como
Three-and-a-Drop is great for the idea of *support*. Since one player must pass to the rear, another player must get open to the rear. When the player to the rear is poorly positioned, freeze the action for a Corrective COMO.

In Scene 9-3, the player providing support is too close to the ball. If he receives a drop pass, opponents will be right on top of him in a dangerous location. The X marks a better spot—back and to the side.

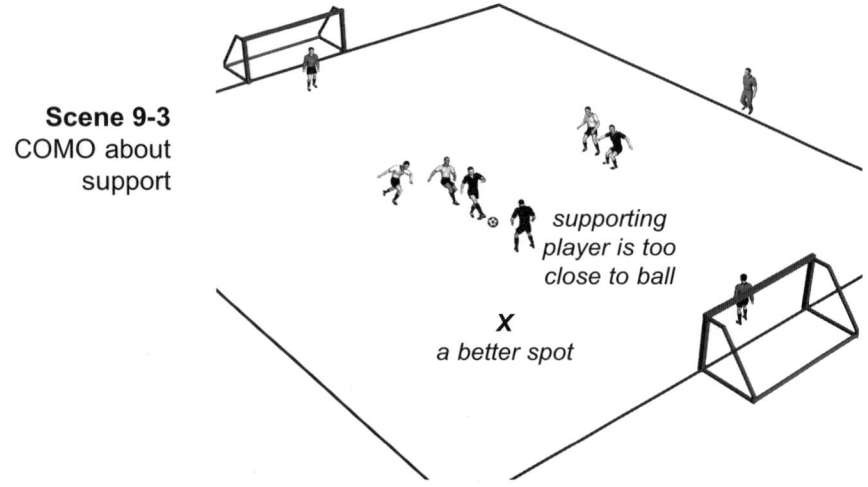

Scene 9-3
COMO about support

First-Time COMO
During First-Time, two players will often position themselves poorly. They'll form a single line with the player who's trying to pass (Scene 9-4). The ball can then be passed in only one direction. Stop the play, and position the players in a triangle. Two passing options are then available.

CHAPTER 9: STEPPING IN TO TEACH

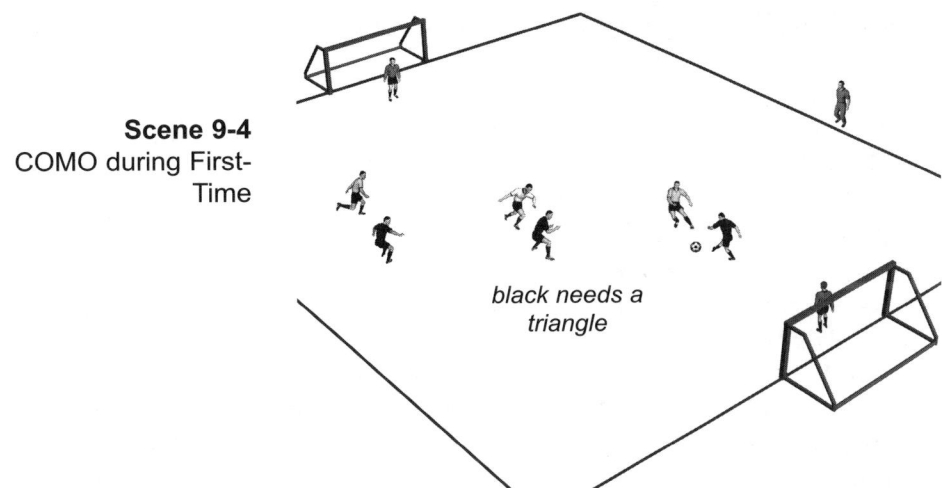

Scene 9-4
COMO during First-Time

black needs a triangle

Side-to-Side COMO
When first playing Side-to-Side, players will try to switch the ball with one long pass. A COMO can then be used to teach players the drop-and-switch maneuver (see page 67). The ball is dropped to a teammate, who switches it to the other side. When players use the maneuver on their own, reward them with an Encouragement COMO.

A COMO From a Large-Sided Scrimmage
Here's a valuable COMO from a large-sided scrimmage. A team moves the ball from one touch line to the other, a major accomplishment. Then, the ball heads straight for the goal and is lost (Scene 9-5).

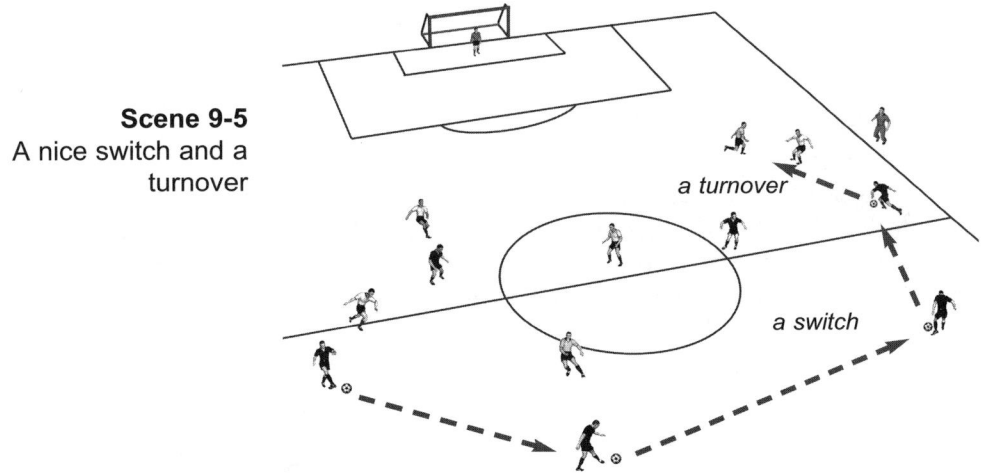

Scene 9-5
A nice switch and a turnover

a turnover

a switch

Freeze the action, and try this spiel:

"That was a great switch from one side to the other. But instead of going forward, let's switch the ball back to the original side. Ray, step in here for a drop pass. Now, swing the ball over to Brian. Look at all the space over

97

PART I: ORGANIZING

a drop pass. Now, swing the ball over to Brian. Look at all the space over there! Play on!"

When a few switches occur during one possession, a high level of thought has been achieved. Not all college teams can do that. But thanks to the COMO teaching style, yours can.

Run the Gauntlet COMO

COMOs also arise in skill activities like Run the Gauntlet (see page 47). New players think they must dribble to the right or the left to get past a defender. But the ball can go to the right while the dribbler goes to the left, or vice versa (Scene 9-6). Ball and dribbler then reunite on the other side of the defender. If you demonstrate the idea with a COMO, your players will try it out.

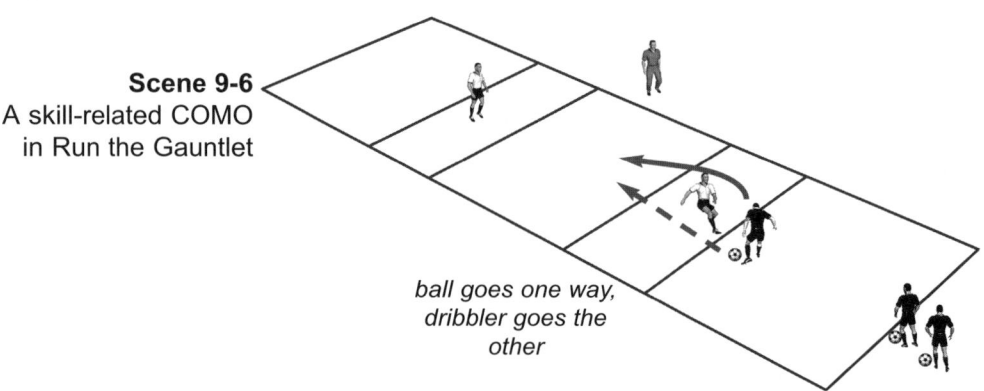

Scene 9-6
A skill-related COMO in Run the Gauntlet

ball goes one way, dribbler goes the other

No Degree Required

Coachable Moments are a clever way to change behavior. A negative pattern is interrupted, and replaced with a positive pattern. The positive pattern is rewarded. Your young sea gulls will hang on your every word. And you don't even need a psychology degree!

PART TWO: COACHING SOCCER'S PARTS

10
SEEING THE PARTS

Ghosts Aghast

The young ghosts weren't learning how to frighten people, and the grownup ghosts were alarmed. The textbooks in the ghost schools just weren't scary enough.

PART II: TEACHING SOCCER'S PARTS

A ghost writer was hired to produce three new stories. A test group of ghost children would read the stories. If the children were frightened, the stories would become required reading.

The stories were finally ready for testing. But the ghosts in the first story were too sensitive. In the second story, nothing terrible happened to the people. And the third story, of all things, had a heartwarming ending!

After reading the stories, the ghost children embraced in a group hug. The adult ghosts were horrified. They ordered the writer to make the stories scary.

Those adult ghosts weren't much help to the writer. They didn't understand the *parts* a story should have: wicked ghosts, suffering humans, and a shocking ending. Without understanding the parts, they couldn't pinpoint the problems.

To pinpoint your team's problems, you must understand soccer's parts. What are those parts? Whatever you want them to be! In a free-flowing sport like soccer, the parts aren't real. They're just figments of your imagination that help you sort out the match. There's no right or wrong way to break soccer into parts. Some ways are just more useful than others.

> **To pinpoint your team's problems, you must understand soccer's parts.**

Here's one useful way. When the other team has the ball, your team must contain the ball to prevent a goal (Contain Part). At some point, your team must win the ball back by pressuring it (Pressure Part). When your team has the ball, it must keep the ball (Possession Part), break through a few obstacles (Breakthrough Part), and score (Finish Part). And since corner kicks, free kicks, and throw-ins don't fit neatly anywhere else, they make up the Restart Part.

Okay, these aren't really separate parts. They're all jumbled together. Your team can't break through without keeping possession. And some defenders can be pressuring while others are containing. Remember— parts are just a useful tool.

Imagine that your team is playing a match. Here are some problems you'll spot if you understand soccer's parts.

CHAPTER 10: SEEING THE PARTS

Where's the Possession Part?

The first part to look for is the Possession Part. Your team should be able to string a few passes together, and keep the ball for a while. When your team wins the ball, notice the direction the ball travels. If the direction is always forward, the problem is clear—weak *Possession Part*!

A weak Possession Part hurts other parts as well. Instead of breaking through and finishing, your team will lose the ball. And your players will have trouble getting back on defense.

If the Possession Part is going well, you'll see the possession secrets at work. Your players will move the ball in different directions, particularly back and to the side. They'll use different numbers of touches on the ball. They'll pass short and long, to teammates and to space. And they'll retreat when no scoring chance is available.

Why Are We Allowing Goals?

When your team allows a goal, which defending part needs work? The problem might have to do with the offside rule, as in Scene 10-1. Your defender is running behind his teammates to cover an opponent. That redraws the offside line, and puts your team at risk. For more on the offside rule, see Chapter 11.

Scene 10-1
Poor use of the offside rule

When the other team is getting easy shots, the *Contain Part* could be the problem. In Scene 10-2, an opponent is dribbling in on your last defender. No other defenders can come to the rescue. To avoid such fiascos, review Chapter 12.

103

PART II: TEACHING SOCCER'S PARTS

Scene 10-2
Contain Part is the problem

What if your team can't win the ball back? The *Pressure Part* might be the problem. In Scene 10-3, your defenders are too spread out, and they're just covering zones. The white team is easily moving through those zones. Chapter 13 shows how to pressure the ball and win it back.

Scene 10-3
Pressure Part is the problem

In Scene 10-4, the problem is the *defensive system*, a 3-3-4. Only one player is in the middle of the field. And there's a big space between your Fullbacks and Halfbacks. For the qualities of a good defensive system, see Chapter 14.

CHAPTER 10: SEEING THE PARTS

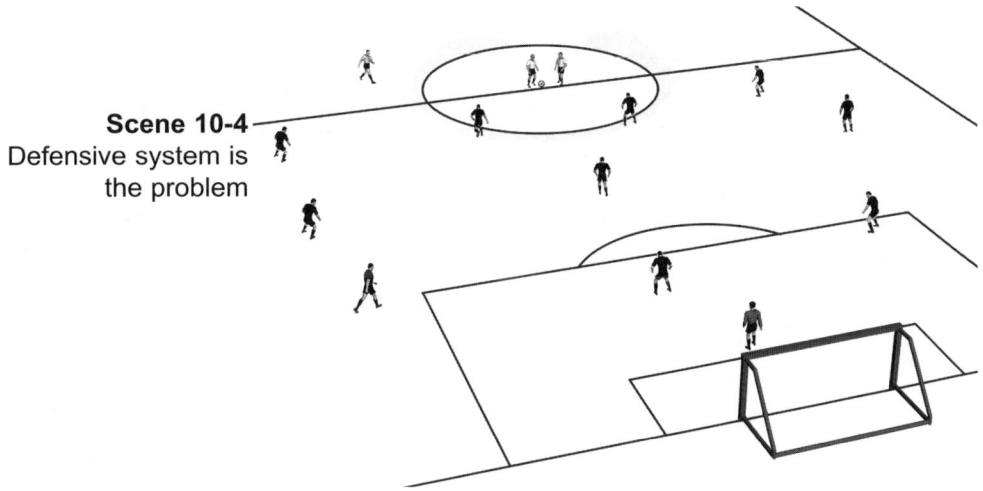

Scene 10-4
Defensive system is the problem

What Is My Keeper Doing?

Keep an eye on your Keeper, who has roles to play in all of soccer's parts. In Scene 10-5, your Keeper is preparing to make a save. That's an important role. But had he played three other roles, he wouldn't be in such trouble.

Scene 10-5
Poor use of the Keeper roles

In Scene 10-6, your Keeper is hurting the Possession Part. He's sending a goal kick deep, where opponents will probably win it. Soon, he'll be making a save again. He should have noticed his teammate in the corner. To expand your Keeper's roles, refer to Chapter 15.

PART II: TEACHING SOCCER'S PARTS

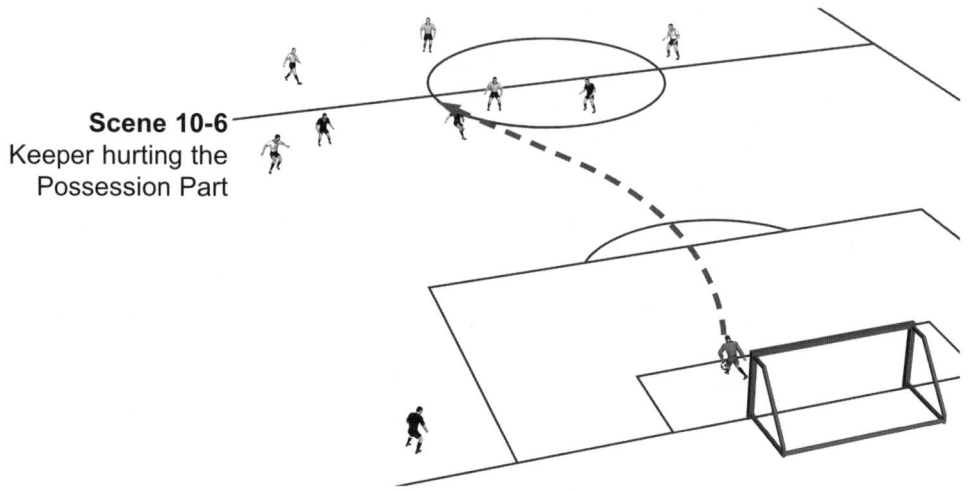

Scene 10-6
Keeper hurting the Possession Part

Why Can't We Break Through?

Suppose your team is keeping possession well, but losing the ball whenever a scoring try is possible. Weak *Breakthrough Part*! Your team must break through a few obstacles before scoring. Here are some possible problems:

- Your team might have only one way to break through—the fast break to goal. For other ways, like the cross from a corner, see Chapter 16.

- Your players might be working separately rather than combining their efforts. For tricky combinations, see Chapter 17.

- Your players might not understand the defensive system they're facing—the problem in Scene 10-7.

Scene 10-7
Poor awareness of the defense

CHAPTER 10: SEEING THE PARTS

Your team is facing a Sweeper system. Each of your Forwards is covered, and the Sweeper must be beaten as well. Your Forwards will be lucky to touch the ball, let alone break through. To get them moving to better spots, refer to Chapter 18.

Why Worry About the Restart Part?

Restart situations like corner kicks and free kicks might seem the least of your problems. But this very brief part can win or lose the match.

In Scene 10-8, your team is defending a free kick. The wall is understaffed and poorly positioned. And that defender in the goal doesn't understand the offside rule.

Scene 10-8
Poor defense on a free kick

Next, your team is taking a corner kick, but the plan is too obvious (Scene 10-9). Your players are outnumbered. They're not moving. And if the ball sails a little long, the other team will win it. Is the Restart Part your Achilles heel? Refer to Chapter 19.

Scene 10-9
Poor attack on a corner kick

PART II: TEACHING SOCCER'S PARTS

Why Did That Shot Sail Into the Parking Lot?

Your team breaks through the defense over and over, only to bungle the shots. You may now make that universal complaint of soccer coaches: "We can't finish!" But careful what you say in your halftime chat. Advice like "Finish your scoring chances!" and "Take more shots!" rarely helps.

The *Finish Part* depends on skillful shooting. Take the pressure off shooters, and encourage better shot selection, with gems like these: "See your teammates, even though you have a shot!" "Make that one extra pass!" "Get the assist, not the goal!" A relaxed shot from close range might finally find the mark.

The only real cure for the Finish Part is shooting practice. As we saw in Chapter 3, many different shots can arise in a match. They all must be practiced regularly.

> **The only real cure for the Finish Part is shooting practice.**

How Can You Mend a Broken Part?

Halftime is the right time to share your ideas. But if those ideas haven't been practiced, you'll get blank stares. Broken parts must be mended in practice.

When the next practice arrives, consider breaking it into three segments. The first segment consists of HISAs, for strengthening skills. The second segment consists of Thoughtscrims, for strengthening the Possession Part. And the final segment is for soccer's others parts. The practice might look like this:

High-Impact Skill Activities (50 minutes)
    Soccer Volley
    Heading Game
    Air Control
    Three shots
    Two dribbling games
Thoughtscrims (35 minutes)
    One-Time
    Three-and-a-Drop
    Side-to-Side
Soccer's other parts (35 minutes)
    Triangle Thoughtscrim (see Chapter 13)
    Doctor Diagnoso Thoughtscrim (see Chapter 19)

CHAPTER 10: SEEING THE PARTS

Such a practice earns top honors for organization. None of the bread-and-butter activities are left out. And within a few practices, all of soccer's parts can be strengthened—not just the broken ones.

See It, Fix It, See It Again

Soccer's parts allow the feedback loop that's behind effective coaching. Watch your team play, and pinpoint the part that's not working. Strengthen that part in practice. And repeat the process over and over until the soccer on the field matches the picture in your mind. Don't be horrified when the soccer comes out wrong. Fix it!

11
THE OFFSIDE RULE, WITH CARE

The Bouncers' Boo-Boo

Vampires were breaking into the bingo club and sucking blood from the players. The manager finally hired some bouncers for protection. At first, the bouncers kept the vampires out in the usual ways—crosses held high, and stakes driven into the heart.

PART II: TEACHING SOCCER'S PARTS

A special trick could also be used. If every single bouncer held a cross up just as a vampire was entering the club, that vampire would instantly vanish—provided that the club's owl hooted at the exact same time. The bouncers were fascinated with the special trick, and began using it over and over. One vampire after another vanished, and the bouncers howled with glee.

Eventually, though, there was a slip-up. A particularly thirsty vampire went past, and all the bouncers but one held up their crosses. The owl was looking the other way, and forgot to hoot. The vampire entered the club. A night of bingo was ruined.

The bouncers were doing fine with crosses and stakes, but they couldn't resist the cross-and-owl trick. It made them feel clever, and got quicker results. They overused the trick, and one mistake was disastrous.

In soccer, the offside rule presents a similar temptation. By relying on the rule, your defenders can quickly end the other team's possession—as long as all your players are in sync, and the referee makes the call. But one mistake can lose the match.

What constitutes thoughtful use of the offside rule? Understanding the rule's benefits and risks. Using the rule with care.

A Quick Review

The offside rule is best explained in four parts. First, an *imaginary offside line* runs from one touch line to the other, parallel to your goal line (Scene 11-1). This imaginary line runs through your second deepest player or players. If your second deepest player is in the other team's half of the field, though, the halfway line becomes the imaginary offside line. In other words, opponents can't be offside unless they're beyond the halfway line.

CHAPTER 11: THE OFFSIDE RULE, WITH CARE

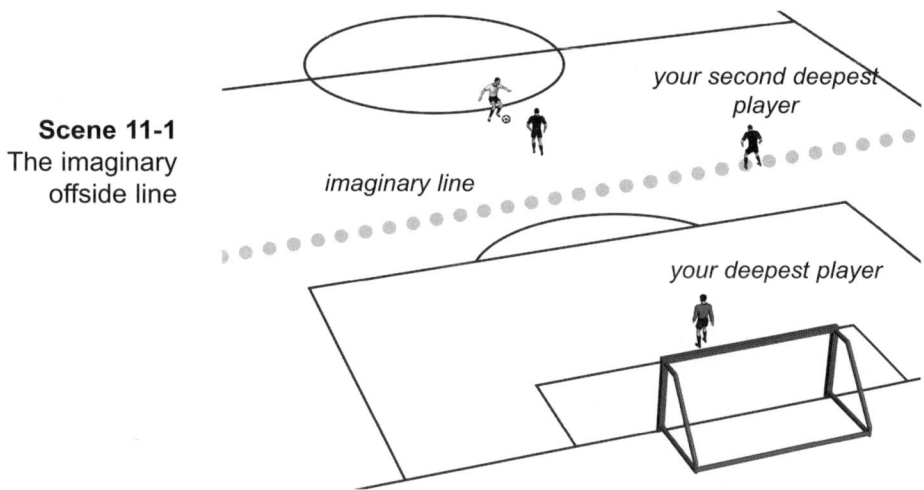

Scene 11-1
The imaginary offside line

Your Keeper will usually be the deepest defender, but not necessarily. In Scene 11-2, your Keeper has scrambled out for the ball, and is only the second deepest defender. The imaginary offside line therefore runs through the Keeper.

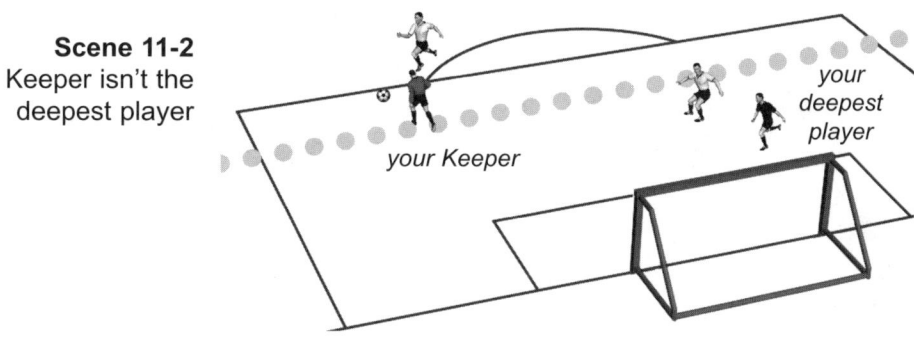

Scene 11-2
Keeper isn't the deepest player

Second, any opponent who is beyond the imaginary offside line and ahead of the ball is in an *offside position* (Scene 11-3). Opponents standing along that line are not in an offside position. In soccer lingo, *even is on*.

PART II: TEACHING SOCCER'S PARTS

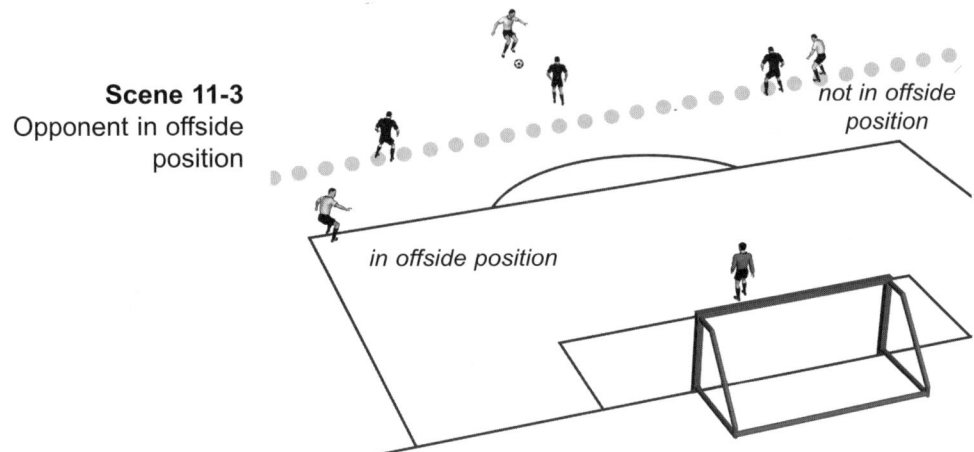

Scene 11-3
Opponent in offside position

not in offside position

in offside position

Third, if the ball is passed toward an opponent in an offside position, that's a violation, and your team should get the ball (Scene 11-4). At the moment the pass is made, the linesman should judge whether or not a violation has occurred. Your team can be given possession even if the pass is blocked or off target.

Scene 11-4
Pass to player in offside position

Fourth, if the opponent in an offside position isn't involved in the play, or isn't the player being passed to, offside usually won't be called. In the above picture, that's the case with the opponent to the right. In rule book lingo, there is no violation unless the opponent is *interfering with play* or *gaining an advantage*.

This fourth part can confuse defenders. Concepts like interfering with play, and gaining an advantage, aren't clear-cut. Consider the scenario in Scene 11-5.

CHAPTER 11: THE OFFSIDE RULE, WITH CARE

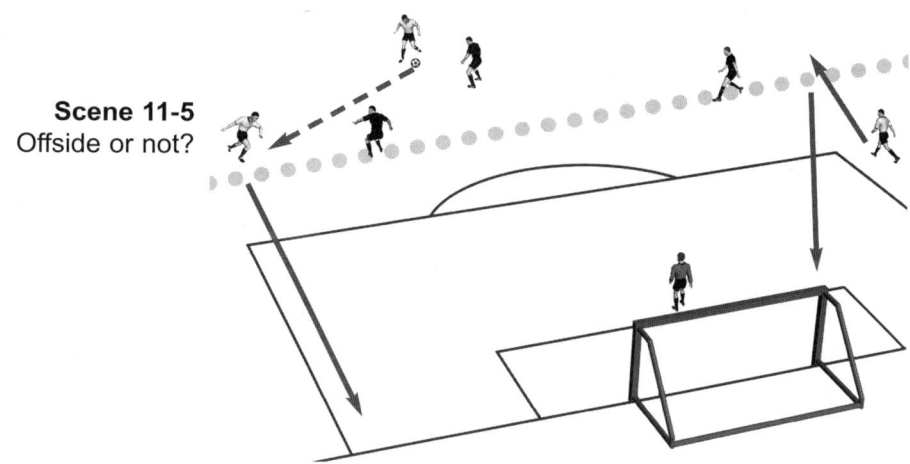

Scene 11-5
Offside or not?

Here, an opponent is in an offside position, but the ball is passed to the other side. Most referees won't make an offside call, because the offside player doesn't seem to be interfering with play as the ball is passed. But what if that player hesitates for a moment, and then runs forward for a crossing pass? Perhaps he was interfering with play after all. But how could the referee have known at the time?

A Tool With Risks

The offside rule can help your defenders in four ways:

- Your defenders can usually ignore opponents who move behind the imaginary offside line, since those opponents are in an offside position.

- By moving the imaginary line further from the goal, your defenders can force opponents further from the goal.

- When the imaginary line is moved further from the goal, your defenders can get closer together, or become more compact.

- By suddenly moving the imaginary line forward, your defenders can win possession through an offside call.

But if your players rely too much on the offside rule, they're asking for trouble. Legal passes can lead to breakaways on your Keeper. Even when an opponent is in an offside position, hoping for a call can be risky. Three things can go wrong:

- The ball might be passed to the opposite side of the field from the offside opponent, as we saw in Scene 11-5. Offside usually won't be called, since that opponent isn't interfering with play.

- The linesman might blow the call, allowing an opponent to break in on your Keeper.

PART II: TEACHING SOCCER'S PARTS

- ♦ The opponent with the ball might fake a pass to an offside teammate, then dribble through the imaginary offside line (Scene 11-6). Offside won't be called while a player is dribbling

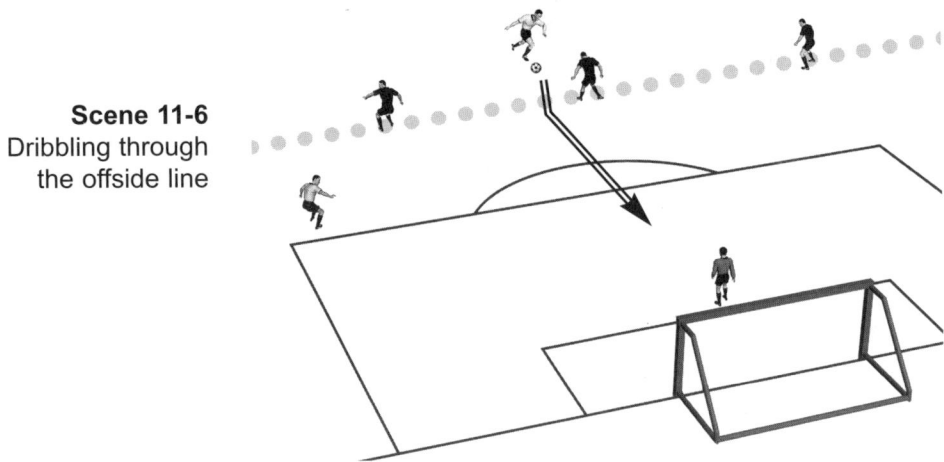

Scene 11-6
Dribbling through the offside line

The offside rule has many ifs, and the cost of a mistake is high. Your players should never assume an offside call will be made. When the ball is passed to an offside opponent, they should assume no call will be made. Usually, they'll have time to hustle back and prevent a goal.

Managing the Risks

Your defenders along the imaginary offside line have an important choice to make. If they sag back, the ball will rarely get past. If they pull forward, they can place opponents in an offside position. Which is better, sagging back or pulling forward?

Both! Your defenders should sometimes sag back and sometimes pull forward, and disguise the choice. They can pretend to sag back and then suddenly pull forward. They can pretend to pull forward and then suddenly sag back. With this *sag/pull option*, they can keep opponents guessing. Here are two examples.

> **Your defenders should sometimes sag back and sometimes pull forward, and disguise the choice.**

In Scene 11-7, your defenders have sagged back to lure opponents ahead of the ball. Now they're pulling forward, to place those opponents in an offside position.

CHAPTER 11: THE OFFSIDE RULE, WITH CARE

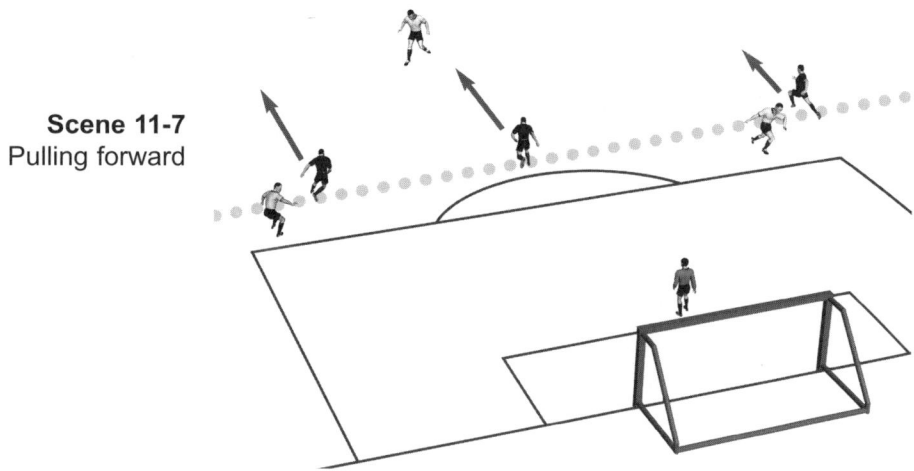

Scene 11-7
Pulling forward

Scene 11-8 shows the process reversed to thwart a direct kick. The kick is about to be taken from midfield. The defenders in white have pulled forward, moving the offside line and opponents further from the goal.

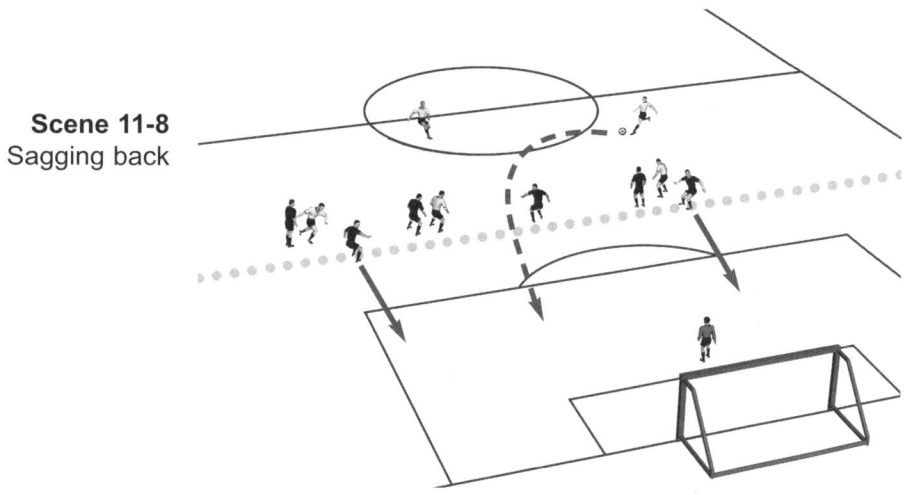

Scene 11-8
Sagging back

Defenders will sometimes hold this line as the ball is kicked, allowing the ball over their heads for a free-for-all in the goal area. In the scene, though, two defenders sag back just as the kick is taken. If they don't let the ball over their heads, the other team probably won't score.

Communicating the Plan
Defenders in the back must communicate about pulling forward and sagging back. If they're not in sync, they'll allow a goal. But yelling "Pull forward!" and "Sag back!" will tip off opponents.

An offside code lets your players communicate without tipping off opponents. Colors are one possibility. Any color beginning with a *b*—black, blue, brown, or burgundy—means pull forward. Any other color means

PART II: TEACHING SOCCER'S PARTS

play it safe. Numbers are another option. Any number with a 1 in it—17, 12, 91—means pull forward. Any other number means play it safe. Defenders, not the coach, must make the calls!

Opponents might laugh at such colors and numbers. But what's more important—playing intelligently or impressing opponents?

Scrimmaging With the Offside Rule

Your players won't be comfortable with the offside rule unless they practice with it. Any scrimmage can include the rule, but who will make the calls? The players themselves!

If a player on the defending team yells "Offside!" the call is assumed to be correct. Play always stops after a call, and the call shouldn't be argued. However, if everyone realizes the call was incorrect, the wronged team may keep the ball with a free kick.

When your players make the offside calls, they must deal with the rule's ambiguities. Who was where when the ball was passed? Was the player interfering with play? Disagreements will occur, but what a great learning experience!

> **When your players make the offside calls, they must deal with the rule's ambiguities.**

Offside COMOs

While scrimmaging with the offside rule, several Coachable Moments will arise. In this example, Fred's team has possession, and Fred is out ahead of the ball (Scene 11-9). A defender is chasing Fred, and that's the mistake. Freeze the action and have the defender pull up toward the ball. Fred will have to follow.

Scene 11-9
An offside-related COMO

CHAPTER 11: THE OFFSIDE RULE, WITH CARE

Coachable moments can also be used to:

- Teach the ambiguities in the offside rule
- Prevent defenders from using the rule too obviously
- Teach the Sag/Pull Option

Don't Count On It

The offside rule baffles new players and coaches at first. And once they understand the rule, they get carried away with it. Don't entrust the match to vampire bouncers and the club owl. Understand the offside rule, but don't count on it.

12

PREVENTING GOALS

A Scrappie Hits the Wall

The village depended on its blinkies. These cuddly animals provided milk and wool, and made great pets as well. The villagers built a wall around their blinkies, and three guards kept watch.

PART II: TEACHING SOCCER'S PARTS

One night, a long-necked scrappie poked its six-foot neck through the wall and looked around. The guards were slow to react. In the wink of an eye, the scrappie jumped through the wall, devoured several blinkies, and escaped.

Heartbroken, the villagers decided on a new plan. They added two more walls around their blinkies. Each wall was five feet from the next—one foot less than a scrappie's neck!

The scrappie returned for another feast, and poked through the first wall. But before it could look around, it bumped its head against the second wall! Stunned, the scrappie was at the mercy of the guards. They pounced on its neck, and trampled it into the ground. The blinkies were saved!

Strong and fast, the scrappie easily got through one layer. Getting through several layers proved more difficult, because the layers were the right distance apart. Had they been too far apart, the scrappie could have broken through one and then the other. Had they been too close, the scrappie could have muscled through both at the same time.

The Contain Part of soccer is like protecting blinkies. Layers, and the distance between them, are the keys. Opponents will often break through a single layer. But your team can usually contain the ball by setting up several layers.

How should players think about the Contain Part? That depends on how many defenders are between the ball and the goal: one, two, three, or more. Before looking at these different numbers, let's ask the zone/man-to-man question.

Zone or Man-to-Man?

With pure man-to-man defense, each of your players would cover one opponent wherever that opponent might go. At some point, your team should have man-to-man defense in its repertoire. When opponents are covered closely, they tend to lose the ball.

But man-to man isn't the best way to contain the ball and prevent goals. If an opponent cuts from one side of the field to the other, a defender must follow—leaving open space behind. And the opponent with the ball has only one defender to get past, since the other defenders are preoccupied (Scene 12-1).

CHAPTER 12: PREVENTING GOALS

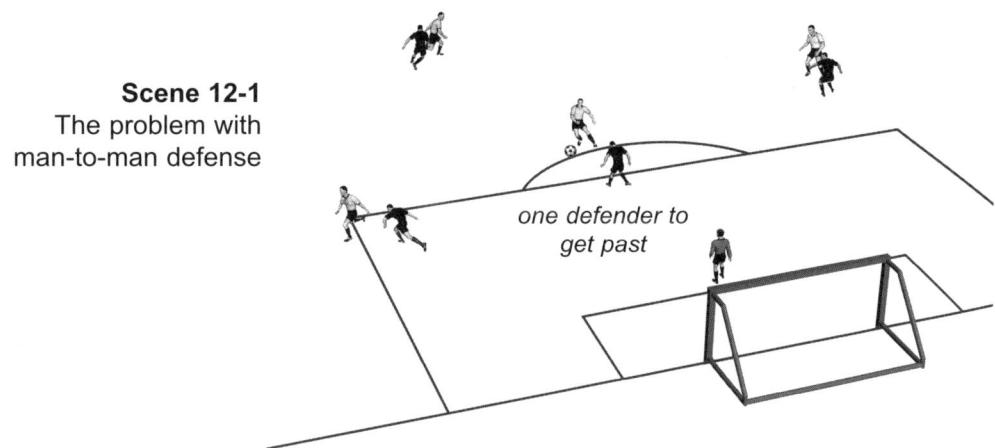

Scene 12-1
The problem with man-to-man defense

one defender to get past

Zone defense, where your players cover areas of the field instead of opponents, is safer. It prevents those big, open spaces. And while one defender stops the ball, other defenders can add layers.

One Lonely Defender

Only one defender is between the ball and the goal. What should that defender be thinking? Something like this:

"No teammates are backing me up! Backpedal and slow the play down until help arrives! Don't go for the ball unless you're sure of winning it! Close in on the shot, but don't fall for that fake!"

Scene 12-2 shows a lone defender at work. The cushion, or space, between the defender and attacker prevents the attacker from pushing the ball past. The defender is forcing the attacker to one side. And the ball can't be pushed between the legs of the defender, who is facing sideways.

Scene 12-2
One defender between ball and goal

cushion

123

PART II: TEACHING SOCCER'S PARTS

A One Versus One HISA

Players experience all these ideas in a HISA called *One To Beat*. A dribbler has eight seconds to beat the defender and score on the Keeper (Scene 12-3). The defender must choose between going for the ball and stalling. The game is great for attacker *and* defender.

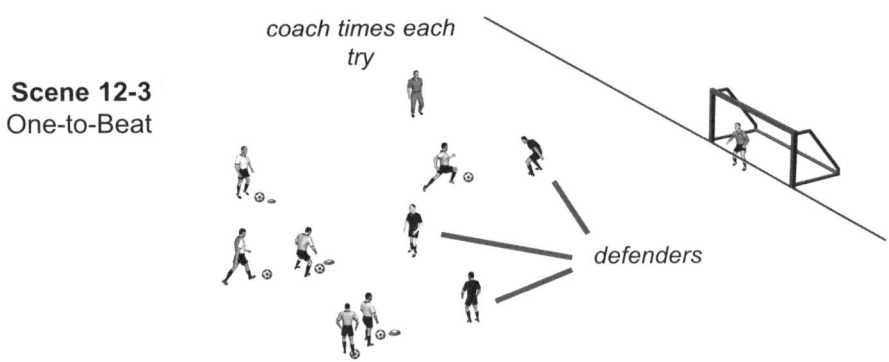

Scene 12-3
One-to-Beat

Rules for One to Beat

Field Setup The field consists of a regulation-size goal and a goal line. Three cones, about thirty paces from the goal, mark the places from which three lines will start.

Starting Positions Up to twelve field players and a Keeper participate. Three of the players begin as defenders, one facing each line. The other players begin as dribblers. They divide into three lines, and each player has a ball.

Object of the Game A dribbler tries to score by defeating a defender and shooting on the Keeper. The ball must be in the net within eight seconds.

How a Try Works A dribbler from the first line begins dribbling toward goal, as the defender there attempts to prevent a goal. The dribbler may dribble past the defender, or shoot from further out. The Keeper may make a save in goal, or come charging out. The coach times the attempt.

How the Game Proceeds After a try, the dribbler gets back in line and the defender awaits the next dribbler. The game proceeds to the second line, where another 1 v 1 duel takes place. The game continues quickly from one line to the next, until each dribbler has had three tries. The defenders then switch places with three dribblers. Players continue rotating until all have had the same number of dribbling tries. The player with the most goals wins.

The time-saving features are commendable. While one line would waste time, two or three lines move quickly. And the eight count prevents dilly-dallying around.

CHAPTER 12: PREVENTING GOALS

With a larger number of players, get two games going on back-to-back goals (Scene 12-4). Ball retrieval is easier, and players get twice as many tries!

Scene 12-4
One-to-Beat on back-to-back goals

Two Defenders Mean Backup

When two defenders are between the ball and goal, one must back the other up—or in soccer lingo, provide *cover*. If both defenders go after the ball at the same time, they might be beaten with a slick dribbling move (Scene 12-5).

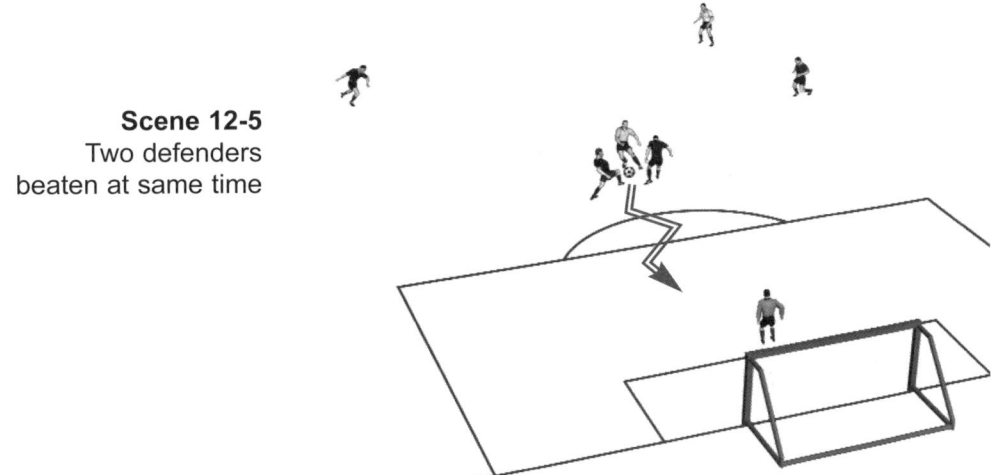

Scene 12-5
Two defenders beaten at same time

Two layers are safer. One defender closes in on the ball while the other provides backup (Scene 12-6). If the ball gets past the first layer, it crashes into the second layer. The layers must be the right distance apart. If they're too close, both can be beaten at the same time. If they're too far apart, one can be beaten and then the other.

125

PART II: TEACHING SOCCER'S PARTS

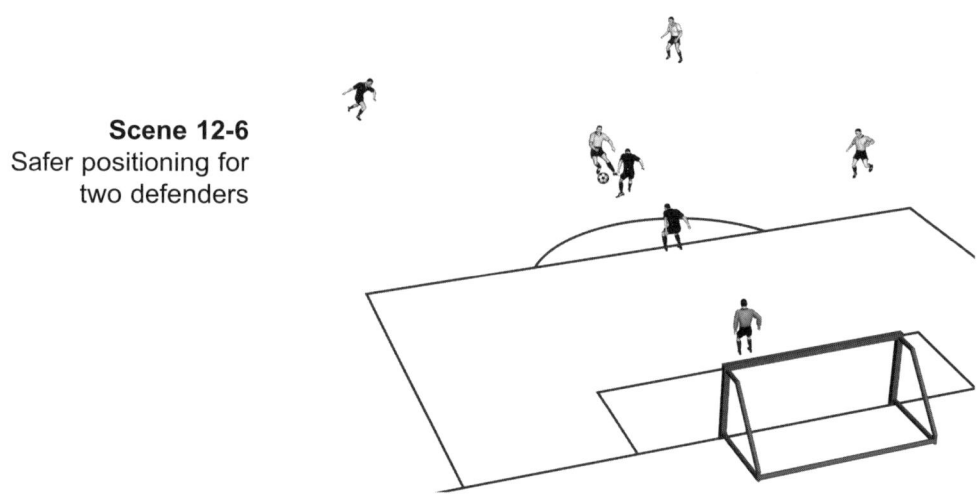

Scene 12-6
Safer positioning for two defenders

The defenders in Scene 12-6 have a problem, though. The backup defender is directly behind the other defender. That moves the offside line further back, and leaves the opponent to the right uncovered.

The problem has been corrected in Scene 12-7. The backup defender is back and to the side. He can still break up the play if his teammate is beaten. He's also covering an opponent and keeping the offside line in place.

Scene 12-7
Safest positioning for two defenders

HISAs for Teaching Backup

Two versions of Run the Gauntlet provide quick backup lessons. In *One-Layer-Two*, the defenders begin side by side in a single layer (Scene 12-8). They work together to keep a lone dribbler from getting through. If one defender backs up the other, the dribbler has little chance.

What if the two defenders go for the ball at the same time? Step in with a Corrective COMO. Have one defender stop the ball while the other pro-

CHAPTER 12: PREVENTING GOALS

vides backup. One defender can yell, "I've got ball!" and the other can yell, "I'll back you up!"

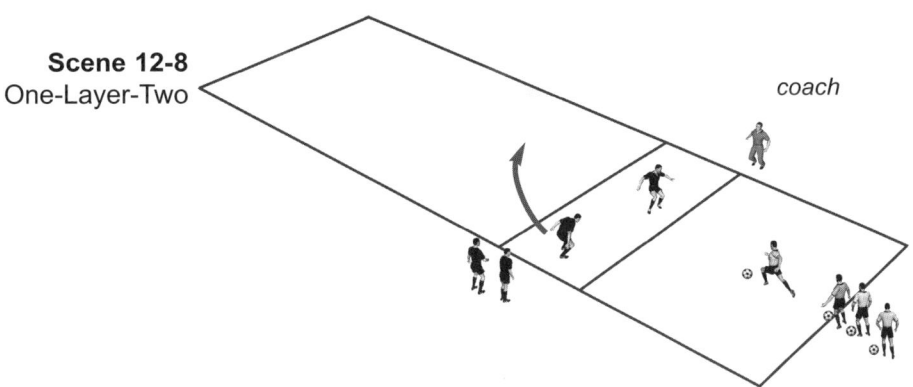

Scene 12-8
One-Layer-Two

Rules for One-Layer-Two

Course Setup The game takes place on a Gauntlet course, thirty paces long and fifteen paces wide. Only one defensive zone is required.

Starting Positions Four to eight players participate, in teams of two. One team begin inside the defensive zone, the players side by side. Another defending team may wait to the side. The other players, each with a ball, form a line at the end of the course.

Object of the Game One dribbler tries to get past two defenders, eliminating them from contention. The last team remaining wins.

How a Try Proceeds The first dribbler begins dribbling forward. The defenders may then move wherever they want to. They may approach the ball, backpedal, or back each other up. The try ends if the ball is stolen or knocked off the course. If the dribbler gets through the course, the defending team is eliminated from contention.

How the Game Proceeds After the first try, the defenders become dribblers, and a new defending team steps in. Teams that have been eliminated continue trying to eliminate others, but may no longer win. The game continues until all but one team has been eliminated, or until the time expires.

The second version is called *Distant Layers*. The defenders begin in two layers, but the layers are too far apart (Scene 12-9). If the problem isn't fixed, the dribbler might get through. The first defender slows the play down, by backpedaling. The second defender moves closer, yelling, "Contain that! I'm behind you! Challenge!"

PART II: TEACHING SOCCER'S PARTS

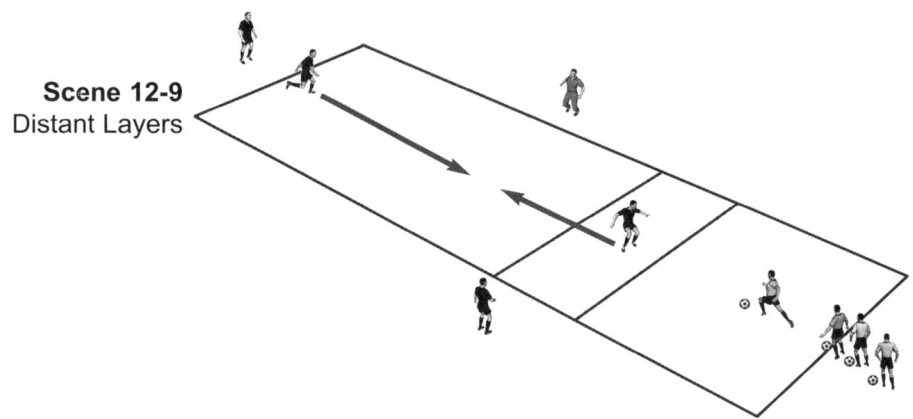

Scene 12-9
Distant Layers

Rules for Distant Layers

Course Setup The game takes place on a Gauntlet course. The course requires only one defensive zone.

Starting Positions The players pair off into teams. One team begins on defense. A defender is in the first defensive zone, and another is twenty-five paces away at the far end of the course. A second defending team awaits the next turn. The other players begin as dribblers.

Object of the Game A dribbler attempts to get through the course safely, by defeating two defenders. A team that allows a dribbler through is eliminated. The last remaining team wins.

How a Try Proceeds As the first dribbler enters the course, the two defenders may alter their positioning. One defender will usually stall until the other gets closer, but this is not required. The try ends if the ball is stolen or knocked off the course.

How the Game Proceeds After the first try, the defending players both become dribblers as the second team defends. Defending teams that allow a dribbler through can no longer win, but continue trying to eliminate other teams. The game continues for six minutes, or until all but one team has been eliminated.

You won't need these two HISAs regularly. After a few games, your players will get the point and never lose it. Backup prevents goals.

After a few games, your players will get the point and never lose it.

CHAPTER 12: PREVENTING GOALS

Three Make a Triangle

Three defenders between the ball and goal should think *triangle*. Three defenders in a triangle can prevent four or more opponents from scoring—if the triangle *points toward the ball* (Scene 12-10).

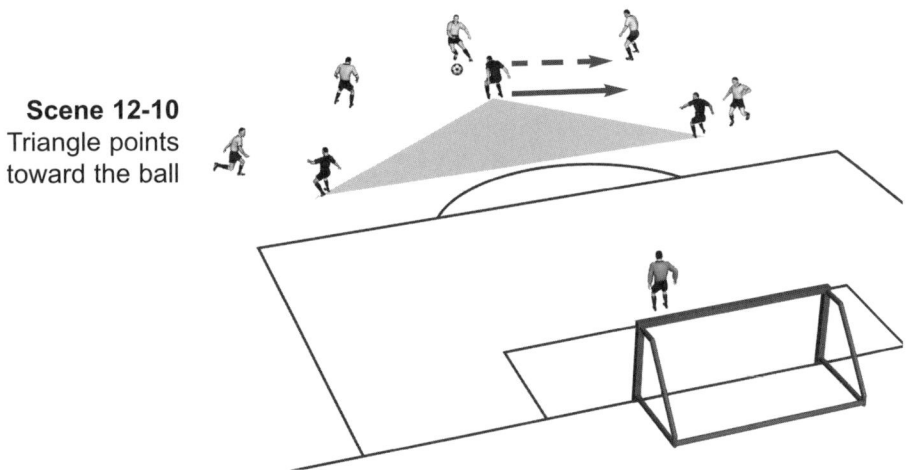

Scene 12-10
Triangle points toward the ball

Here's how the triangle works. One defender, the triangle's point, stays on the line between the ball and the goal. As the ball moves from one side to the other, so moves that defender. Two defenders create the triangle's base, providing a second layer in case the ball gets past the point. Those two also cover the field's width, should the ball be passed to one side or the other.

A defensive triangle needs the correct shape. Poorly shaped triangles come in four varieties, and each spells trouble.

> **Poorly shaped triangles come in four varieties, and each spells trouble.**

Triangle Too Flat

If the defenders in the base move too far forward, or spread too wide, the triangle will be too flat (Scene 12-11). Now, the base can't back up the point. The defender with the ball has only one defender to beat.

Scene 12-11
Triangle too flat

Triangle Too Steep

If the defenders in the base move too close together, the triangle will be too steep (Scene 12-12). The base is backing up the point, but isn't helping with the field's width. A pass to either side will cause trouble.

Scene 12-12
Triangle too steep

Base of Triangle Uneven

Usually, the defenders in the base should be the same distance from their own goal line. If one sags back further than the other, the base of the triangle will be uneven—a problem because of the offside rule (Scene 12-13). In the picture, the uneven base has allowed an opponent to move forward without being in an offside position.

CHAPTER 12: PREVENTING GOALS

Scene 12-13
Base of triangle uneven

opponent not in offside position

Triangle Pointing Away

If one defender sags behind two others, the triangle will point *away* from the ball (Scene 12-14). Such triangles have three serious flaws:

- An opponent can dribble right through the middle, with only the rear defender to beat.
- If the rear defender is beaten, the other two defenders can't back up the play.
- There's only one defender in the rear to cover the field's width. If that defender is drawn to one side, the other side might be wide open.

Scene 12-14
Triangle pointing away from ball

Defensive setups that use a Sweeper—one defender backing up the others—suffer from these three flaws. Sweeper-bashing will resume in Chapter 14.

PART II: TEACHING SOCCER'S PARTS

A Thoughtscrim for Triangles

How might you teach the power of a triangle? A Thoughtscrim called *Triangulation* makes the required points. The defending team must always have a triangle in place (Scene 12-15).

Scene 12-15
Triangulation Thoughtscrim

Rules for Triangulation

Field Setup and Teams The scrimmage field requires a halfway line so that offside calls can be made. Each team has either three or five players. Four-player teams are not recommended, because the natural shape is a square or diamond. Keepers are optional.

The Triangle Rule The team with the ball has no special conditions imposed, and may play as it pleases. The defending team must either have a triangle in place or be in the process of setting up one. The triangle must point toward the ball. When such a triangle isn't present, the coach begins counting out loud to three. If the triangle isn't in place by the count of three, the other team receives a penalty kick.

Trading Positions Players may trade off positions within the triangle. One player may be the point for a while, and then switch to the base. Players must communicate about such trades, however.

Before Triangulation, conduct a triangle walk through. In particular, show how the point of the triangle swings from side to side as opponents pass the ball. To perform this duty, the point defender must visualize a large box within the field, and stay inside it. If the defender wanders from the box, the triangle will soon break down (Scene 12-16).

CHAPTER 12: PREVENTING GOALS

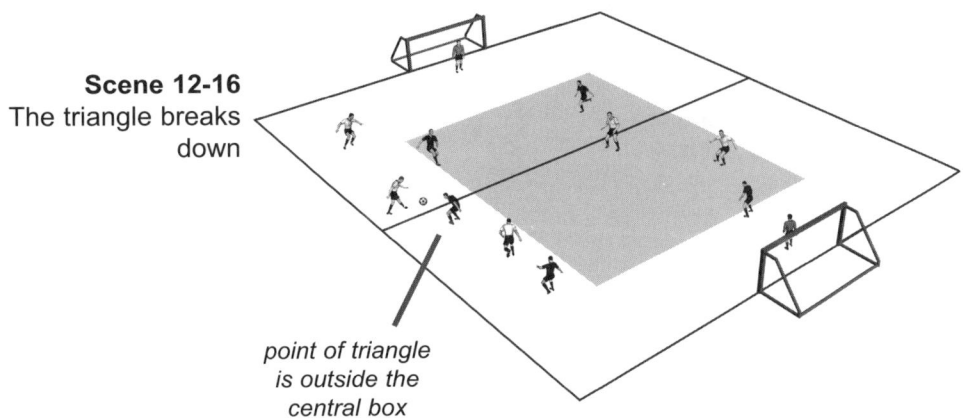

Scene 12-16
The triangle breaks down

point of triangle is outside the central box

During Triangulation, many triangle-related COMOs will arise. Corrective COMOs can be used when:

- The point defender covers one opponent, and forgets to swing from side to side
- The point defender wanders from the central box, and can't swing from side to side
- The base of the triangle becomes flat, steep, or uneven

Spot the problem, freeze the action, and walk through a solution.

Four Defenders and Beyond

The risk of a goal decreases once four, five, or six defenders get back. Those defenders must create several layers, though. The six defenders in Scene 12-17 are in one layer, which isn't much help. They're all beaten with one pass.

PART II: TEACHING SOCCER'S PARTS

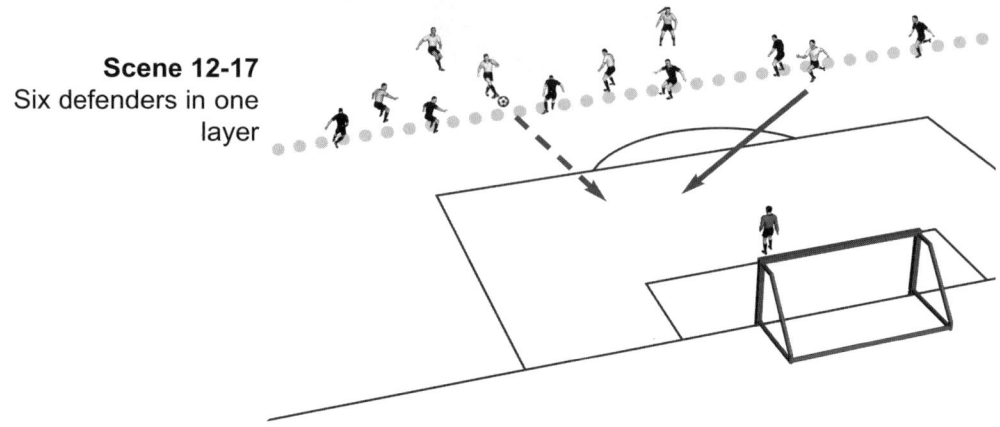

Scene 12-17
Six defenders in one layer

Scene 12-18 shows a safer positioning of six defenders—in four different layers. The layers are the right distance apart. Opponents won't be scoring anytime soon.

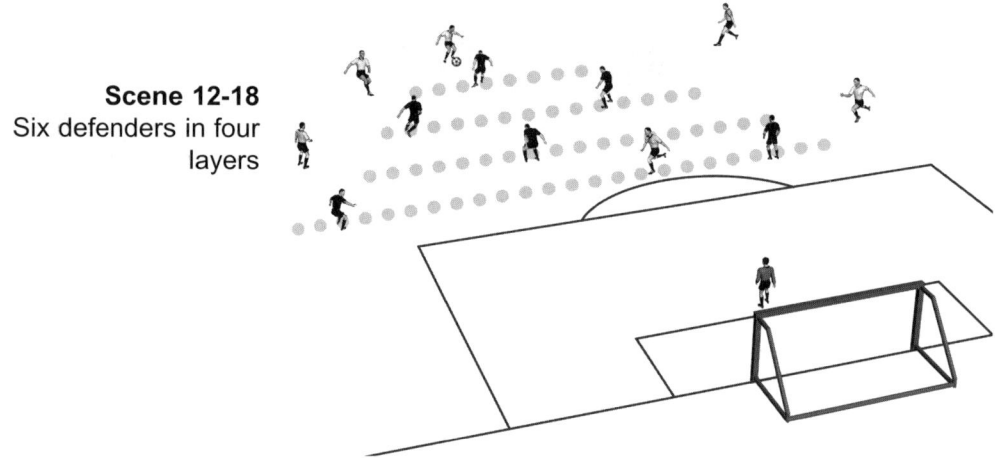

Scene 12-18
Six defenders in four layers

Layers, the Main Suspect

Most goals can be prevented by setting up multiple layers. When your team gives up a goal, don't assume someone made a skill mistake. Look closely, and you'll usually find a layer mistake.

As your team defends, ask these questions. Is there backup? Is a triangle pointing toward the ball? Are there a few layers for the ball to get past? If an answer is no, your team is about to lose a blinkie.

13

WINNING BACK THE BALL

Revenge of the Scrappies

The other long-necked scrappies were devastated by their comrade's demise in the previous chapter. They vowed revenge, and planned an attack in greater numbers against the three-layered wall and the blinkies inside it.

PART II: TEACHING SOCCER'S PARTS

Here was their plan. One scrappie would poke through the first wall, and retreat when the guards rushed there. Another would poke through at a different spot, and retreat. The guards would be confused. The other scrappies would break through three walls and steal the blinkies.

On their way to the village, the scrappies stopped for a cookout. As they sang around the campfire, villagers suddenly rushed from the woods. Taken by surprise, the scrappies got their necks trampled. Back at the village, the blinkies slumbered peacefully — without a single guard.

The scrappies had a great plan, but so did the villagers. Instead of hanging back at the village, they went after the scrappies aggressively. The blinkies were unprotected, but the scrappies had more immediate concerns.

That's how defending works in soccer. If your players always hang back in zones, look out. Opponents can overload the zones and pass right through them—the problem in Scene 13-1. Opponents will keep the ball and create scoring threats as well.

Scene 13-1
Overloading a zone

By playing man-to-man, and going after the ball aggressively, your team can win the ball before trouble materializes. Your goal might be less well protected, but the other team probably won't notice. That's the point of the Pressure Part.

136

CHAPTER 13: WINNING BACK THE BALL

Ripe for Pressure

To pressure the ball effectively, your team must get enough players near the ball. The black team in Scene 13-2 can't apply pressure yet, because it has only one player near the ball.

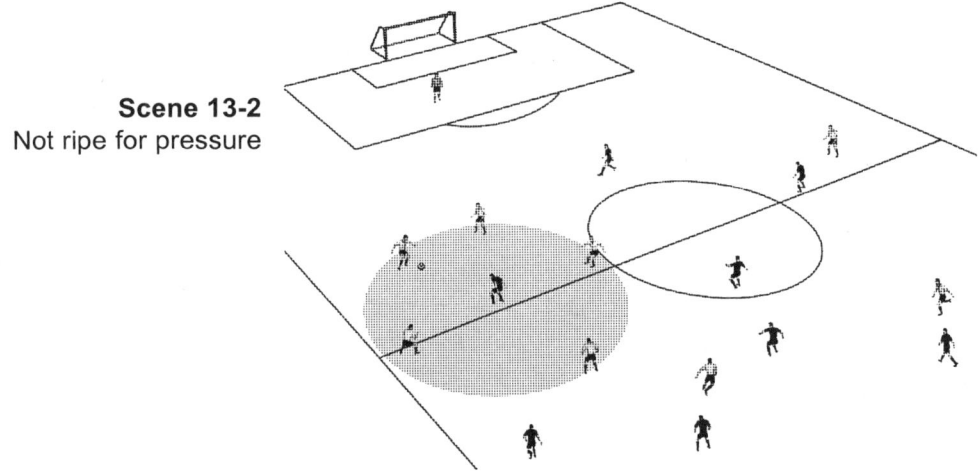

Scene 13-2
Not ripe for pressure

The situation in Scene 13-3 is ripe for applying pressure. A few of the black players have moved further from their goal and closer to the ball. There are as many black players near the ball as white players.

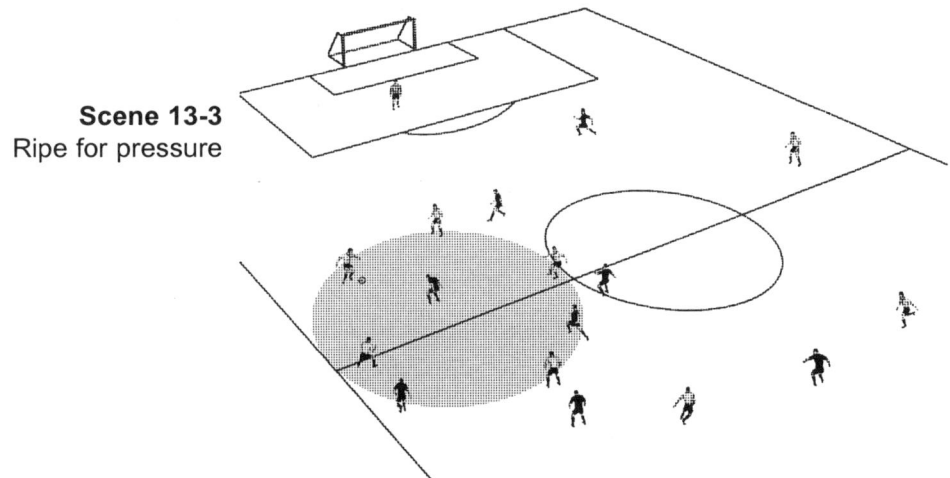

Scene 13-3
Ripe for pressure

Scene 13-4 shows effective pressure in action. One defender has closed in on the ball, and a second is about to join in. Every opponent near the ball is covered, so short passes will be difficult. Even the Keeper is covered. The white team will soon lose the ball.

PART II: TEACHING SOCCER'S PARTS

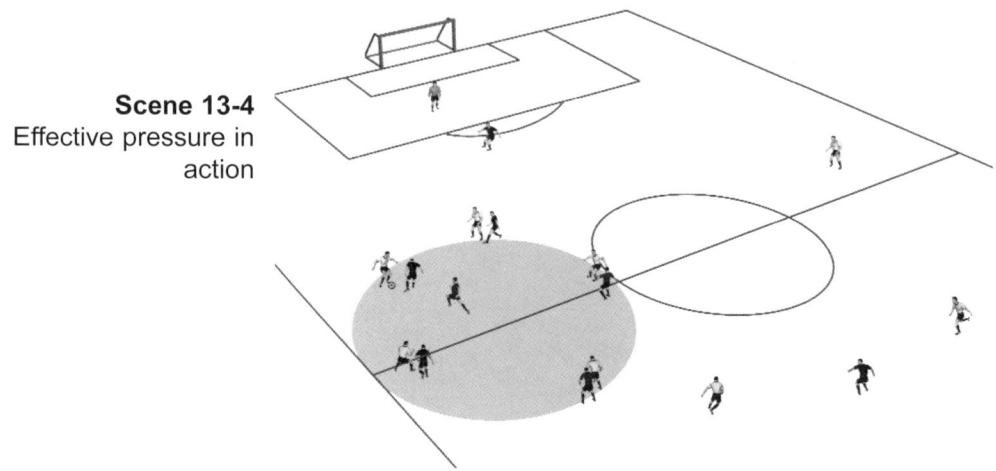

Scene 13-4
Effective pressure in action

The situation further from the ball might look risky. Only one defender is watching over three opponents. But since the ball is under pressure, it probably won't reach those opponents.

When your team uses pressure effectively, three good things happen:

- Opponents have trouble keeping the ball.
- Opponents are so worried about keeping the ball that they can't mount scoring threats.
- Your players win the ball closer to the other team's goal.

Teaching Pressure

If that's what pressure looks like, how can you teach it? Special rules, as always, provide the method. In a Thoughtscrim called *Pressure Cooker*, the defending team must pressure the ball man-to-man.

Rules for Pressure Cooker

Field Setup The field requires touch lines and goal lines. Use of the offside rule is optional. If the offside rule is used, a halfway line is also required.

Teams Teams consist of three or more field players. Keepers are optional.

The Pressure Rule The team with the ball has no conditions imposed, and may play as it pleases. The defending team must at all times use man-to-man defense, and pressure the ball. At least one defender must close in on the ball, while other defenders cover opponents near the ball. If no defenders are within three steps of the ball, the coach begins counting out loud. If the count of three is reached, and there are still no defenders near the ball, the attacking team is awarded a penalty kick.

CHAPTER 13: WINNING BACK THE BALL

If defenders continue hanging back in zones, freeze the action and walk through the correct use of pressure. Move one defender up to the ball, and put other defenders on opponents close to the ball—even if distant opponents are uncovered (Scene 13-5). When you shout, "Play on!" a turnover will occur quickly, and your players will get the point.

Scene 13-5
Pressure Cooker, with repositioned players

Pressure Cooker teaches the advantages of pressure, but also the risks. Now and then, those uncovered opponents will score.

From Layers to Pressure

Your team knows how to set up layers, and how to pressure the ball. What's next? Shifting between the two! One moment, your defenders are covering zones. Suddenly, they're scrambling after the ball, with man-to-man pressure. The Thoughtscrim for teaching these shifts is *Plan-to-Plan*.

Rules for Plan-to-Plan

Field Setup The field requires touch lines and goal lines. Use of the offside rule is optional. If the offside rule is used, a halfway line is also required.

Teams Teams consist of three or more field players. Keepers are again optional.

The Zone/Man-to-Man Rule The team with the ball has no conditions imposed, and may play as it pleases. The defending team must switch back and forth between zone defense and man-to-man. It may begin with zone and switch to man-to-man, or vice versa. The switch must be executed by all the defenders, and be clear to the coach. The attacking team earns a penalty kick by completing eight passes before the defending team switches defenses.

Usually, the defending team will start out with zone defense (Scene 13-6). Layers and triangles are a great way to conserve energy and prevent goals.

PART II: TEACHING SOCCER'S PARTS

Usually, the defending team will start out with zone defense (Scene 13-6). Layers and triangles are a great way to conserve energy and prevent goals.

Scene 13-6
From zone . . .

Once enough defenders are around the ball, one can yell, "Pressure!" Defenders then play man-to-man, closing in on the ball and nearby opponents, until a turnover is forced (Scene 13-7).

Scene 13-7
. . . to man-to-man

In your first game of Plan to Plan, decide the sequence yourself. When you shout "Zone!," the defending team must use zone. When you shout "Pressure!," man-to-man is required. After a while, let players read the situation, communicate, and decide for themselves.

Learn Both Approaches

Most soccer teams take an either/or approach to defending. Either they play a strict man-to-man and allow unnecessary goals. Or they play a

CHAPTER 13: WINNING BACK THE BALL

strict zone and have trouble winning the ball back. If your players learn both approaches, they'll pick the best one for the situation. Don't let those long-necked scrappies attack your goal at their leisure. Keep them guessing!

14

DEFENDING WITH A SYSTEM

Penny Goes to Work

Penny entered Oodles of Poodles for her first day of work. After graduating from the poodle hair styling academy, she had finally found a job. Soon, she'd be cutting the hair of her fellow poodles.

PART II: TEACHING SOCCER'S PARTS

When the shampoo pooch dumped hair clippings on the floor, Penny began to have doubts about the shop. She also noticed an unusual sign in the window: "No Tips, No Clips." And the shop manager informed her that hair must be cut and *then* shampooed. What a strange place!

Business was slow, but Penny finally had her first customer. She hacked through the poodle's hair as best she could, and sent him back for a shampoo. He soon returned, and Penny held up her mirror for the final okay.

The butchered beast howled, and the manager came running. Penny was fired on the spot, despite her protests. From the shop door, a Help Wanted sign again hangs upside down.

Clippings on the floor? Enforced tipping? Haircuts before shampoos? No wonder the shop was always hiring. It had serious system problems.

System problems might also be to blame for those 7-0 losses you've endured. Poorly positioned players? Confusing responsibilities? Not enough layers? You need a thoughtful defensive system.

A thoughtful system puts players where they're needed most. The responsibilities fit together like the parts of a machine. When one part of the machine breaks down, another kicks in.

There's no such thing as a perfect defensive system. Every system has weak spots. And you might use different systems on different days, depending on your players, your opponents, and the match situation.

Not all defensive systems are created equal, though. Some have more weak spots than others. To choose wisely between systems, you must understand the qualities a system should have.

Imagine the Possibilities

A defensive system begins with who plays where, but includes more. Three numbers spell out how many players are in each position. The first number is for Fullbacks, the second for Halfbacks, and the third for Forwards. In Scene 14-1, a 4-4-2 is to the left, and a 3-5-2 to the right.

CHAPTER 14: DEFENDING WITH A SYSTEM

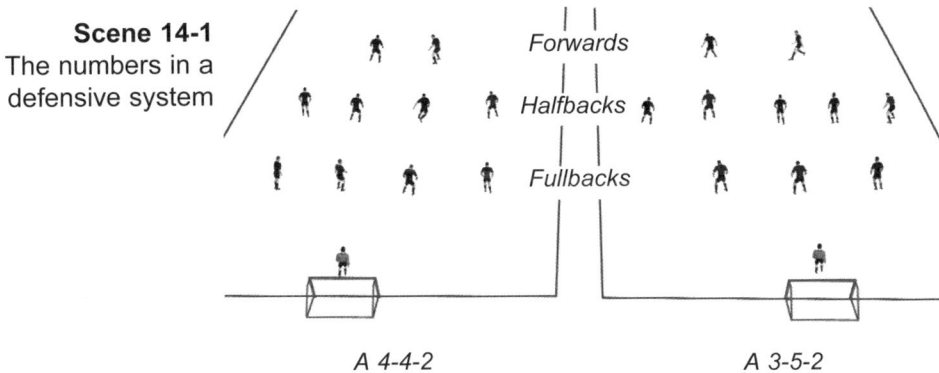

Scene 14-1
The numbers in a defensive system

A 4-4-2   A 3-5-2

Not every 4-4-2 or 3-5-2 is the same, though. As the 4-4-2's below show, players in each position can be *staggered* differently, producing different systems (Scene 14-2). To the left, the four Fullbacks are staggered, with one (a Sweeper) positioned behind the other three. (You could call the system a 1-3-4-2, but most soccer people don't.) To the right, the Fullbacks are lined straight across the field (a Flat Back Four) while the Halfbacks are staggered.

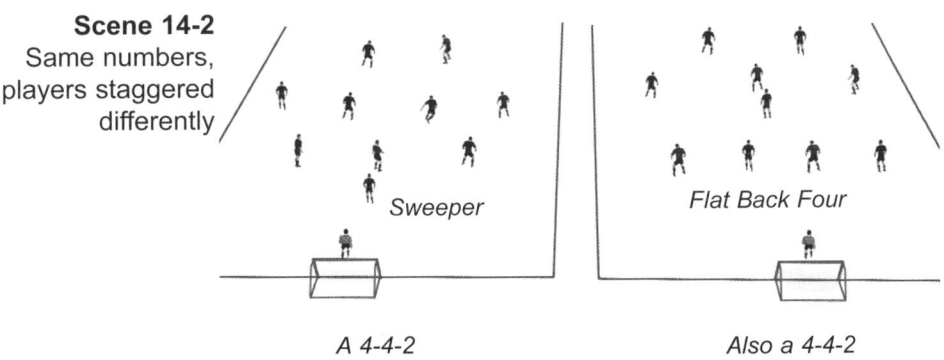

Scene 14-2
Same numbers, players staggered differently

A 4-4-2   Also a 4-4-2

Here's one more variable to consider. Two systems might stagger players the same way, but assign entirely different *responsibilities*. The 4-4-2's below look the same, because each has a Sweeper behind three Fullbacks (Scene 14-3). But to the left, the Fullbacks are covering zones. To the right, they're covering specific opponents and would be called *Marking Backs*.

PART II: TEACHING SOCCER'S PARTS

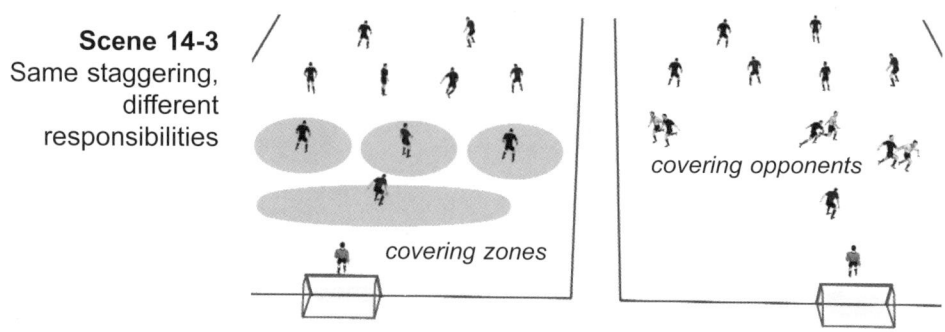

Scene 14-3
Same staggering, different responsibilities

covering opponents

covering zones

Don't Neglect the Middle

Your defensive system should place enough players in the middle areas of the field. Middle players are always close to the action, while players near the edge get left out now and then. Middle players can more easily shift between offense and defense. And they can protect your goal from two serious threats: the dribble up the middle, and the shot from the middle.

> **Middle players are always close to the action, while players near the edge get left out now and then.**

You might want to rule out the 3-3-4 in Scene 14-4. Only the Center Halfback is positioned in the middle. The other Halfbacks are spread wide, and the Center Fullback is sagging back. The Center Halfback has too much to do and too little help.

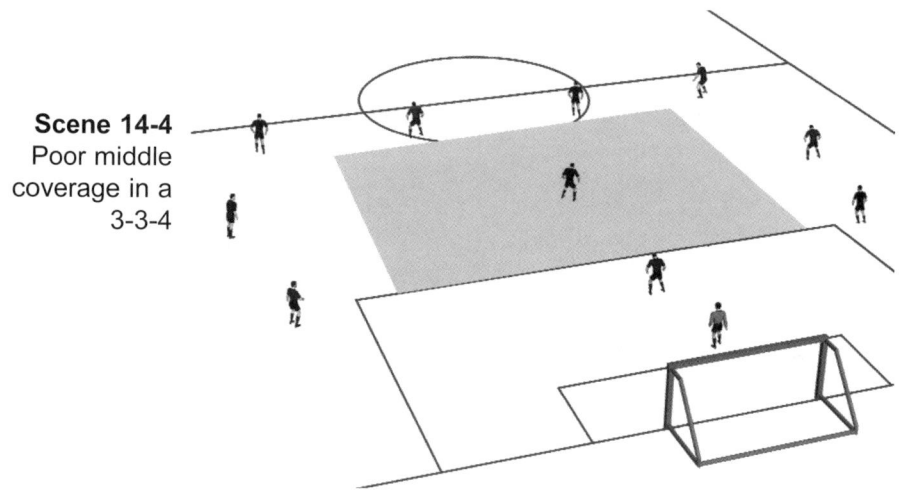

Scene 14-4
Poor middle coverage in a 3-3-4

CHAPTER 14: DEFENDING WITH A SYSTEM

Reconsider That Sweeper

Many coaches believe a defensive system *must* have a Sweeper—that defender behind the other Fullbacks. But a defensive system should allow an effective triangle in the back. The triangle created by a Sweeper tends to point in the wrong direction (Scene 14-5)!

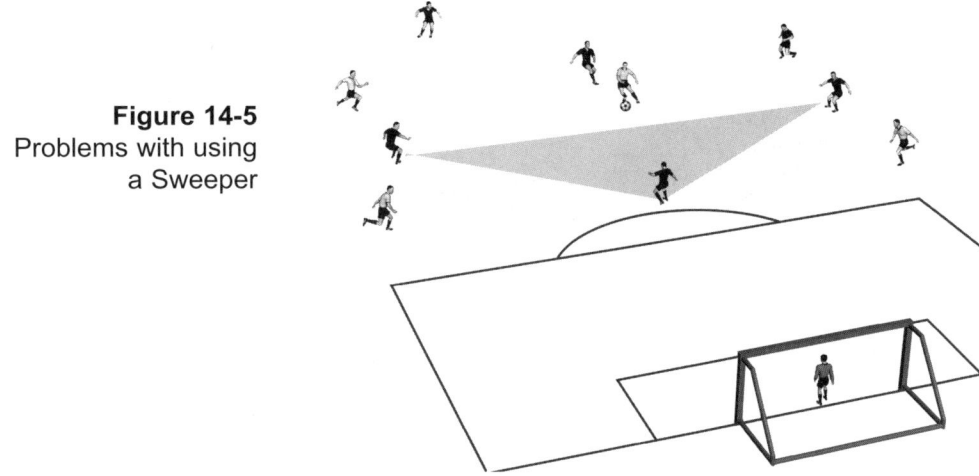

Figure 14-5
Problems with using a Sweeper

A triangle like that creates three problems:

- Opponents dribbling through the middle have only the Sweeper to beat. The other Fullbacks are too far forward to provide backup.

- Opponents can move behind the other Fullbacks without being in an offside position, since the Sweeper determines the offside line.

- Only the Sweeper is covering the width of the field in the back. If the Sweeper is pulled to one side, the other side is unguarded.

Such problems can be overcome if your players know how, or if your Sweeper is outstanding. But if a Sweeper makes more problems than it solves, why use one? Maybe you can find a better spot for that player.

> **But if a Sweeper makes more problems than it solves, why use one?**

The Problem With Marking Backs

What about a defensive system with Marking Backs and a Sweeper? The Marking Backs cover specific opponents—Forwards, usually—until the ball is regained. The Sweeper provides backup. Sounds reasonable, but here are two problems.

PART II: TEACHING SOCCER'S PARTS

First, opponents can create open spaces too easily. Forwards aren't required to stay in set positions. If a Forward cuts to the other side of the field, and your Marking Back follows, an open space has been created (Scene 14-6). The same is true if a Forward swaps locations with a Halfback.

Scene 14-6
Marking Backs allowing open space

Second, keeping possession is a challenge. Since your Marking Backs follow opponents all over the field, they won't be in the best spots once your team has the ball (Scene 14-7). And before they reach the best spots, your team might lose the ball again. Run to your opponent, run to your best spot, run to your opponent—is all that running really necessary?

Scene 14-7
Defenders in poor spots for keeping possession

Think Twice About a Flat Back Line

Your defensive system should set up layers between the ball and the goal. That can be tricky with Flat Back systems, where the Fullbacks are aligned

CHAPTER 14: DEFENDING WITH A SYSTEM

flat across the field. The Flat Back Four is the most popular variation, with the Flat Back Three a distant second.

In the Flat Back Four below (Scene 14-8), the Sweeper and its related problems are gone. The space behind the Fullbacks is off limits because of the offside rule. Four Fullbacks can easily cover the field's width. And players are well situated for keeping possession. Now for the problems.

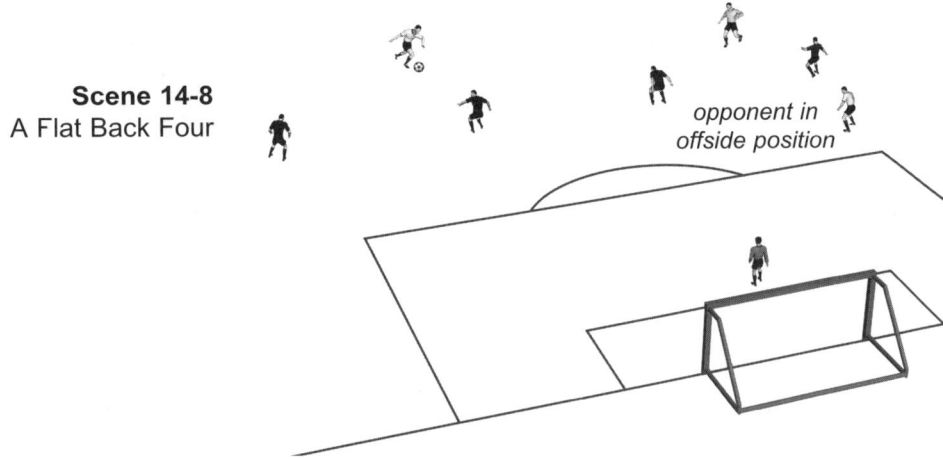

Scene 14-8
A Flat Back Four

opponent in offside position

First, the offside line can easily get out of sync. If one of the four Fullbacks sags too far behind the others, a goal might be allowed.

Second, there's only one layer of defenders. Defenders along a flat line have trouble backing each other up. A nice pass or dribbling move can beat all four at the same time (Scene 14-9).

Scene 14-9
One layer to beat in Flat Back Four

Fortunately, Flat Back is just a name and not a rigid requirement. One Fullback can step forward to the ball, while others prepare for backup duty.

PART II: TEACHING SOCCER'S PARTS

As Scene 14-10 shows, a triangle is even possible. In this 4-4-2, one of the Halfbacks is a defensive Halfback in front of the Fullbacks. That player can swing from side to side, like the point of a triangle, as the two Center Fullbacks provide the base.

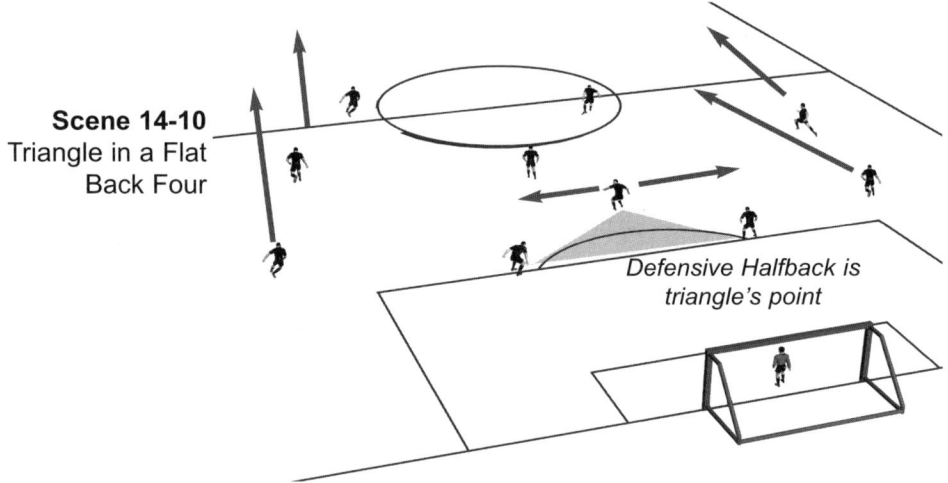

Scene 14-10
Triangle in a Flat Back Four

Defensive Halfback is triangle's point

This picture shows another advantage of a Flat Back Four. When the Outside Fullbacks and Outside Fullbacks push forward, eight players can join in the attack—a 2-4-4, in effect!

The Unique, Logical Triangle Three

So far, we've mentioned six qualities a defensive system should have:

- Players in the middle areas
- A triangle in the back
- Width coverage in the back
- An easy-to-move offside line
- Players well situated for keeping possession
- Players free to join in the attack

The Triangle Three is a Thoughtful Soccer favorite because it has all these qualities. The system is named after the three Fullbacks, who aim a triangle at the ball. The basic setup is a 3-5-2 (Scene 14-11). Two of the Halfbacks are staggered behind the other three. Each position has responsibilities attached.

CHAPTER 14: DEFENDING WITH A SYSTEM

Scene 14-11
Triangle Three
defensive system

The Fullbacks

The Left Fullback and Right Fullback sag behind the Center Fullback, creating the triangle. The base of the triangle should usually be even. In other words, the Left and Right Fullbacks should be at the same level, forming a two-player offside line. A two-player line is easily pulled up and back. Two players can also handle the field's width.

The triangle shifts with the location of the ball (Scene 14-12). The Middle Fullback is usually the point, swinging from side to side as the ball is passed, and the Outside Fullbacks are usually the base. These players may swap roles at times, but doing so invites confusion. The system works best when the Middle Fullback is the point . . . with one exception.

Scene 14-12
The shifting triangle

In the triangle to the lower left, an Outside Fullback is confronting the ball near a corner. The Middle Fullback keeps focusing on the ball, though. If the opponent dribbles back toward the middle, the Middle Fullback must prevent a shot.

PART II: TEACHING SOCCER'S PARTS

The Left and Right Fullbacks mustn't be too far apart. If one is beaten, the other must cut across and break up the play (Scene 14-13). This maneuver allows the Left and Right Fullbacks to back each other up. Unlike a Sweeper system, there are always two layers to beat.

Scene 14-13
Cutting across to break up the play

The Outside Halfbacks

Let's follow the above example a few seconds into the future. The Right Fullback has cut across to the left. Won't the right side be wide open? Right *Halfback* to the rescue! (Scene 14-14).

When the ball is on one side, the Halfback on the opposite side must cover the *back door*, that dangerous area near the far post. Since the ball is on the left side, the Right Halfback has back-door duty. An opponent has run there, hoping for a crossing pass. Only the back-door defender can prevent an easy goal.

Scene 14-14
Covering the back door

CHAPTER 14: DEFENDING WITH A SYSTEM

Outside Halfback has strict job requirements: speed, fitness, and a sense of responsibility. Lazy players who only want to score need not apply.

The Defensive Halfbacks (Stoppers)
The two Halfbacks to the rear are nicknamed *Stoppers*. That name is a good reminder of the position's responsibilities: stopping the ball, and stopping up holes.

Stopping the ball is priority number one. The Stoppers must never allow an open shot from the middle, and never allow a dribble through the middle. Much like the Center Fullback, they swing from side to side as the ball is passed, rather than latching onto specific opponents.

Priority number two is stopping up holes. If a Halfback can't get back, a Stopper can jump into the open space (Scene 14-15). In fact, a Stopper can transform into any missing player, and take over that player's duties.

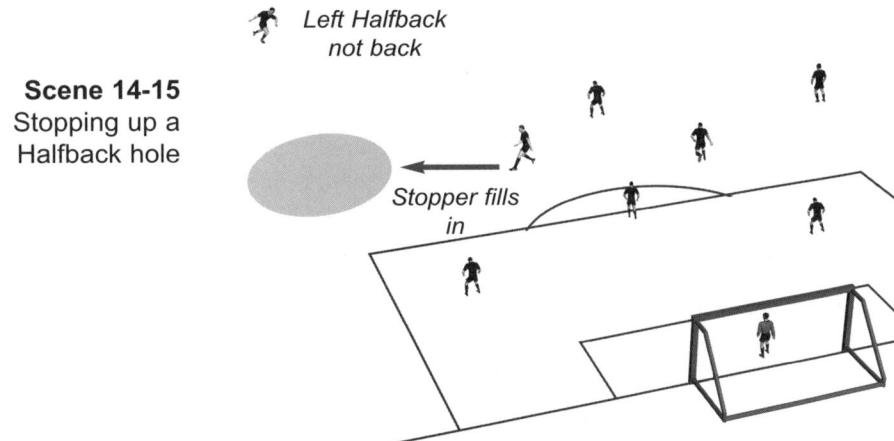

Scene 14-15
Stopping up a Halfback hole

The Center Halfback
The Center Halfback is another player who gravitates toward the ball rather than covering a specific opponent. Four players now control the middle in this way: a Center Halfback, two Stoppers, and a Center Fullback. The middle won't be a breeding ground for scoring threats.

The Forwards
The Forwards add the finishing touches to this defensive system. When they set up the first layer between the ball and goal, the other team probably won't score. The Forwards can also look for chances to pressure the ball, and win it near the other team's goal.

PART II: TEACHING SOCCER'S PARTS

Keeping Possession

The Triangle Three is great for keeping possession. Scene 14-16 shows a typical possession moment. The Right Fullback has the ball. The middle players provide passing targets. The Left Fullback is in great position for a drop pass. And on the other side waits the Left Halfback. Time for a drop-and-switch maneuver!

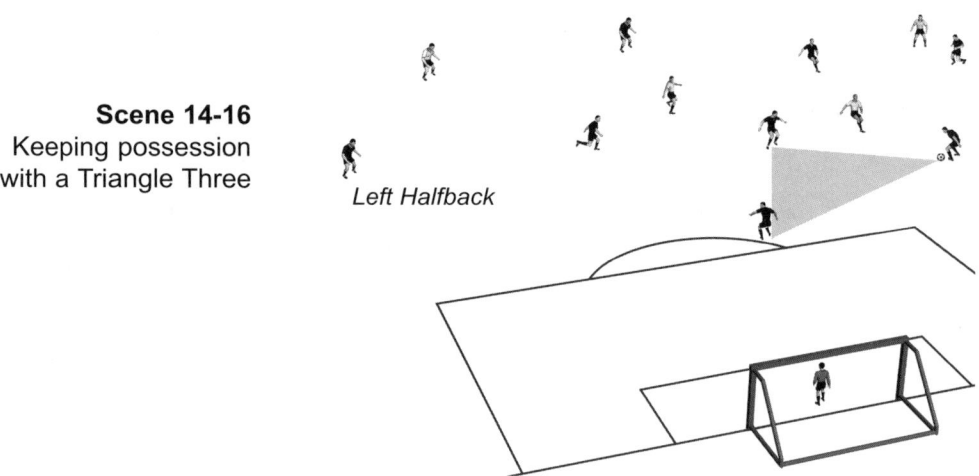

Scene 14-16
Keeping possession with a Triangle Three

Triangle Three Variations

Once you've got a system, devise a few variations as well. Then, you can choose the best variation for each situation. Triangle Three variations keep the triangle, but relocate a player or two.

3-5-2 With One Stopper

Of the five Halfbacks, only one is a Stopper (Scene 14-17). The attack is a little stronger, but the Stopper has many holes to fill.

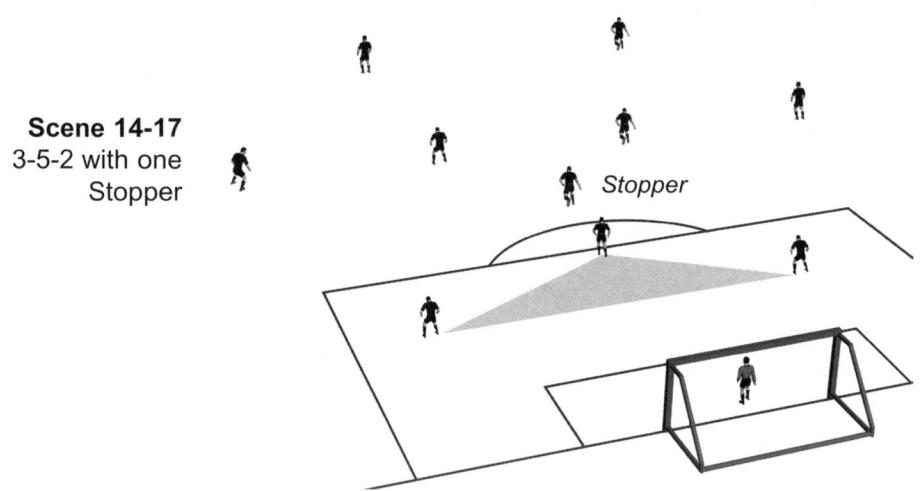

Scene 14-17
3-5-2 with one Stopper

CHAPTER 14: DEFENDING WITH A SYSTEM

3-4-3 With One Stopper
Moving three players to Forward can create a stronger attack. Three Forwards can also pressure the ball well in the other team's end. Although fewer middle players are left, the risk is acceptable if you're playing a weaker team or losing the match.

3-4-2 With Shadow
Does the other team have a superstar who always scores three goals and beats your team? You need the *3-4-2 With Shadow*. The numbers add up to nine, because the tenth field player is the Shadow (Scene 14-18).

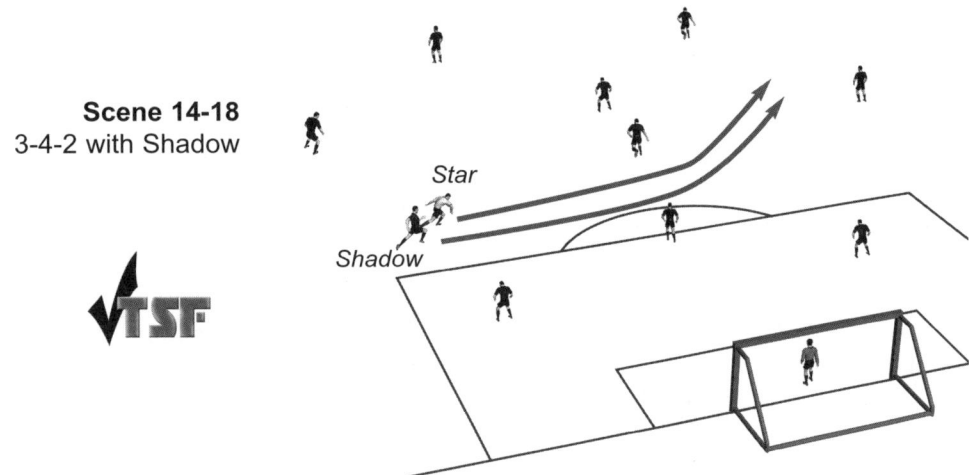

Scene 14-18
3-4-2 with Shadow

The Shadow covers the star all over the field, even when your team has the ball. What's the point? The star works hard just to touch the ball, and tires quickly. And when the star finally gets the ball, at least two layers are in the way—the Shadow, plus the defender of a particular zone. A star without open space is just a night light!

What if the star runs behind the other Fullbacks? If the Shadow were to follow, the offside line would be ruined and only one player would be guarding the star. The Shadow should stay level with the deepest Fullback, forcing the star to come back onside.

Don't put your best player on the star. Any fit, responsible player will do, since that player will always have help. You'll think the star and one of your weaker players were both thrown out of the match—not a bad deal!

Systems for Smaller Numbers

If you coach indoor soccer, or work with younger players, you'll need a system for smaller numbers. The qualities for eleven-a-side systems also apply to smaller numbers.

PART II: TEACHING SOCCER'S PARTS

When five players are out in the field, here are some possibilities. The first number, as always, refers to the Fullbacks.

- 2-3 and 3-2 are both very weak. Nobody is assigned to the middle.

- 1-3-1 and 1-2-2 are both weak. One player in the back can't cover the field's width.

- 2-2-1 is workable, if at least one Halfback controls the middle and stops the ball. But if both Halfbacks are wide, the middle is wide open.

- 2-1-2 is the Thoughtful Soccer favorite (Scene 14-19). The Halfback controls the middle, and provides the point of a triangle.

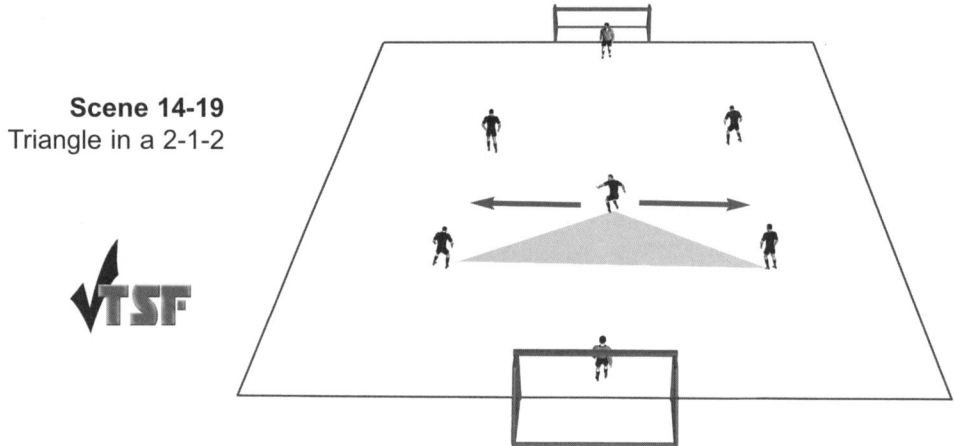

Scene 14-19
Triangle in a 2-1-2

What about six players in the field?

- Anything beginning with a 1 provides no width coverage in the back, and is weak.

- 2-2-2, also known as the spaghetti system, is long, thin, and weak. Only two of the six players are centrally located.

- 2-3-1 is the logical choice (Scene 14-20). It provides width coverage in the back, three central players, and a nice defensive triangle.

CHAPTER 14: DEFENDING WITH A SYSTEM

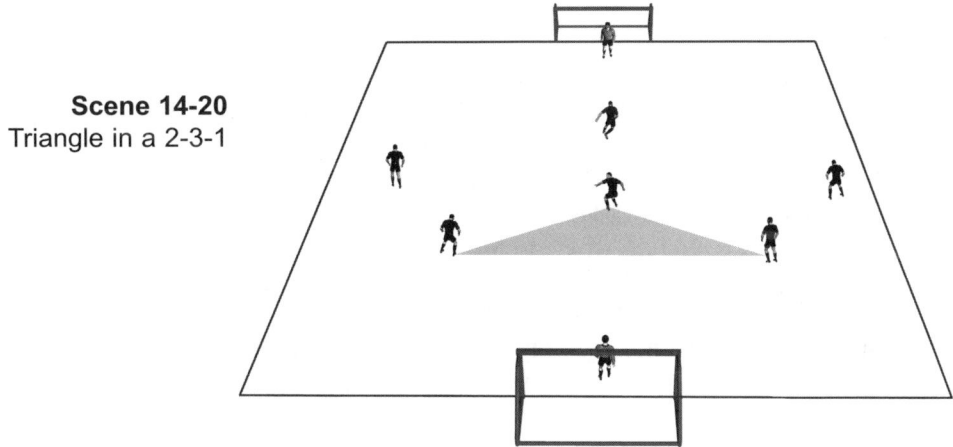

Scene 14-20
Triangle in a 2-3-1

Try applying the system qualities to some other player numbers: 3, 4 (very tricky!), 7, 8, and up.

Teaching Your System

Once you've got a defensive system in mind, how can you teach it to your players? Three steps are required. Walk through the positions and responsibilities. Test drive the system in a scrimmage. And freeze the scrimmage to get the system right.

For the walk through, add a few players at a time. Bring the Fullbacks out first, as the other players watch. With a soccer ball at your feet, move to different spots and have the Fullbacks react. Dribble slowly past one Fullback, and show how another Fullback should back the play up.

> **For the walk through, add a few players at a time.**

Next, add the Outside Halfbacks, and walk through the back-door idea. Bring on the Stoppers, and show how they close in on the ball and stop up holes. And so on. Your players will begin to see the logic.

Now take the system for a test drive. Set up a scrimmage where one team has an extra player or two, and the smaller team is usually on defense—9 v 7, for example. Watch how the smaller team uses the defensive system.

Soon, the system will break down somewhere. A shot from the middle will be allowed, the back door will be uncovered, or the triangle will fall apart. Freeze the action, correct the problem, and play on.

PART II: TEACHING SOCCER'S PARTS

Trust the Qualities

Don't be so sure about that system you grew up with, or that everyone else is using. It might have more problems than a poodle barbershop.

Place your trust in the qualities a system should have. Your system *must* put players in the middle. It *must* allow players to back each other up. Ignore such qualities at your own risk.

Once you understand the qualities, you can choose wisely between systems. Better yet, invent a system that other coaches don't understand!

15
THE FOUR-ROLES-IN-ONE KEEPER

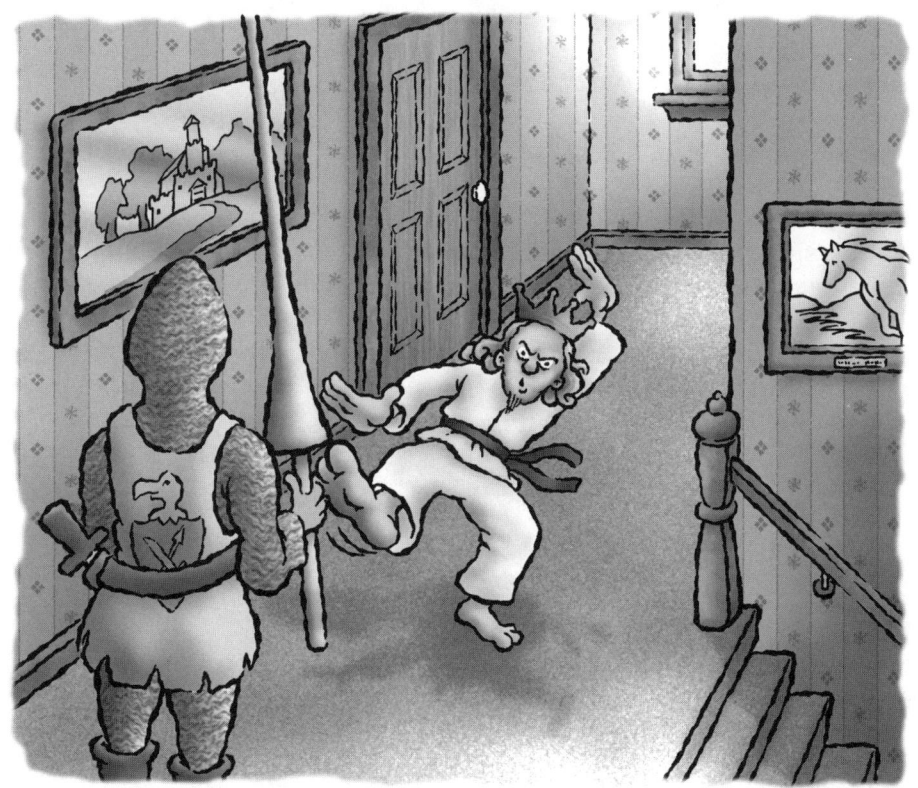

The Overprotective King

Alex knocked nervously on the king's front door. Many other knights had sought the hand of the princess, only to be thwarted by her overprotective father. Would Alex's courtship end in failure, too?

PART II: TEACHING SOCCER'S PARTS

The king opened the door. "I'm here to date your daughter," proclaimed Alex. "In keeping with the traditions of our land, I shall marry her if the date goes well."

"Not so fast," replied the king, in his scholar's cap. "To date the princess, you must first solve my tricky math problem." Being a math major, Alex solved the problem easily. He entered the door and walked down the hall. The king stood in the way, now dressed in a magician's outfit.

"Just one minute," said the king. "To date the princess, you must also figure out my brilliant magic trick." Alex pointed out the card up the king's sleeve, and climbed to the top of the stairs.

There stood the king again, dressed in his karate outfit. "Now," he announced, "I'm going to kick your butt!"

Nobody could date the princess without getting past the king's three roles: mathematician, magician, and karate expert. If one role failed, the king slipped into the next one. No wonder his daughter was single!

The Keeper position works the same way. To score, opponents must get past your Keeper's four roles: Possession Helper, System Organizer, Extra Fullback, and Savemaker. When one role fails, your Keeper can slip into the next one. When one role goes well, the next role won't be necessary.

When one role goes well, the next one won't be necessary.

Those new to soccer see only the Savemaker role. What do the other roles look like, and how can you develop them?

The Four Keeper Roles

The four Keeper roles follow each other in a logical way. Each role has its own secrets.

The Possession Helper Role
Possession Helper is the feature role when *your* team has the ball. Your Keeper helps by:

CHAPTER 15: THE FOUR-ROLES-IN-ONE KEEPER

- Coming out of the goal for a drop pass, rather than standing in one place
- Telling teammates where to pass the ball, rather than just watching
- Making smart outlet passes—throws, punts, and goal kicks—rather than sending every ball deep

In the logical sequence, Possession Helper comes first. While your team has possession, no other Keeper roles—and no saves—are needed.

> **While your team has possession, no other Keeper roles—and no saves—are needed.**

The System Organizer Role

Once your team loses the ball, System Organizer is the role of choice. Your Keeper spots weaknesses in the defensive system, and patches them up with a shout or two.

Your Keeper is in a great spot for organizing the defense. Are there two layers to get through? Is the defensive triangle in good shape? Is the back door covered? From behind the other players, your Keeper can tell.

The Extra Fullback Role

If System Organizer fails, Extra Fullback might be required. For this role, your Keeper should move as far from the goal as possible (Scene 15-1). From this advanced location, your Keeper can:

- Clear away balls that get through or over defenders
- Back up the defender who is on the ball
- Stop a breakaway as far from the goal as possible

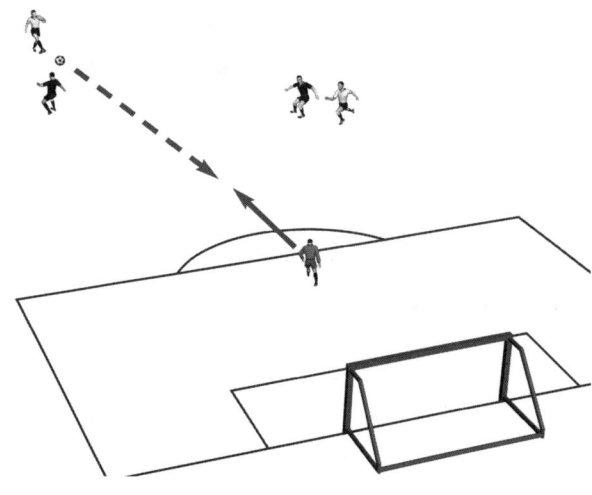

Scene 15-1
Ready for the Extra Fullback role

PART II: TEACHING SOCCER'S PARTS

The Savemaker Role

If the first three roles fail, your Keeper can finally make that brilliant save. Making saves, the skill side of playing Keeper, is obviously important. But the thoughtful Keeper avoids making saves—by passing, organizing, and charging out of the goal. Savemaker is a role of last resort!

Savemaker is a role of last resort!

Those are the four roles. How can you develop them?

Coaching Possession Helpers

Keepers learn the Possession Helper role through Thoughtscrims like Three-and-a-Drop and Reset. During these games, keep your Keepers out in the field a good part of the time. They'll become all-around soccer players, and learn the possession secrets more quickly

Halfway through, let your Keepers be Keepers again. Then, they can help with possession by receiving drop passes, making outlet passes, and communicating. Passing to the Keeper is critical for keeping possession, particularly in small-sided situations. The Keeper is almost always uncovered.

Passes to the Keeper will backfire at times, though. The pass might be stolen, or the Keeper might flub the ball away. Two groundrules will prevent such tragedies:

- When a pass to the Keeper would be risky, the Keeper must yell, "No Keeper!"
- When under any kind of pressure, the Keeper must pass or clear the ball with only one touch

In Scene 15-2, the ball has been passed to the Keeper, and opponents are too close for comfort. The ball might be stolen and deposited in the goal if the Keeper uses more than one touch. The Keeper therefore clears the ball with one touch.

You can teach the two ground rules during any scrimmage. When a Keeper fails to communicate, or uses the wrong number of touches, it's COMO time.

CHAPTER 15: THE FOUR-ROLES-IN-ONE KEEPER

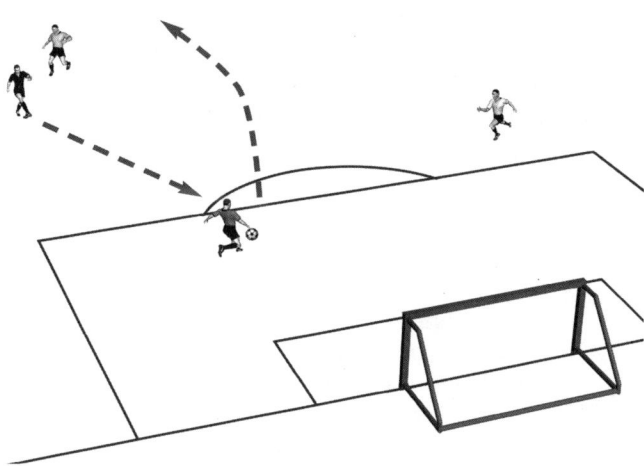

Scene 15-2
Keeper has time for only one touch

Outlet Passes

Keeper outlet passes—throws, punts, and goal kicks—are an important part of the Possession Helper role. If your Keeper sends every pass deep, possession will usually be lost. Here are some alternatives to the long boot. You can teach each one with a walk through, a scrimmage, and a COMO.

The Old Trusty Pass to a Corner

Who should your Keeper pass to in Scene 15-3? The Fullback in the middle is not a safe target. Opponents from every direction can converge there. Your team will lose the ball in the worst possible spot.

The Fullback in the corner, though, makes a very safe target. After receiving the ball, he might dribble thirty yards before an opponent comes near. And even if the ball is stolen, the corner provides a poor shooting angle.

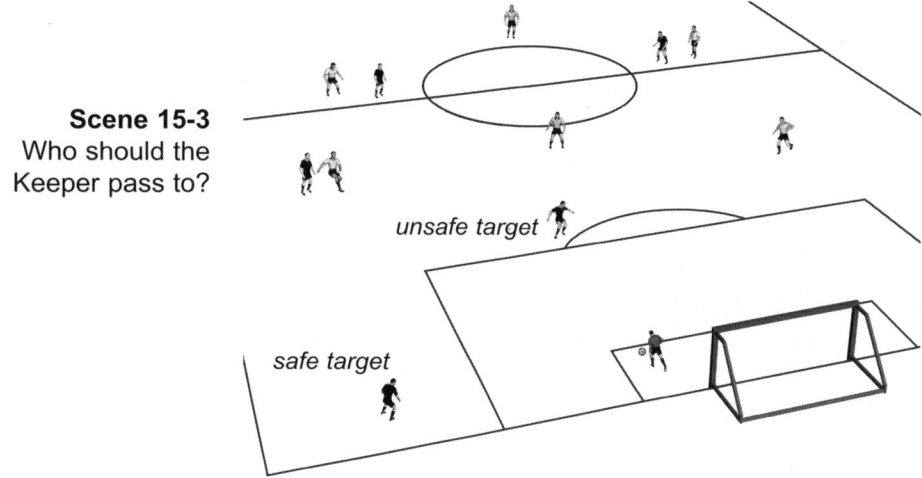

Scene 15-3
Who should the Keeper pass to?

163

PART II: TEACHING SOCCER'S PARTS

The Corner Clear-Out

If opponents prevent those passes into the corner, a long punt, kick, or throw is called for—depending on your Keeper's strength, of course (Scene 15-4). Opponents might win the ball, but they'll have a long way to travel.

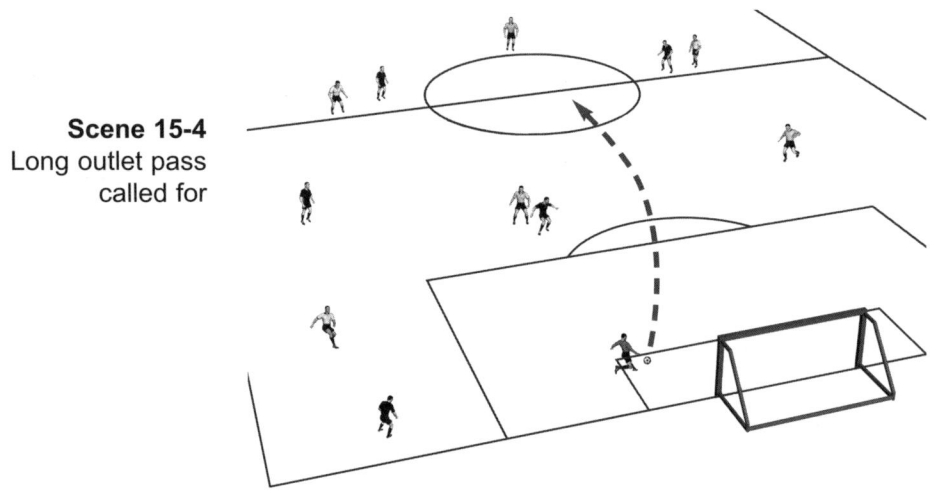

Scene 15-4
Long outlet pass called for

When a Fullback in the corner is covered, the *Corner Clear-Out* is another option. The Fullback sprints from the corner to the middle of the field. The opponent will usually follow, clearing out the corner (Scene 15-5). A Halfback then runs there for a short pass.

Scene 15-5
Corner Clear-Out

The Wave and Loop Trick

Before kicking deep, a Keeper will often wave teammates away from the goal. Players from both teams then hike to the halfway line, anticipating the long kick.

After waving, though, the Keeper doesn't have to send the ball deep. The *Wave and Loop Trick* is another possibility (Scene 15-6). As players walk to the halfway line, the Keeper's partner-in-crime loops back for a shorter pass—and dribbles forty yards before anyone notices.

Scene 15-6
Wave and Loop trick

Coaching System Organizers

How can you coach the System Organizer role? During a scrimmage, stand back with your Keeper and spot system weaknesses as your Keeper should. Only one layer might be present, or the back door might be uncovered. Freeze the problem, and have your Keeper fix it.

In Scene 15-7, the triangle is too flat. The defender on the ball has no backup, and a dribble through the middle might lead to a goal. Your COMO might go like this:

Scene 15-7
Keeper sees that triangle is too flat

coach

PART II: TEACHING SOCCER'S PARTS

"Freeze! As you can see, the Left and Right Fullbacks are spread too wide. They can't back up the play if a ball gets through the middle. We'd like our Keeper to fix the triangle, by yelling something. Give it a try."

Your Keeper commands the Left and Right Fullbacks to sag back and pinch in to the middle—not bad for a first attempt. The Fullbacks respond, the triangle is restored, and the scrimmage continues.

Here are some other problems your Keeper can fix.

Base of Triangle Uneven

In Scene 15-8, the triangle's base is uneven. Since the Left Fullback is further back than the Right Fullback, the opponent behind the Right Fullback is not in an offside position. Your Keeper must either get the Right Fullback to sag back, or the Left Fullback to pull forward.

Scene 15-8
Keeper sees that triangle's base is uneven

No back door coverage

The triangle is fine in Scene 15-9, but the back door is uncovered. An opponent there is hoping for a crossing pass. Your Keeper *must* get a teammate to cover the back door, and the Right Halfback is the most likely candidate.

CHAPTER 15: THE FOUR-ROLES-IN-ONE KEEPER

Scene 15-9
Keeper sees that back door is uncovered

Right Halfback

Layers too far apart

Your Keeper can also correct layer problems. In Scene 15-10, the first layer and second layer are too far apart. The opponent with the ball might beat one layer and then the other. The defender in the first layer must stall until the second layer moves closer.

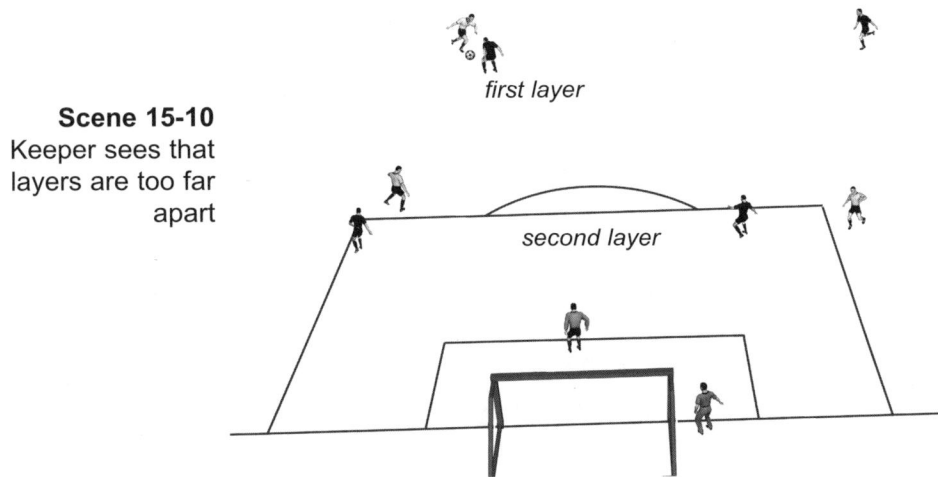

Scene 15-10
Keeper sees that layers are too far apart

first layer

second layer

Coaching Extra Fullbacks

Scrimmages create many COMOs for the Extra Fullback role. If your Keeper is glued to the goal line, or forgets to charge out, jump in with a COMO. You can also coach the role using the three HISAs below.

Breakaway Shot

With the Breakaway Shot (see page 36), a dribbler breaks in on the Keeper and has eight seconds to score. If the Keeper just stands in goal, the dribbler has an easy time. The Keeper should hustle toward the ball

PART II: TEACHING SOCCER'S PARTS

the dribbler has an easy time. The Keeper should hustle toward the ball as a Fullback might, and slow down at the last moment (Scene 15-11).

Scene 15-11
Keeper on a
Breakaway Shot

One to Beat

In One to Beat (see page 124), a dribbler must beat a defender and then shoot on the Keeper. If the Keeper just stands in goal, the dribbler can dispense with defender and Keeper one after the other. But if the Keeper sneaks out of goal to become an Extra Fullback, two layers are in place (Scene 15-12). When the ball is pushed past the defender, the Keeper can intercept it.

Scene 15-12
Extra Fullback Role
in One to Beat

Dizzy Miss Lizzy

In *Dizzy Miss Lizzy*, two players try to score against a defender and a Keeper (Scene 15-13). By passing repeatedly back and forth, the attackers can make the defender dizzy. They can also find a wide open shot. Time for the Extra Fullback role.

CHAPTER 15: THE FOUR-ROLES-IN-ONE KEEPER

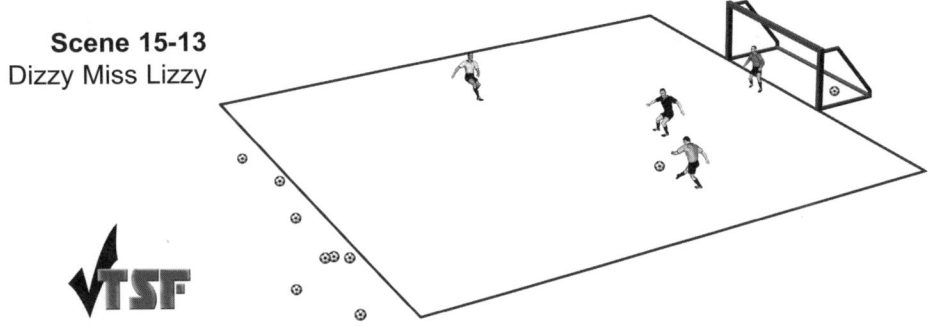

Scene 15-13
Dizzy Miss Lizzy

Rules for Dizzy Miss Lizzy

Field Setup The field is set up around one regulation size goal. Extra soccer balls are placed along the side opposite the goal. Each side of the field is about thirty paces long.

Teams Four players compete, in teams of two. One team defends the goal, providing a Keeper and a defender. The other team attacks. Additional players may rotate into the game.

Object of the Game Each team gets ten tries to score goals. The team with the most goals wins.

How a Try Proceeds The attacking team brings the first ball into play, and attempts to score. The players may pass as often as they like before shooting. They may dribble in on the Keeper, or shoot from further out. The offside rule is not in effect.

The defending team tries to prevent a goal, by knocking the ball out of bounds, stealing it, or making a save. The Keeper may stay in the goal, or charge out of the goal. A shot that is blocked or punched away is still in play.

How the Game Proceeds When the first try ends, the attacking team immediately brings in the second ball. After the fifth try, the defender and Keeper may switch roles. After the last try, the two teams switch roles.

Find a moment when the Keeper is standing in goal and the defender is gasping for breath. Freeze the action, and have the Keeper sneak out to the uncovered player (Scene 15-14). This Extra Fullback maneuver might seem risky, but it can lead to a steal or blocked shot.

PART II: TEACHING SOCCER'S PARTS

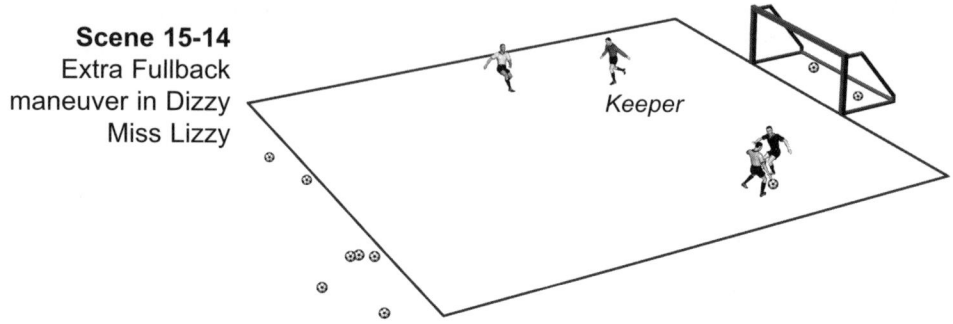

Scene 15-14
Extra Fullback maneuver in Dizzy Miss Lizzy

Although Dizzy Miss Lizzy is designed for four players, larger numbers can also play. One player can rotate in on defense, and another on offense. Two Keepers can alternate. And several games can be going at the same time. The game is great for field players, also. They must choose unpredictably between passing and shooting. And they must shoot under pressure.

Coaching Savemakers

How can you coach the Savemaker role if you don't know any save techniques? There's no substitute for expert instruction, but Thoughtful Soccer can help. While field players practice different shots, Keepers must save those shots. After a few thousand saves, Keepers can't help but improve.

> **While field players practice different shots, Keepers must save those shots.**

Be sure to make save practice like the real thing. In a match, shots could come from any angle or distance, on the ground or through the air. Chips and crosses could come floating in. And a dribbler could break in alone on your Keeper. Include all these scenarios in practice.

A Surprisingly Fun Position

When only the Savemaker role matters, Keeper can be a dreary position. Very few saves might be required in a match. If the other team is weak, *no* saves might be required. Your Keepers will wonder why they became Keepers.

CHAPTER 15: THE FOUR-ROLES-IN-ONE KEEPER

Once you coach all four roles, Keeper becomes a fun position. Like field players, Keepers must pass, receive, communicate, and think. They participate in every moment of the match. And few brave knights will get past your four-roles-in-one Keeper.

16
BREAKING THROUGH TO SCORE

The Great Water Balloon Battle

The armies glared across the field through the wall of clear glob that separated them. The great water balloon battle would soon begin. Soldiers would charge across the field and leap through the glob. Those who still had their water balloons would then bombard the enemy.

PART II: TEACHING SOCCER'S PARTS

A captain suddenly yelled, "Charge!" His troops sprang from their trenches and charged toward the glob. Many lost their balloons because of the field's rough terrain. Many more lost their balloons while leaping through the glob.

Only a few soldiers got through with water balloons in one piece. They heaved their balloons, but without accuracy. The troops returned to their trenches.

"Those throws were terrible," complained the captain. "You've got to bend your elbow when you throw a water balloon, and follow through to the target."

The soldiers had trouble breaking through the glob. By comparison, balloon throwing was a minor problem. But that was the only problem the captain saw.

Don't make the same mistake when your team can't score. You might think your players have a finishing problem, when their real problem involves breaking through.

Before finishing, your players must break through a few defensive obstacles (Scene 16-1). One obstacle is the other team's defensive system, which might confuse your players. Another is the offside line, which proclaims, "No trespassing!" And a third is the Keeper, who can gobble up balls that get through.

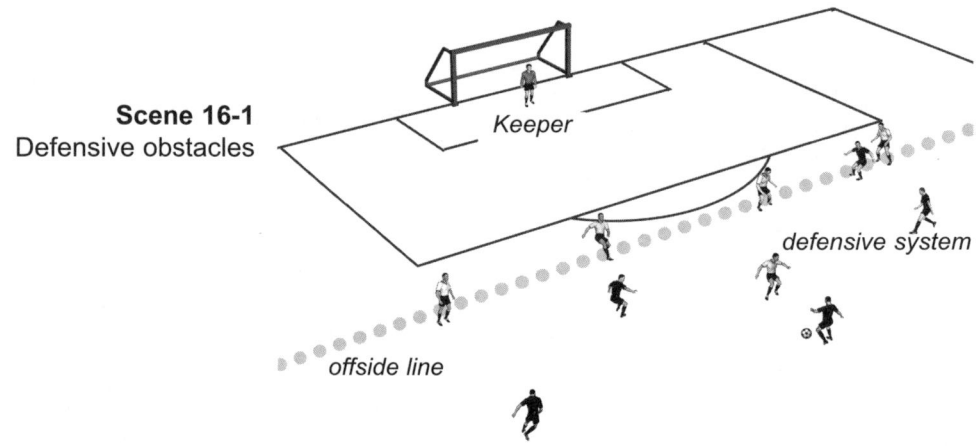

Scene 16-1
Defensive obstacles

The next three chapters look at the Breakthrough Part and how to coach it. This chapter presents a few basic ideas for breaking through. Chapter 17

CHAPTER 16: BREAKING THROUGH TO SCORE

shows how two players can combine to break through. And Chapter 18 shows how to break through different defensive systems.

Quickstart for the Breakthrough Part

Before getting theoretical, let's head to the practice field. A HISA called *Space Cowboy* brings the Breakthrough Part to life. The game is challenging, but can be played by brand new players—a rare combination!

The playing area is like a large Run the Gauntlet course (Figure 16-2). Each defensive zone holds two or three defenders rather than one. Those defenders create offside lines for the attackers to break through. The team with the most breakthroughs wins.

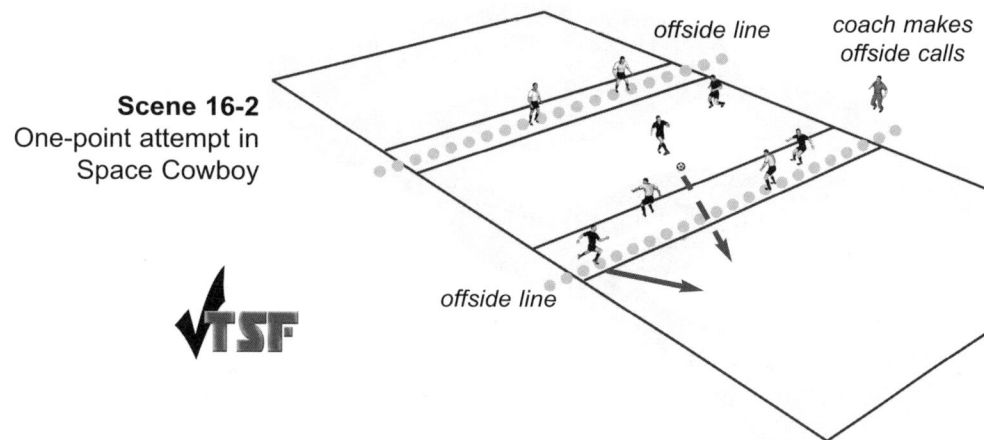

Scene 16-2
One-point attempt in Space Cowboy

Rules for Space Cowboy

Course Setup The course is approximately seventy-five paces long and thirty paces wide. It contains three attacking zones, separated by two narrow defensive zones.

Teams and Starting Positions Eight to twelve players may play, divided into two teams. One team begins on defense, with two or three of its players in each defensive zone. The other team begins on offense. Its players may go anywhere on the course. The offensive team has one ball.

Object of the Game While on offense, a team tries to score points by passing through the defensive zones. The team scores as many points as possible in three minutes, and then becomes the defending team. The team with the most points wins.

How the Game Proceeds As the coach keeps time, the offensive team begins scoring points. To earn one point, the ball must be passed through a defensive zone. The receiving player may not be in an offside position, as explained below, and must get two touches on the ball before it goes out of bounds.

PART II: TEACHING SOCCER'S PARTS

The defending team tries to prevent points, by kicking the ball of the course, stealing it, and earning offside calls. The ball must be returned immediately to an attacker after a steal or offside call. The clock keeps running, and the attacking team continues scoring points.

The ball may be moved in any direction to score points. Attackers may dribble or pass as often as they like. Every pass does not have to be a scoring attempt.

Offside Calls As the ball approaches a defensive zone, the deepest defender in that zone represents the offside line. The attacker receiving a pass may not be behind that line at the moment the ball is passed. In other words, that player must run through the offside line as the ball is passed, and gather in the ball on the other side.

Two-Point Attempts A pass that travels over both defensive zones earns two points (Scene 16-3). For these longer passes, the offside line is in the distant defensive zone.

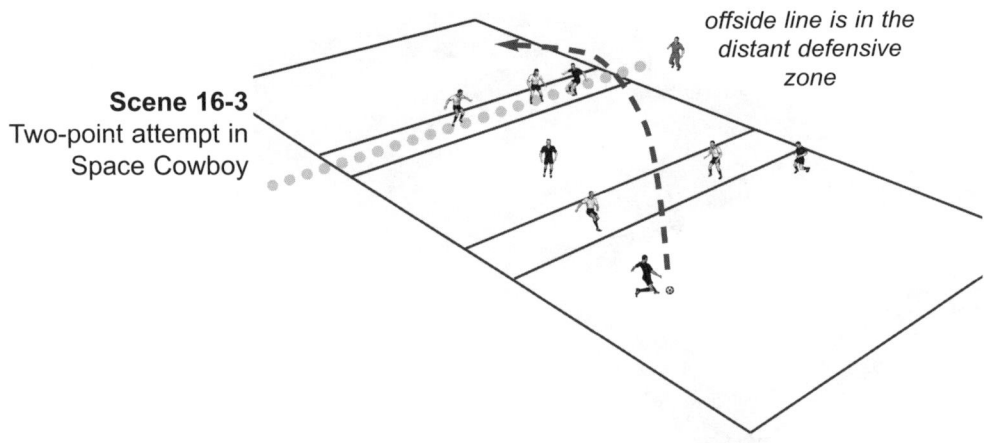

Scene 16-3
Two-point attempt in Space Cowboy

offside line is in the distant defensive zone

Note that the offside line depends entirely on which direction the ball is travelling. The attacking team may move the ball back and forth through the same defensive zone, or fake toward one zone and attack the other. The ball may even be passed *intentionally* to an offside player, setting up a pass in the opposite direction.

What makes Space Cowboy worthwhile? It provides many tries at breaking through an offside line. It requires no sophisticated coaching. It takes only a few minutes. And it's fun!

CHAPTER 16: BREAKING THROUGH TO SCORE

Taking the Indirect Path

Players can attempt a breakthrough along two different paths (Scene 16-4). New players almost always take the *direct path*, which leads straight to the goal. Experienced players often prefer the *indirect path*. They move the ball toward a corner, and then toward the goal.

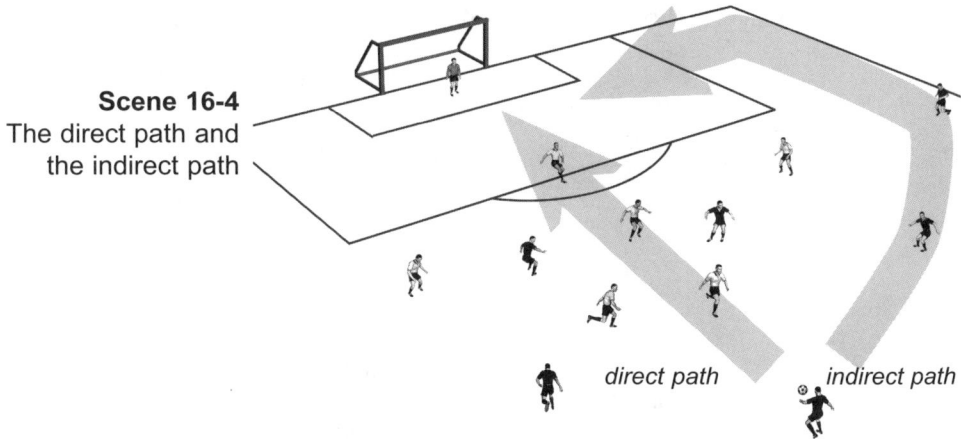

Scene 16-4
The direct path and the indirect path

direct path *indirect path*

The indirect path has four advantages:

- It's usually less crowded than the direct path.
- The Keeper can't gobble up the ball when it's moving toward a corner.
- Once the ball reaches a corner, the offside rule is no longer a barrier. Players may move as close to the goal as they like.
- Balls crossed into the goal area often lead to close-range shots.

The secret is to choose unpredictably between the two paths. Start down the direct path and switch to the indirect path, or vice versa. When opponents worry about two paths, both become more open.

Remember the Big Goal/Small Goal setup in Chapter 7? Now you can fully appreciate its value. It rewards players for taking the indirect path, and gets them choosing unpredictably between the two paths.

The Counterattack Choice

With a *counterattack*, a team wins the ball and attacks right away—before any obstacles are in place. Counterattacks can be launched from anywhere on the field. Some begin near the other team's goal. Others begin in the middle of the field. And a long pass can start a counterattack from

PART II: TEACHING SOCCER'S PARTS

the defensive end of the field (Figure 16-5).

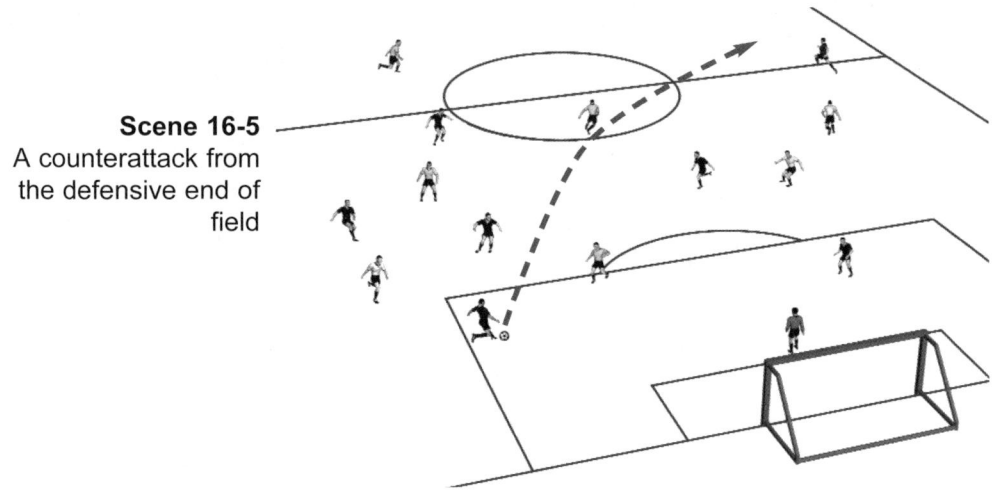

Scene 16-5
A counterattack from the defensive end of field

To counterattack or not to counterattack, that is the question. If the path forward is clear, a counterattack might work. But if the path forward is crowded, a counterattack will lose the ball.

How can your players practice counterattacking? Thoughtscrims aren't much help, at least in their pure form. Their rules usually *prevent* counterattacks.

Here's one solution. To any Thoughtscrim except One-Time, add a special *Counterattack Exception*. If a team steals the ball, the Thoughtscrim's conditions are lifted temporarily. The ball may be taken straight to the goal, without a drop pass, side-to-side maneuver, and so on. When the scoring attempt stalls, the regular conditions are reinstated.

Defensive Thoughtscrims like Plan-to-Plan (see page 139) also allow counterattacking. The defending team has conditions imposed, but the attacking team may play as it pleases.

When counterattacks are allowed, use COMOs to encourage good decisions. If a team overlooks a counterattack chance, freeze the moment. If a team counterattacks into a crowd, correct the mistake. And when a good decision is made, throw in an Encouragement COMO.

Moving Players Forward

At all levels of soccer, some players stay back on defense while others move forward to attack. But new players take this trend too far. The Forwards *always* attempt the breakthroughs, while the Halfbacks only help

CHAPTER 16: BREAKING THROUGH TO SCORE

now and then. The Fullbacks *never* help, and with good reason. By the time they could get forward, the ball will already be lost.

As your team improves at keeping possession, more players can move forward. Halfbacks, and even a Fullback or two, have time to join the breakthrough attempt.

When players move forward, one good thing leads to another. More passing targets mean more openings in the defense. Opponents are less likely to counterattack, because they must all defend. And with no counterattack to worry about, even more of your players can move forward.

> **When players move forward, one good thing leads to another.**

Pass-and-Move (see page 71) is a great Thoughtscrim for moving players forward. Players must move somewhere, and more often than not, they move forward. Once they experience the thrill of the breakthrough, they want that feeling again.

Count Your Blessings

Attacking has a Breakthrough Part and a Finish Part. If your team misses shot after shot in the match, count your blessings. The Breakthrough Part is going well.

If possession is the most important part of soccer, breaking through is probably the most challenging part. Don't leave your players plastered against a wall of glob. Be aware of the Breakthrough Part, and find ways to practice it.

17

BREAKING THROUGH WITH COMBINATIONS

Sid Makes the Team

The spiders were starving. Unable to find food on the dry plain, they sent an expedition into the jungle. Only the strongest and most aggressive spiders were selected. Sid, a bright but weaker spider, was allowed to tag along.

PART II: TEACHING SOCCER'S PARTS

In the jungle, the spiders built webs to catch moths and mosquitoes. But the webs glistened in the sunlight, and the spiders were too easily spotted. Not a single bug was caught. With nothing to lose, the spiders asked Sid for help.

At one web, Sid held up a Free Barbecue sign while the other spider donned a chef's hat and spatula. At another, he masqueraded as a wounded mosquito while his comrade dialed Mosquito 911. And at another, a spider danced while Sid sang a popular moth musical. At day's end, the expedition headed home with an impressive haul of bugs.

The spiders were strong and aggressive, but relied completely on their individual skills. Sid was successful because he *combined* with other spiders.

In soccer, that's how the Breakthrough Part works. Strong, aggressive players might score in beginning soccer. But to break through sophisticated defenses, players must combine their efforts. Clever ways of combining are called *combinations*.

Combinations make defenders hesitate for a moment. Where will the ball go, and who should cover whom? That moment of hesitation allows the breakthrough. Here's how to teach some basic combinations.

The Run-On Combination

A *run-on* isn't a grammatical error but a way to break through the offside line. A player runs toward the offside line, and reaches it just as a teammate passes (Scene 17-1).

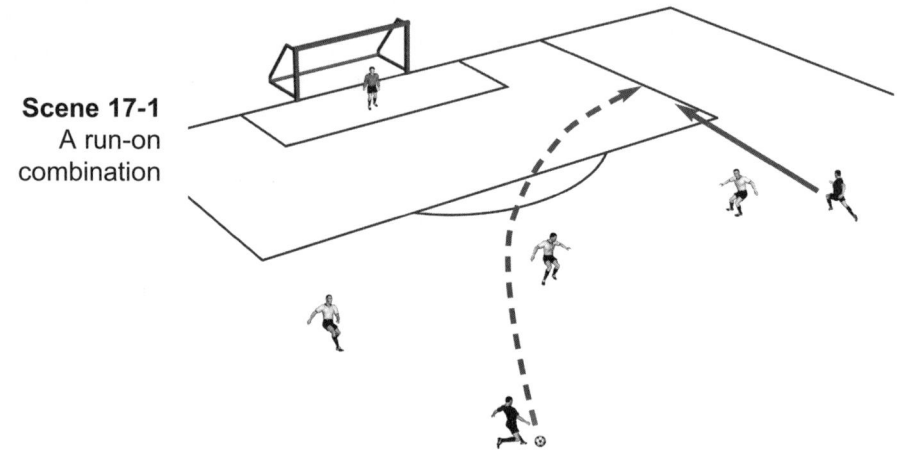

Scene 17-1
A run-on combination

CHAPTER 17: BREAKING THROUGH WITH COMBINATIONS

The timing between run and pass is the key. If the ball is passed too soon, defenders will reach it first. If the ball is passed too late, the running player will be offside.

> **The timing between run and pass is the key.**

The run-on should look familiar. It's the primary way to score in Space Cowboy, from the previous chapter.

The Give-and-Go Combination

The *give-and-go*, also known as the wall pass, is another way to break through the offside line (Scene 17-2). It's actually a type of run-on. A player passes to a teammate, runs past the offside line, and gathers in the teammate's one-touch pass.

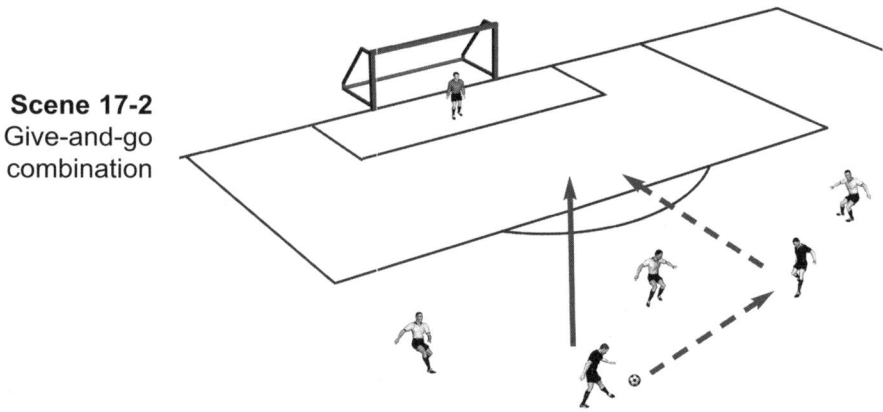

Scene 17-2
Give-and-go combination

A give-and-go relies on an attention lapse. When the ball is passed, defenders pay attention to its flight rather than to the passer. Suddenly, the passer is behind them and dribbling in on the Keeper. Like all combinations, a give-and-go works in other parts of the field as well.

The give-and-go is another way to score in Space Cowboy. But the easiest way to teach the combination is on a Gauntlet Course (Scene 17-3). A neutral player to the side is required. Each dribbler can either take on the first defender or pass to the neutral player, who one-touches the ball behind the defender. The dribbler gathers the ball in, and takes on the second defender without help.

PART II: TEACHING SOCCER'S PARTS

Scene 17-3
Give-and-go in Run the Gauntlet

neutral player gets one touch

The Creative Runs

The *creative runs* aren't a digestive problem, and they're not really combinations. They're a building block for several combinations.

Players who run forward in straight lines can't combine well, because they're too easily covered. Creative runs such as *overlaps* and *diagonals* are the remedy.

The Overlap Run

With the *overlap run*, one player overtakes and runs past the player with the ball. Two variations are shown in Scene 17-4. The running player can loop behind and around the ball. Or the running player can run straight past the ball. While making an overlap run, a player will usually yell, "Overlap!" or "Hold!"

The player making the overlap run will often find open space on the other side of the ball. The ball can either be passed to that player, or faked.

Scene 17-4
Two examples of overlap runs

CHAPTER 17: BREAKING THROUGH WITH COMBINATIONS

The Diagonal Run
With a diagonal run, a player slants from one section of the field to another (Scene 17-5). The run could be made toward a touch line, or toward the middle. Once again, the player with the ball may either pass it or keep it.

As with an overlap run, opponents must quickly decide whom to cover. If uncovered, the running player can receive a pass in open space. If an opponent follows the running player, a space might become open for someone else.

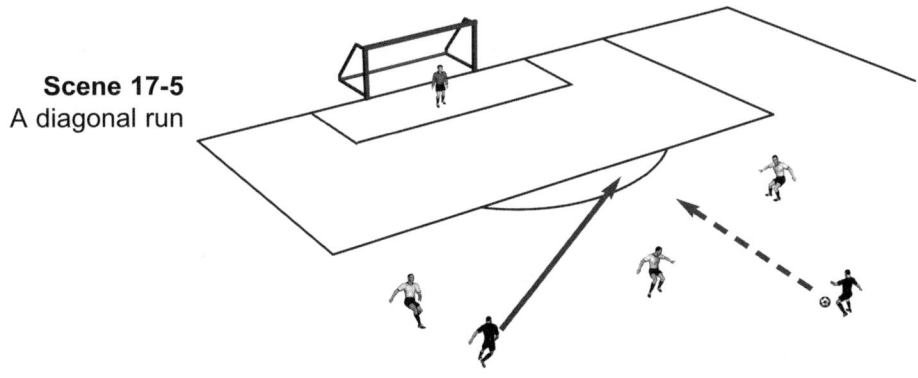

Scene 17-5
A diagonal run

Creative Runs in Team Gauntlet
Team Gauntlet (see page 48) is a quick way to introduce creative runs. In Scene 17-6, players are using overlaps and diagonals to get past the two defenders.

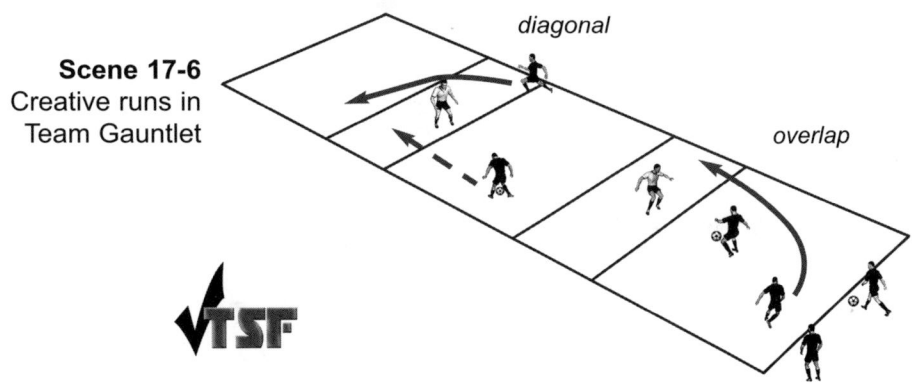

Scene 17-6
Creative runs in
Team Gauntlet

Introduce each run with a walk through. Then require teams to use one of the runs at the start of every try. Finally, let teams use either run at any

185

PART II: TEACHING SOCCER'S PARTS

point during the try. After a while, you'll see interesting mixtures of the two runs.

Takeovers and Dummies

Here are two more combinations to teach with Team Gauntlet. In the *takeover* combination, a dribbler and a teammate move past each other in opposite directions. The teammate may either take the ball or leave it. Defenders must figure out who has the ball and whom to cover (Scene 17-7).

Scene 17-7
A takeover combination

In the *dummy* combination, a player pretends to receive the ball, but lets it run through to a teammate (Scene 17-8). Two typical dummy scenarios are shown. In one, your player pretends to shoot the ball, but lets it run through to an awaiting teammate. In the other, your player lets the ball roll past the offside line to a running teammate.

Scene 17-8
Two examples of dummy combinations

186

CHAPTER 17: BREAKING THROUGH WITH COMBINATIONS

Takeovers and Dummies in Team Gauntlet

In this version of Team Gauntlet, the attacking players begin a few steps from the first defender (Scene 17-9). The coach kicks or rolls the ball from eight yards away, and the try begins with a dummy combination. The closest player may either receive the ball or let it run by as the defender tries to read the play. After getting past the first defender, players may beat the second defender any way they like.

Scene 17-9
Dummy combination in Team Gauntlet

The journey back through the course must begin with a takeover combination (Scene 17-10). The players move past each other in opposite directions. The player without the ball might take it or leave it, and the choice should be disguised.

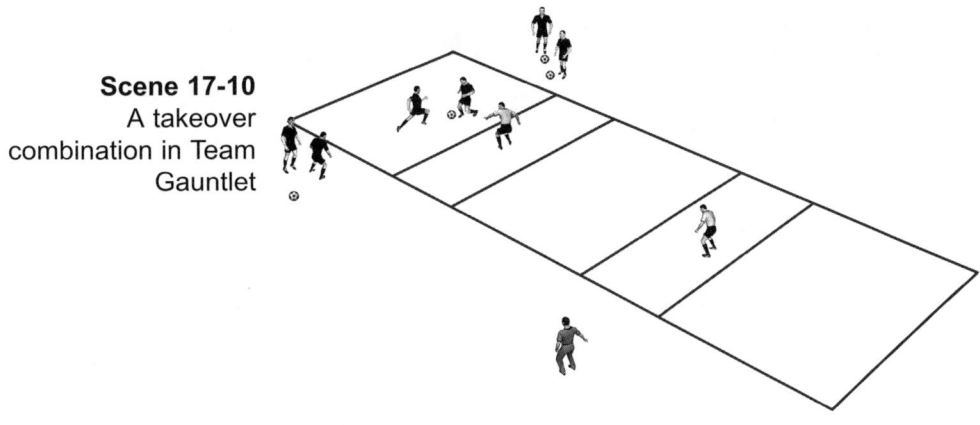

Scene 17-10
A takeover combination in Team Gauntlet

PART II: TEACHING SOCCER'S PARTS

Check-To and Check-To Fake

Passes forward are risky if the receiving player just stands there. An opponent might cut in front, steal the pass, and begin a counterattack. The *check-to* and *check-to fake* prevent such steals (Scene 17-11). And they're great for disrupting an offside line.

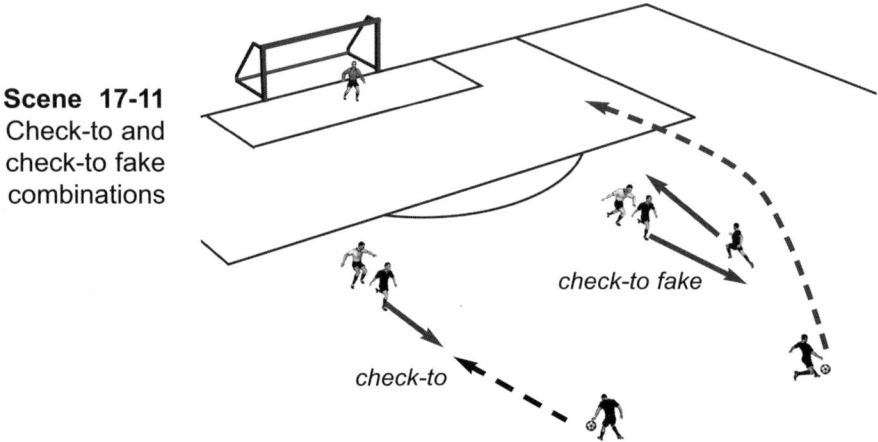

Scene 17-11
Check-to and check-to fake combinations

In the check-to, the receiving player cuts back to the ball, leaving the opponent behind. When the ball is passed forward, it probably won't be stolen. If the opponent follows the run too closely, as in the scene, the check-to fake is possible. The pass is faked, the opponent falls for the fake, and the runner breaks away from the ball for a longer pass.

You don't need a new activity for these two combinations. They can be experienced in Pass-and-Move (see page 71). In this Thoughtscrim, a player must be moving somewhere when receiving a pass. If the player is moving toward the passer, that's a check-to. And every check-to can become a check-to fake.

CHAPTER 17: BREAKING THROUGH WITH COMBINATIONS

Crossing Combinations

When one player crosses the ball and another shoots, the players are performing a simple crossing combination. Bombs Away develops that combination (see page 28). But crosses allow other combinations as well, some involving three players. Players in the goal area can make creative runs. The ball can be crossed to the far post or near post, on the ground or through the air. And the player receiving the ball can either shoot it or pass to a teammate.

In Scene 17-12, the ball has been crossed to the far post. Instead of shooting, the attacker heads the ball to the opposite post.

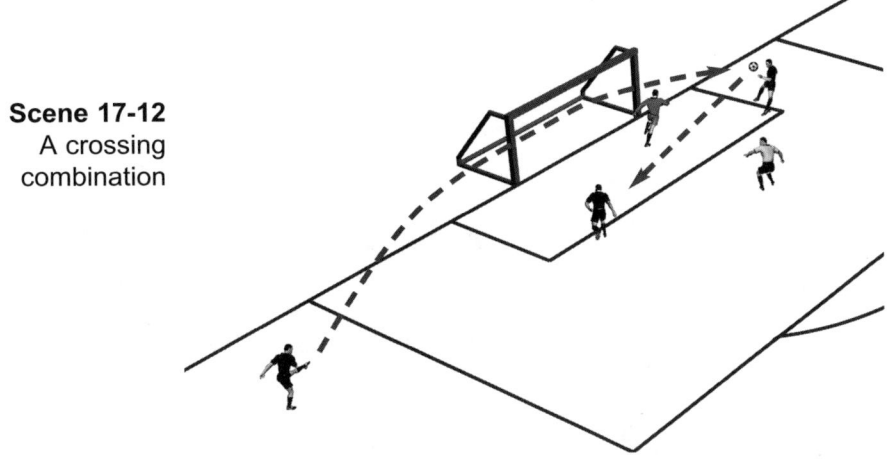

Scene 17-12
A crossing combination

In Scene 17-13, one attacker overlaps the other, and the ball is crossed to the near post. Instead of shooting, the attacker deflects the ball to the far post—a *glancing header*.

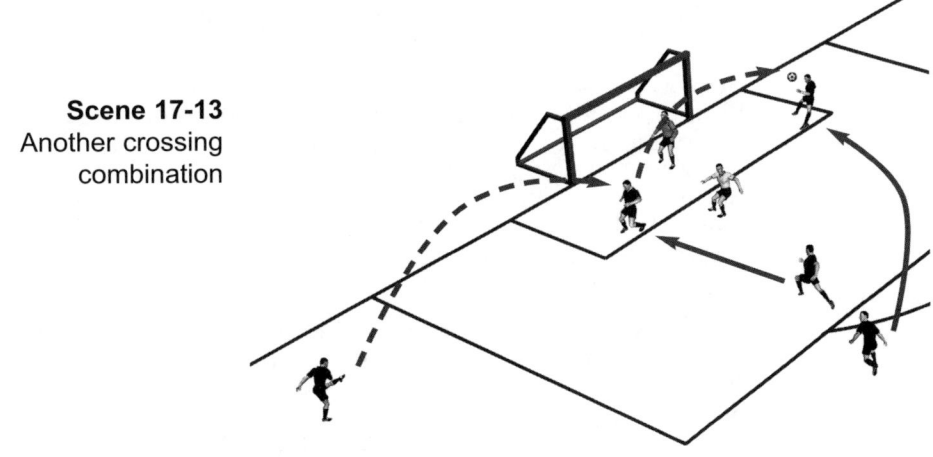

Scene 17-13
Another crossing combination

PART II: TEACHING SOCCER'S PARTS

Crossing combinations like these can be experienced in *Combo Bombs Away*—a challenging HISA for experienced chippers (Scene 17-14). The chips may be delivered to the near post or the far post. And rather than standing in one place, the receiving players run and combine.

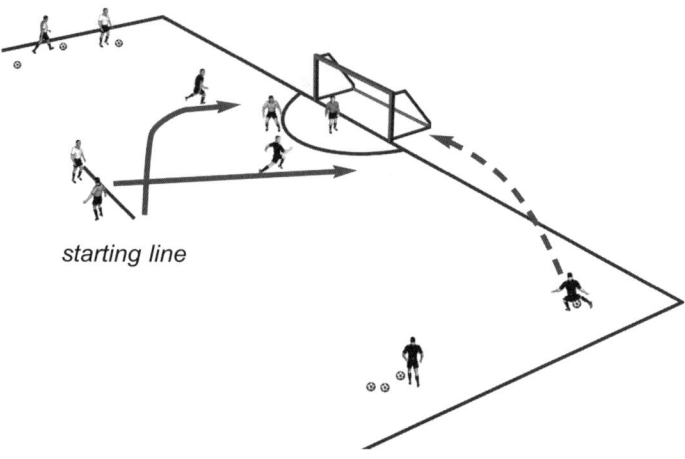

Scene 17-14
Combo Bombs Away

starting line

Rules for Combo Bombs Away

Field Setup The field is set up around a regulation-size goal. The corners are thirty to forty paces away. An arc-shaped Keeper area surrounds the goal. Two cones about thirty paces from the goal represent a starting line.

Teams and Starting Positions Each team has four to eight players, divided evenly between Crossers and Shooters. A team's Crossers line up along one touch line, with several soccer balls. Shooters from both teams begin behind the starting line, outside the penalty area. Shooters may not enter the Keeper area, and the Keeper may not leave that area. A neutral defender outside the Keeper area helps the Keeper prevent goals.

Object of the Game Teams score as many points as possible by crossing balls and shooting on goal. Headers count two points, while other shots count one point.

How a Try Works A Crosser gets the ball moving as two Shooters break toward the goal. The Shooters may run in straight lines, or overlap and crisscross creatively. After the Crosser crosses the ball, the Shooters attempt to score. The Shooter receiving the ball may either shoot, or pass to the teammate. Both players are allowed only one touch. The neutral player attempts to clear the ball, and the Keeper attempts to make a save.

How a Round Proceeds After the first try, the Crosser returns to the original line and the Shooters move back behind the starting line. The other team then crosses from the opposite side as its Shooters try to score. The round continues for three minutes, with one team crossing and then the other. Each Crosser must alternate crossing with the right foot and the left foot, pulling the

CHAPTER 17: BREAKING THROUGH WITH COMBINATIONS

ball back as necessary. After scoring, a team must announce its point total.

Rotating to Other Stations A new round begins every three minutes, as players rotate to new stations. For the second round, players switch places with their teammates. Then, they rotate to the remaining two stations. After four rounds, the team with the most points wins.

Scrimmaging With Combinations

After introducing a few combinations, include them all in a Thoughtscrim called *Mambo Combo* (Scene 17-15). One team has more players than the other, and gets many combination opportunities. Combinations are further encouraged by the scoring system.

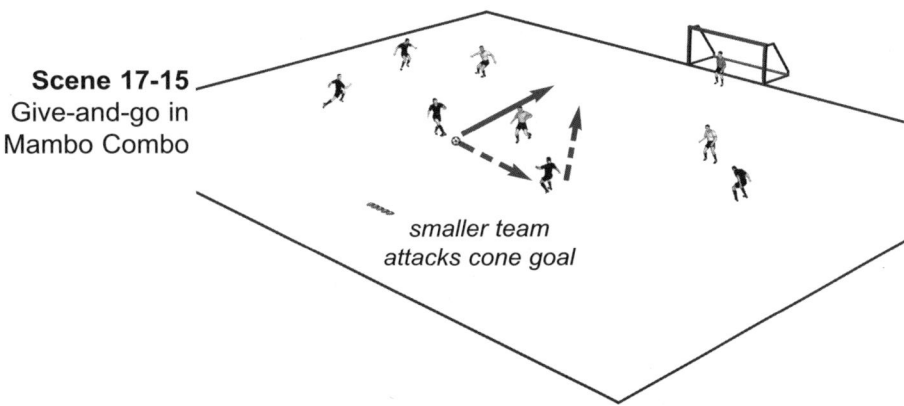

Scene 17-15
Give-and-go in Mambo Combo

smaller team attacks cone goal

Rules for Mambo Combo

Field Setup The field has a regulation size goal at one end, and a small goal at the other end. The size of the field depends on the number of players participating.

Teams and Starting Positions One team has several more players than the other team: 4 v 2, 5 v 3, 7 v 4, or 8 v 5. The smaller team also has a Keeper, and defends the small goal. The larger team has no Keeper, and defends the regulation-size goal.

Object of the Game The teams try to score on their respective goals. Goals by the larger team count as one point, while goals for the smaller team count as two points. However, if a combination is involved in the goal—a run-on, give-and-go, takeover, dummy, etc.—the points are doubled.

How the Game Proceeds The scrimmage continues for approximately eight minutes. The coach declares when a combination has occurred, and resolves all scoring controversies. The offside rule is in effect, and any player on the defending team may call offside. Players may rotate from one team to the other.

PART II: TEACHING SOCCER'S PARTS

Mambo Combo creates many Coachable Moments. When you see a situation where a dummy, run-on, or other combination would fit, freeze the action, walk through the combination, and play on. Your players will begin seeing the opportunities on their own.

Greater Than the Parts

When evaluating players, look beyond speed, strength, and skill. The players who combine usually have an edge. And eleven Sid the Spiders can't be beat!

18
BREAKING THROUGH DEFENSIVE SYSTEMS

A Bridge Too Short

Krimpo was a small island with a mountain. Three rivers flowed from the mountain to the sea. The first river wound its way through a thick forest. The second carved out a deep canyon. And the third flowed across a swampy plain.

PART II: TEACHING SOCCER'S PARTS

For centuries, the Krimpions had no need to travel around the entire island. But when an annual Parade Around Krimpo was approved, three bridges were required. Every day, islanders met at the Bridge Construction Center to build the bridges.

Eventually, three strong but identical bridges had been built. Each was hauled to a different river. The first bridge wasn't high enough to pass over the trees. The second bridge wasn't long enough to reach across the canyon. And the third sank slowly into the swamp. The Parade Around Krimpo was cancelled.

Surely, you've identified the islanders' mistake. Bridges can't be built at a bridge construction center. They must be built on location, and adapted to the terrain.

Breakthrough attempts must also be adapted to the terrain—the other team's defensive system. What works against a Sweeper won't necessarily work against a Flat Back Four. And zone defense has different weaknesses than man-to-man. Your players must recognize different systems and know how to attack them.

How can you coach this? You'll need an idea or two for attacking each defensive system, and a Thoughtscrim like *Doctor Diagnoso*.

A Doctor for the Breakthrough Part

In *Doctor Diagnoso*, the smaller of two teams poses in different defensive systems. The larger team must diagnose each system, and exploit its weaknesses. In Scene 18-1, the smaller white team is using a Sweeper system. The coach has already walked through that system and some ideas for beating it. The larger black team is applying those ideas.

Scene 18-1
Attacking a Sweeper
in Doctor Diagnoso
(7 v 5)

CHAPTER 18: BREAKING THROUGH DEFENSIVE SYSTEMS

Rules for Doctor Diagnoso

Field Setup The field is as wide as a regular soccer field, and about half as long. The exact size will depend on the size of the teams. A regulation-size goal is at one end of the field, and a small goal is at the other end.

Teams Lopsided teams are created by giving one team more players than the other—6 v 4, 7 v 5, 9 v 6, or 10 v 7. The smaller team has a Keeper, and defends the regulation-size goal. The larger team has no Keeper, and defends the small goal.

Preparatory Phase Before play begins, the coach walks through at least three *feature defenses,* and at least two ideas for exploiting each defense. The coach then huddles privately with the smaller team, and assigns one of the defenses: Sweeper with Marking Backs, Flat Back Four, etc.

How the Game Proceeds As play begins, both teams attempt to score goals. The regular rules of soccer apply, including the offside rule. The smaller team must use the assigned defense.

Before scoring, the larger team must figure out the defense it's facing—by moving, passing, and watching the smaller team's responses. At least one player on the larger team must correctly identify the defense, by calling out its name. Goals scored before this happens don't count.

After three minutes, the coach huddles with the smaller team again, and assigns a different defense. When play resumes, the larger team must identify the new defense. The game continues until at least three defenses have been attacked. Players may rotate from one team to the other.

Doctor Diagnoso is an every-now-and-then activity. Continue adding feature defenses. And let the smaller team change defenses on its own, while the game is in progress. The larger team must then diagnose each change before scoring.

Now you need some ideas for attacking the defenses. Think up your own ideas, or try the ones below. Walk through the ideas before a game of Doctor Diagnoso, and bring them to life with COMOs. Soon, your players will recognize defenses and attack them thoughtfully.

Sweeper Headaches

Many teams you face will use a Sweeper, despite the weaknesses in that system (see page 151). In Scene 18-2, your Forwards are arrayed across the field. They're covered closely, and the Sweeper provides a second layer. The chance of a breakthrough is slim.

PART II: TEACHING SOCCER'S PARTS

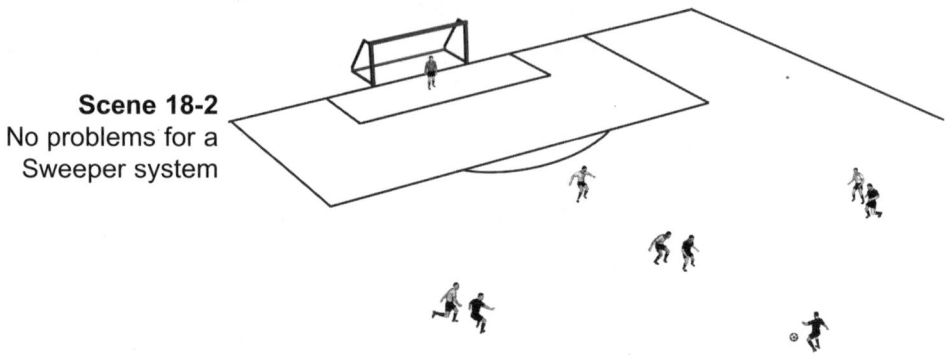

Scene 18-2
No problems for a Sweeper system

Fortunately, your players don't have to stay in set positions. One Forward can move up while another sags back. Two Forwards can operate on the same side of the field. And players can make creative runs from one side to the other. Such movements can give the Sweeper headaches.

Idea: Push Up to the Sweeper

In Scene 18-3, one of your Forwards has pushed up to the Sweeper's level. The others are hanging back. The defense has three possible responses, and each is flawed:

- The Sweeper might continue covering your Forward, who then has only one layer to beat.

- The Sweeper might pull forward, to put your Forward in an offside position. But that would change the defense to a Flat Back line with layer problems of its own (see page 190).

- The other defenders might drop back to your Forward's level, so that the Sweeper can drop back even further. But your Forward can just keep pushing up to the Sweeper. If the Sweeper keeps dropping back, the offside line is rendered useless.

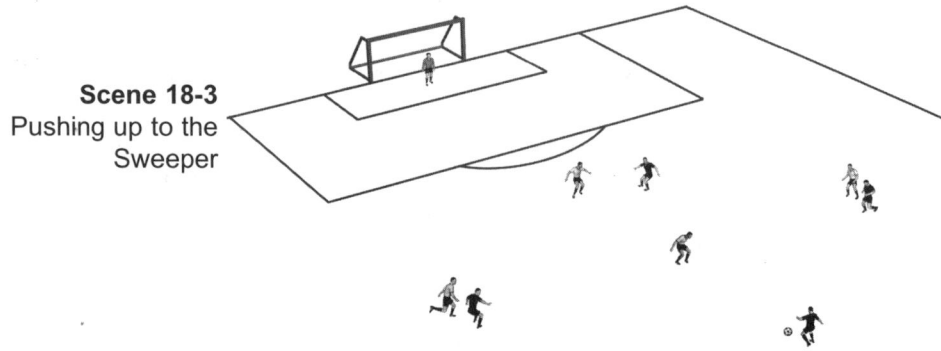

Scene 18-3
Pushing up to the Sweeper

CHAPTER 18: BREAKING THROUGH DEFENSIVE SYSTEMS

Idea: Two Forwards on the Same Side

Scene 18-4 shows another way to confuse the Sweeper. Your two Forwards are working the right side of the field. One is near midfield, while the other has pushed up to the Sweeper's level and isn't in an offside position.

What will the defenders do? The ball is about to be passed behind the Left Fullback. But if that Fullback sags back, your other Forward will be open. And if the Sweeper cuts over to help, the other side of the field will be open.

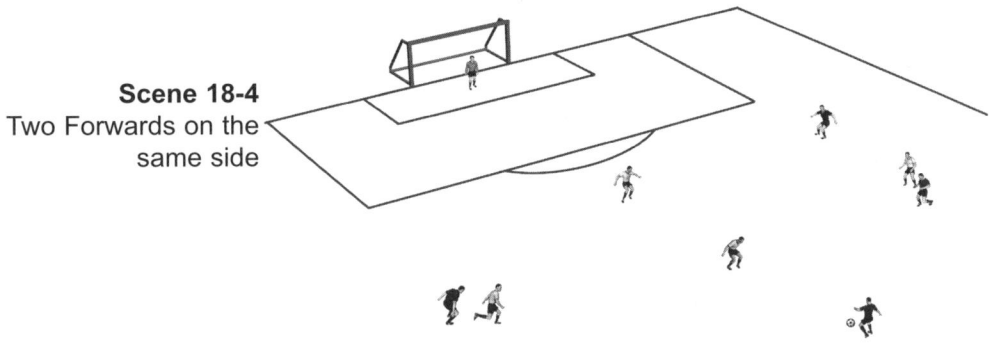

Scene 18-4
Two Forwards on the same side

Idea: An Offside Ploy

The last anti-Sweeper idea is an offside ploy in three steps (Scene 18-5). First, your Forward makes a diagonal run to the right, behind the Left Fullback. The Sweeper could cover the run, but the other side of the field would be open. The Left Fullback could cover the run, but he's already covering someone.

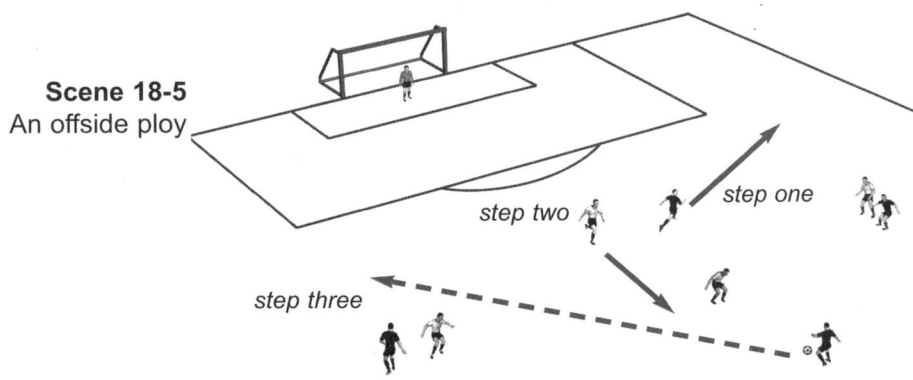

Scene 18-5
An offside ploy

PART II: TEACHING SOCCER'S PARTS

Instead, the Sweeper pulls up to put your Forward offside—step two. That allows step three, the offside ploy. A long pass is sent to the left side of the field, where a Halfback is sprinting through the offside line. The Sweeper is out of position. And offside probably won't be called, because your Forward to the right isn't interfering with the play.

Disrupting a Flat Back Line

A Flat Back line is easy to recognize. As your team works the ball forward, the opposition will have three or four Fullbacks across the back, at the same level. Those Fullbacks will usually move up and back together, and they'll have no Sweeper behind them (Scene 18-6).

In the scene, your Forwards are straight across the field causing few problems for the defense. Each Forward is stationary, facing the ball, and covered. A pass through the defense is unlikely. What might work?

Scene 18-6
No problems for a Flat Back Line

Idea: Try a Run-On Combination
The main weakness in a Flat Back line is the lack of layers (see page 148). A run-on combination is the way to take advantage. In Scene 18-7, one of your Forwards is running toward the offside line. Another is at the level of the offside line, ready to burst through. A pass through the offside line to either player looks promising.

CHAPTER 18: BREAKING THROUGH DEFENSIVE SYSTEMS

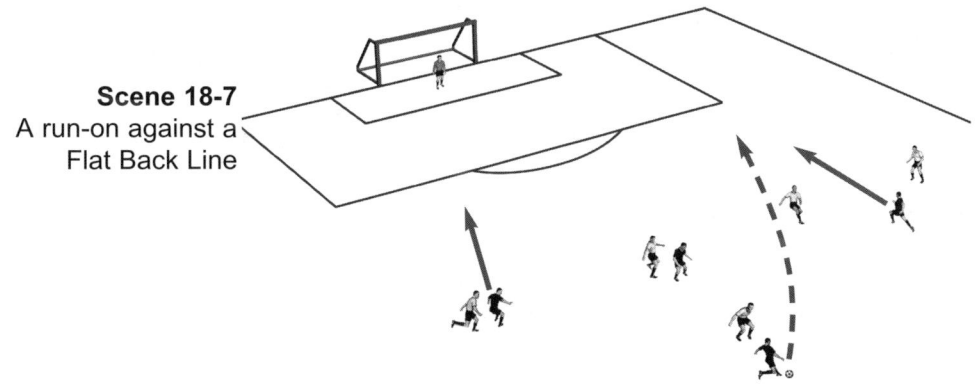

Scene 18-7
A run-on against a Flat Back Line

Idea: Check To and From the Ball

Flat Back lines have trouble staying flat, and that's another weakness to exploit. The Fullbacks are supposed to move up and back together—no easy task when three or four are involved.

In Scene 18-8, one of your Forwards is checking back to the ball, while the other is moving away from the ball. What might the Fullbacks do? If they stay where they are, the Forward checking back will be open in a dangerous spot.

Probably, they'll move their offside line up toward the ball. But that requires the coordination of four players. If one lags behind, the Forward moving away from the ball won't be offside. A pass through the left side, toying with the offside rule, is also possible. When your players continually check to the ball and away from the ball, life is more difficult for a Flat Back line.

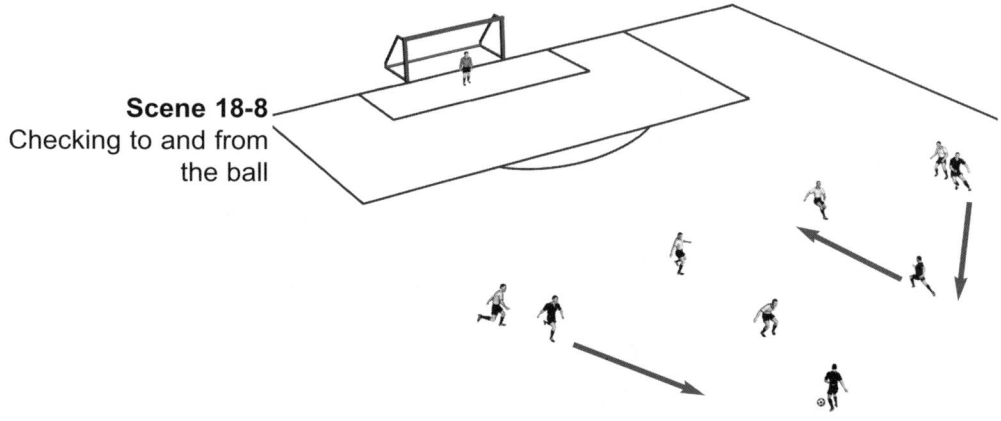

Scene 18-8
Checking to and from the ball

PART II: TEACHING SOCCER'S PARTS

Creating Space Against Man-to-Man

Early in the match, your team should determine whether man-to-man defense is being used. Open space might be hard to find. But your Forwards can drag defenders from side to side, or up and back, to create space for teammates.

Scene 18-9 shows an easy way to diagnose man-to-man defense. Your Forward cuts from the left side to the right. With zone defense, the opposing Fullback would follow part of the way, and then entrust your Forward to someone else.

In the example, though, the Fullback follows your Forward to the other side of the field. Man-to-man defense is clearly being used, and a large space has been created where the Fullback once roamed. One of your Halfbacks sprints into the space, and receives a pass.

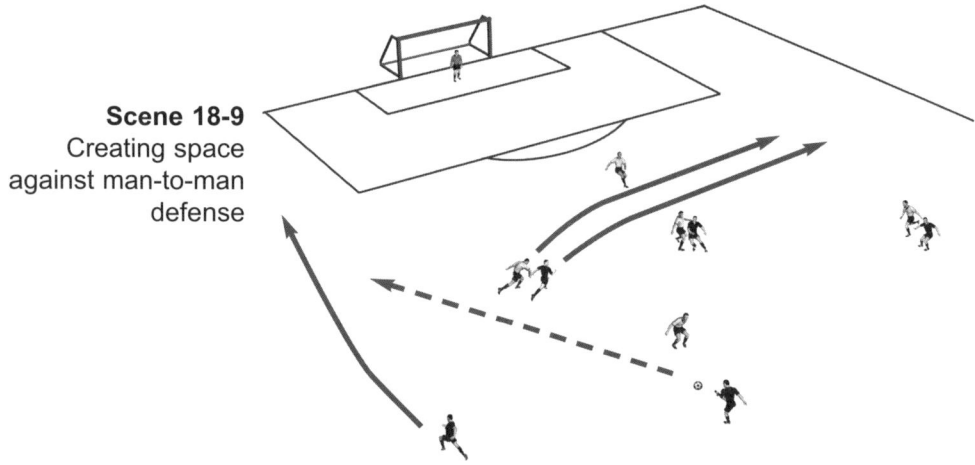

Scene 18-9
Creating space against man-to-man defense

Against man-to-man, players mustn't feel tied to their positions. Your Left Forward isn't required to stay on the left, or even to stay at Forward. When Forwards cut from one side to the other, and swap with Halfbacks, man-to-man unravels.

> **Against man-to-man, players mustn't feel tied to their positions.**

Swapping With a Marked Star

Don't be surprised when your star Forward is marked. One defender might shadow your star the entire match, regardless of which team has the ball. Unless your team adjusts, your star will become a spectator.

CHAPTER 18: BREAKING THROUGH DEFENSIVE SYSTEMS

A marked Forward doesn't have to remain a Forward, and that's the key. In Scene 18-10, your marked Forward is swapping positions with a Halfback. How might opponents respond?

- The marking player might cover a different Forward. But marking a weaker player doesn't accomplish much, and leaves your star free in midfield.

- The marking player might stick with your star. But marking is less bothersome to a Halfback. Your star can still influence the match by winning loose balls, passing, and defending.

If marked as a Halfback, your star has the option of moving to Fullback. That will probably end the marking altogether, because marking a Fullback is silly. Then, your star can sneak back to Forward!

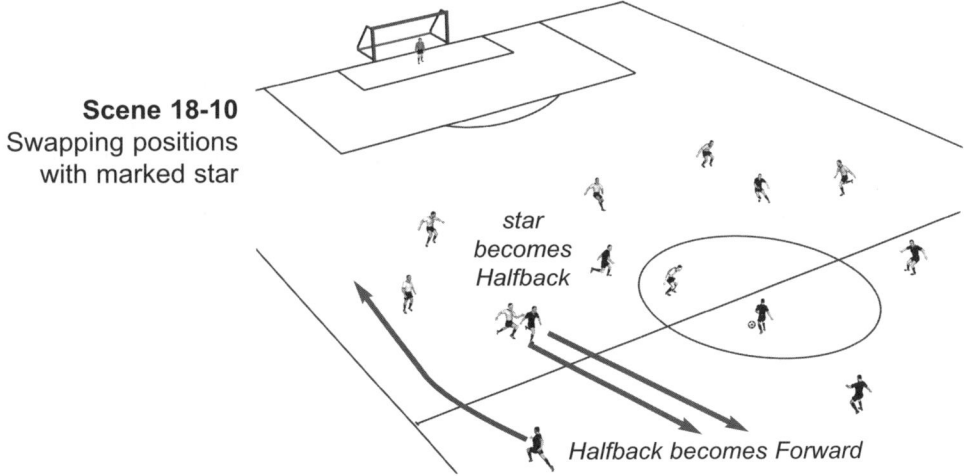

Scene 18-10
Swapping positions with marked star

star becomes Halfback

Halfback becomes Forward

Disrupting a Triangle Three

If enough coaches read this book, you might face a Triangle Three one day. The three Fullbacks form a triangle, with the Middle Fullback in line with the ball and goal, and the other Fullbacks sagging behind.

Scene 18-11 shows a Triangle Three at its best. Your player with the ball has been stopped, and has two layers to get past. Teammates to either side could receive a pass, but the triangle will just swing to that side. A run-on won't work, because the rear defenders will sag back and win the ball.

The system does have weaknesses, though. A player can get behind the triangle's point without being offside. The triangle's point can be overworked. And two players can take on the point together. For more ideas, you're on your own!

PART II: TEACHING SOCCER'S PARTS

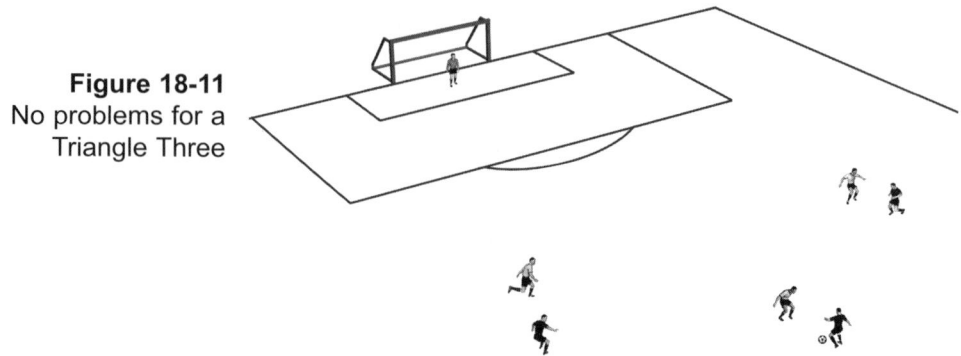

Figure 18-11
No problems for a
Triangle Three

A Higher Level of Thought

Players can be so concerned about what to do that they don't notice what opponents are doing. Is there a Flat Back line or a Sweeper, zone or man-to-man? If players don't know, they can't exploit the weaknesses.

A Thoughtscrim like Doctor Diagnoso takes thoughtful play to a higher level. Not only do players have many options. They fit those options to the situation at hand. Like effective bridge-builders, they adapt to the terrain!

19

AN OPTION APPROACH TO THE RESTART PART

Juliet, Juliet, Where Art Though?

The king hired an acting company to help him with his moods. When he was sad, a comedy would cheer him up. When he was nervous, a philosophical play would calm him down. And when he was lonely, a love story would make him feel warm and fuzzy.

PART II: TEACHING SOCCER'S PARTS

With the first performance a week away, the actors began rehearsing Shakespeare plays. They would perform Midsummer Night's Dream when the king was sad, King Lear when he was nervous, and Romeo and Juliet when he was lonely. Actors not in the play would have the night off.

On opening night, the actors launched into Midsummer Night's Dream. But in the front row, to their horror, sat a very lonely-looking king. The shift to Romeo and Juliet was awkward, because Juliet had the night off. The king began sobbing as the curtain closed.

The next night, the actors tried a different plan. When the curtain opened, a hero, a villain, a comedian, a wise old man, and two lovers were on the stage. They noted the king's mood, and invented a play on the spot. At last, the king could smile.

The Shakespeare plan had three problems. The plays took a long time to learn. One was chosen without knowing the king's mood. And when a different play was needed, the required actors weren't around.

You'll have similar problems if you call specific corner kick and free kick plays in a match. Several plays must be memorized, and that takes up practice time. A play must be called without knowing where opponents will be. And the required players might not even be in the match. The Restart Part becomes a burden.

The actors found an easier way, and so can you. You only need one corner kick play and one free kick play, if they branch into different options. Your players can look over the defense and choose the option that fits.

Corner Kick Roles

Whether taking a corner kick or defending against one, your players have roles to fill. One approach is described below. The roles have catchy names that suggest their purposes. If each player learns a few different roles, you won't have to worry about who's in the match.

Roles for Defending Against a Corner Kick
What's better for defending against a corner kick—zone or man-to-man? Strict man-to-man is risky, and Scene 19-1 shows why. A defender is covering an opponent at the far post, the most dangerous of areas. When the opponent runs somewhere else, the defender follows and the far post is unprotected.

CHAPTER 19: AN OPTION APPROACH TO THE RESTART PART

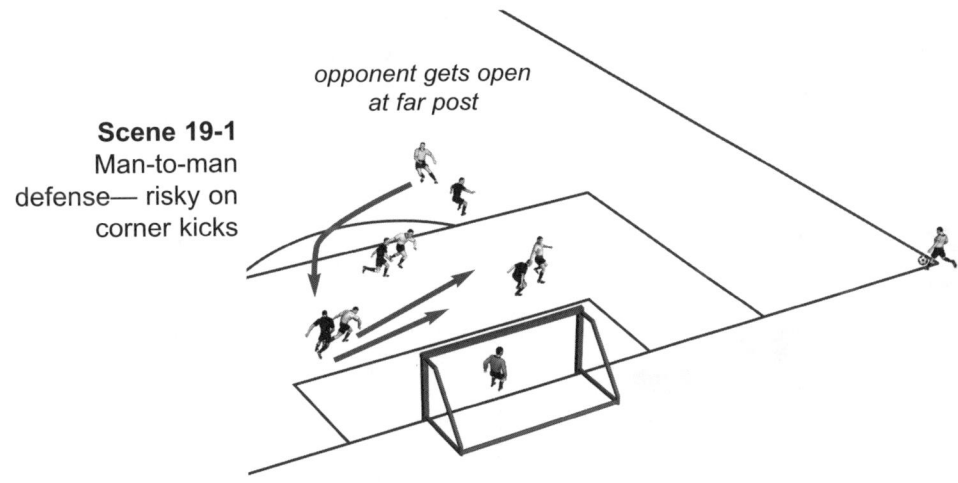

Scene 19-1
Man-to-man defense— risky on corner kicks

opponent gets open at far post

The zone approach below is safer (Scene 19-2). All eleven players are defending against the corner kick, and each has a role:

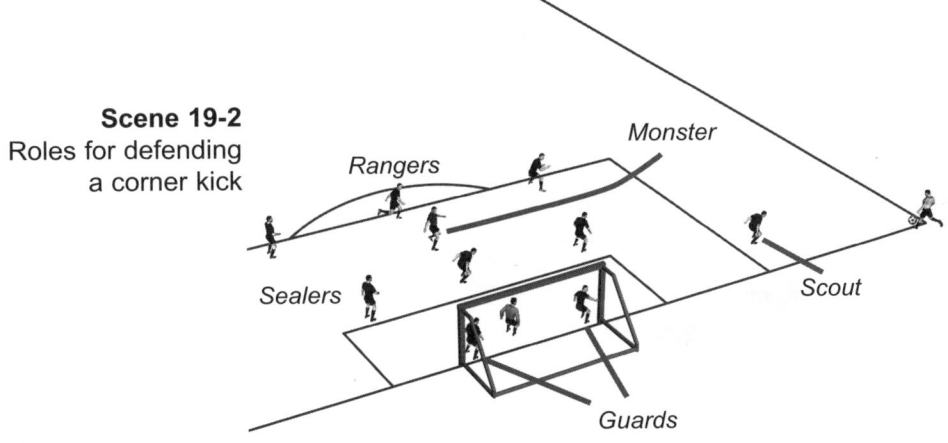

Scene 19-2
Roles for defending a corner kick

- One *Scout* moves toward the ball, to get in the kick's way and watch out for tricks.

- Two *Guards* stand in the goal, one at each post. They can block a shot that gets past the Keeper.

- Three *Sealers* are aligned about five yards in front of the goal. They cover zones rather than opponents, and clear away a ball the Keeper can't reach.

- Three *Rangers* form a second layer of defenders. They prevent a shot or header from further out.

- One *Monster* begins in the middle, and has one assignment—pursue the ball until the play is over. When a Monster is used, at least two players will always be closing in on the ball.

PART II: TEACHING SOCCER'S PARTS

The Keeper must decide quickly between caution and bravery. If the Keeper stays in the goal cautiously, the odds of a score might by fifty/fifty. If the Keeper snares the ball or punches it away bravely, the play is over. When in doubt, the Keeper should go bravely for the ball.

Roles for Taking a Corner Kick

Here are some possible roles when *your* team is taking the corner kick (Scene 19-3). For clarity, only your players and the Keeper are shown.

- One *Kicker* begins over the ball. If a long chip is called for, the Kicker will take it.

- One *Starter* joins the Kicker near the ball, so that a few tricks can be considered. The Starter also starts up the play, by breaking onto the field.

- Two *Cloggers* move very close to the goal, distracting the Keeper.

- Three *Breakers* begin ten yards or more from the goal. As the play unfolds, they break or loop to different areas—one to the far post, one to the near post, and one up the middle.

- One *Pounder* lurks outside the penalty area, hoping to receive a pass or rebound and pound it into the goal.

- One *Recycler* moves out beyond the far post. If the corner kick sails too far, the Recycler sends it back into the fray.

- One *Container* (not shown) stays back near the halfway line to prevent a counterattack. Don't give up a goal on *your* corner kick!

- The Keeper comes far out of the goal to back up the Container.

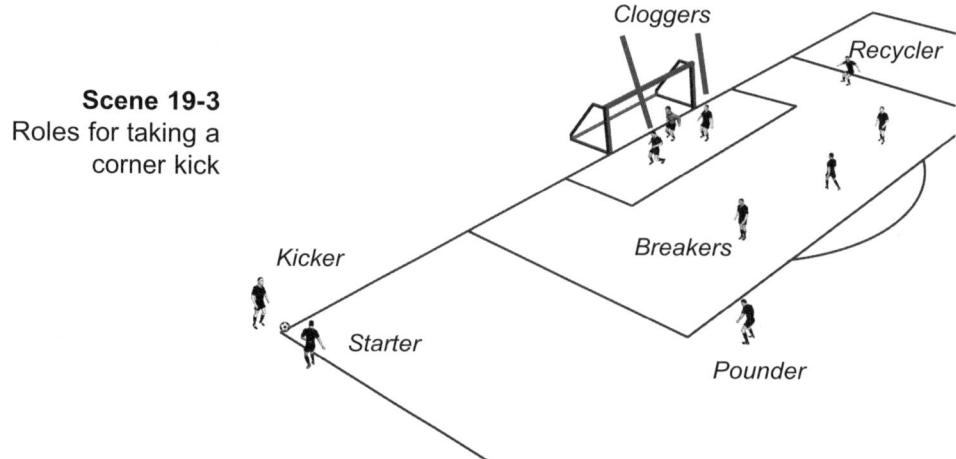

Scene 19-3
Roles for taking a corner kick

Players must communicate to make sure all the roles are filled: "I'm the Recycler!" "I've got Pounder!" and so on. But they shouldn't stand in

CHAPTER 19: AN OPTION APPROACH TO THE RESTART PART

assigned locations, advertising their roles. They should start in one place and cut to their final destinations as the play unfolds (Scene 19-4).

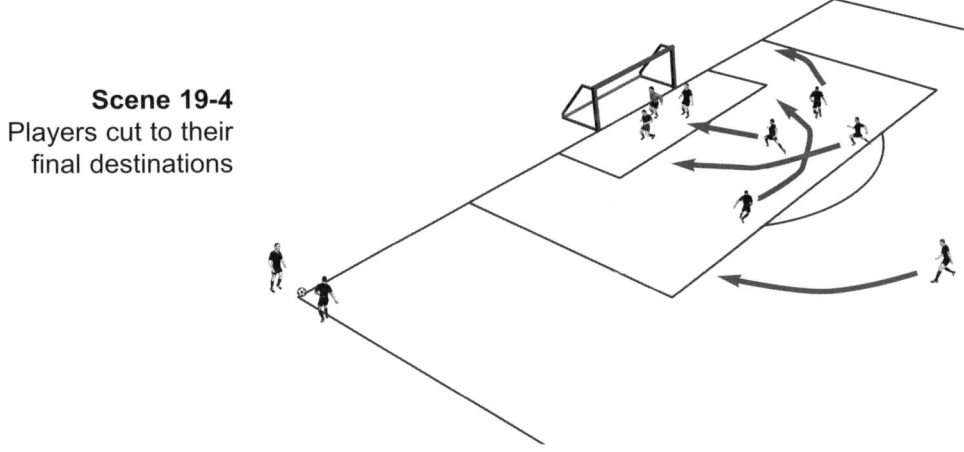

Scene 19-4
Players cut to their final destinations

A Corner Kick Option Play

When your team has earned a corner kick, players hustle to fill the required roles. The Kicker and the Starter move over to the ball, and consider the available options.

The Dribble-In

If defenders aren't paying attention, the *Dribble-In* (Scene 19-5) is a deadly option. The Kicker taps the ball to the Starter (or vice versa), who dribbles in for a cross or a shot.

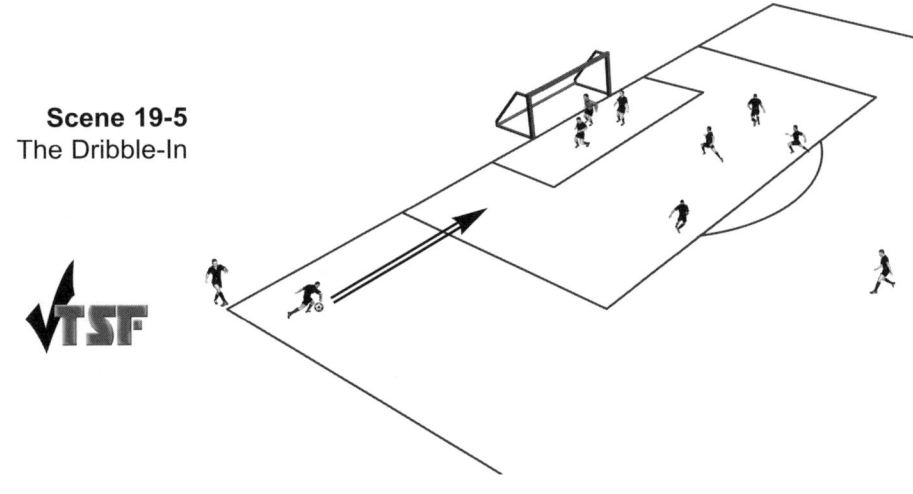

Scene 19-5
The Dribble-In

PART II: TEACHING SOCCER'S PARTS

The Set and Chip

The Starter and Kicker can also try the *Set and Chip* option (Scene 19-6). The Starter runs onto the field, receives a pass from the Kicker, and settles the ball. The Kicker then chips the ball into the goal area from a better distance and angle.

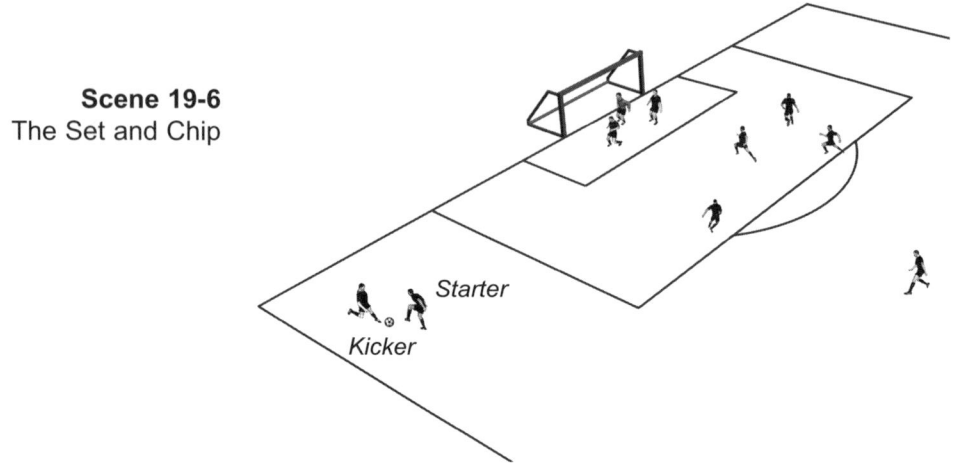

Scene 19-6
The Set and Chip

The Loop Back

What if the first two options aren't promising? The Starter then runs toward the near post, prompting the other players to head for their final destinations. Opponents will now expect a long chip, but two other tricks are still possible.

In the *Loop Back* (Scene 19-7), the Starter runs toward the near post but loops back suddenly toward the Kicker. The Kicker passes, the Starter one-touches the ball back, and the Kicker dribbles, passes, or chips.

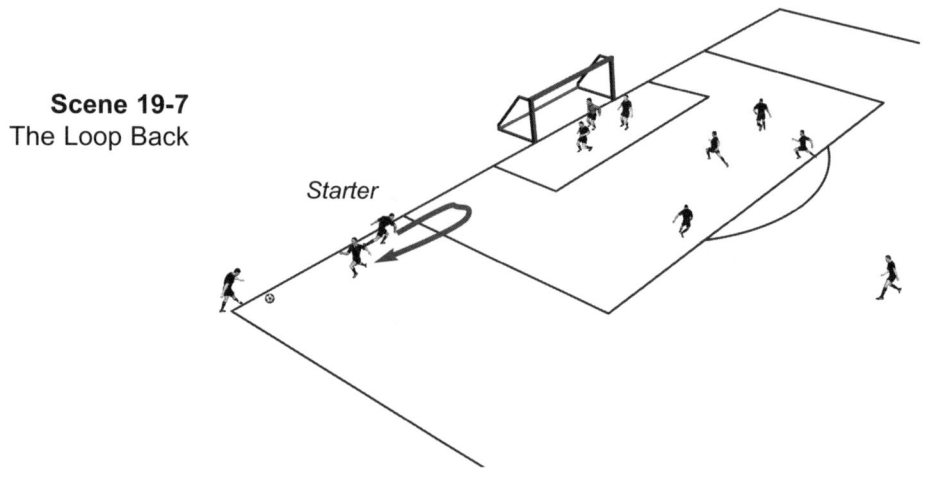

Scene 19-7
The Loop Back

Pounder Play

The other trick is the *Pounder Play* (Figure 19-8). As the Starter breaks in, the Pounder sneaks into open space outside the penalty area. The Pounder receives the ball, and shoots with the first or second touch. If no shot is available, the Pounder may pass—the Kicker being a prime target!

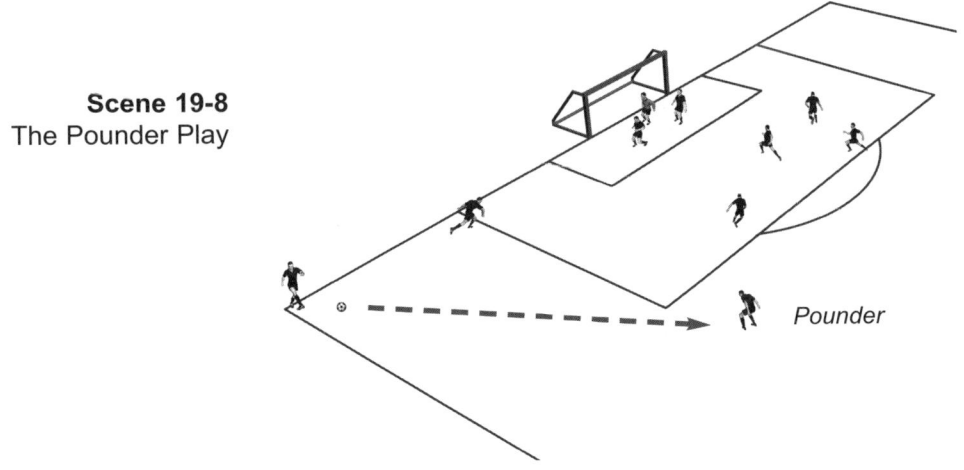

Scene 19-8
The Pounder Play

The Standard Chip

If no tricks are possible, the *Standard Chip* is sent in as players complete their runs (Scene 19-9). The chip may be directed toward the far post, near post, or center, whichever looks promising. Someone will be in each area, so even an off-target chip has a chance. The chip may be lofted, or driven on a line. A lofted chip is easier to run under, but a driven chip is harder for the Keeper to snare.

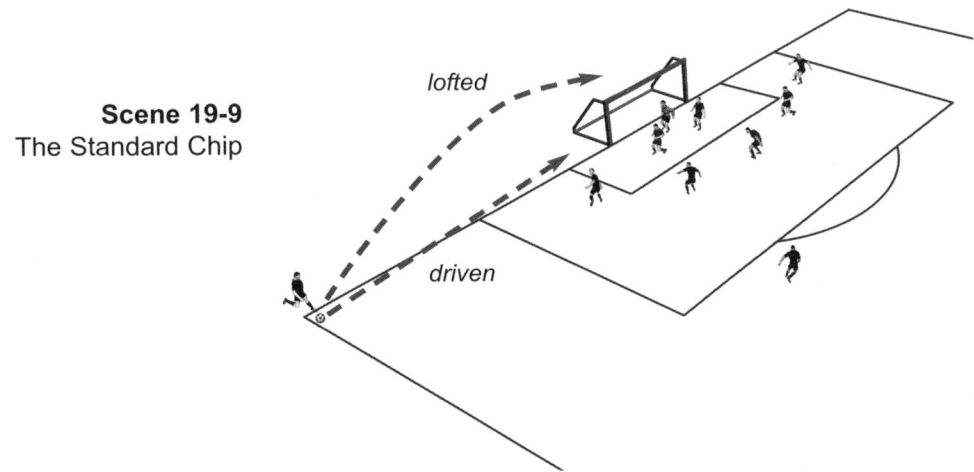

Scene 19-9
The Standard Chip

As the ball sails into the goal area, another option arises. The player arriving at the ball may either shoot, or pass to a teammate for a more dangerous shot. In Scene 19-10, the ball has reached the Recycler, who has a

PART II: TEACHING SOCCER'S PARTS

poor shooting angle. The Recycler heads the ball to the opposite post, where two open teammates lurk. A pass back to the Pounder, who has arrived at the top of the penalty area, is also possible.

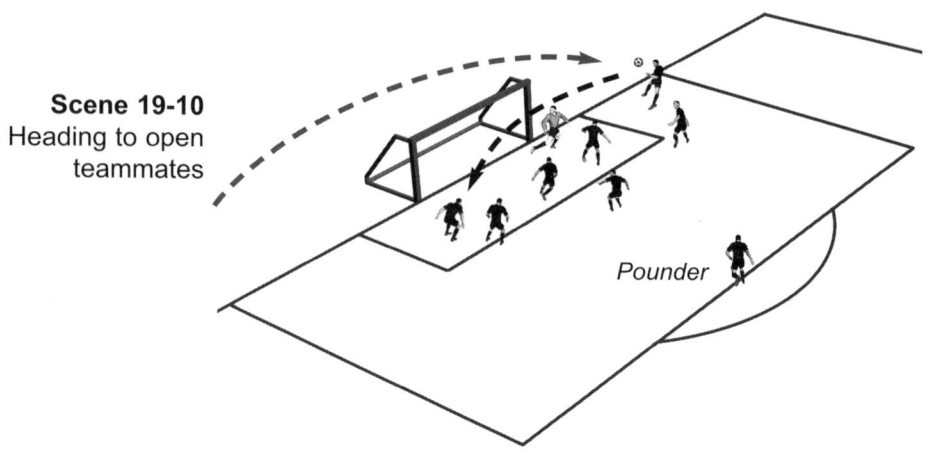

Scene 19-10
Heading to open teammates

Free Kick Roles

Free kicks can be managed much like corner kicks. Each player learns a few roles and one play branches into options.

Roles for Defending a Free Kick

This approach to defending a free kick requires four roles. The number of players in each role will depend on the ball's location. In Scene 19-11, the kick is being taken from a central location.[1]

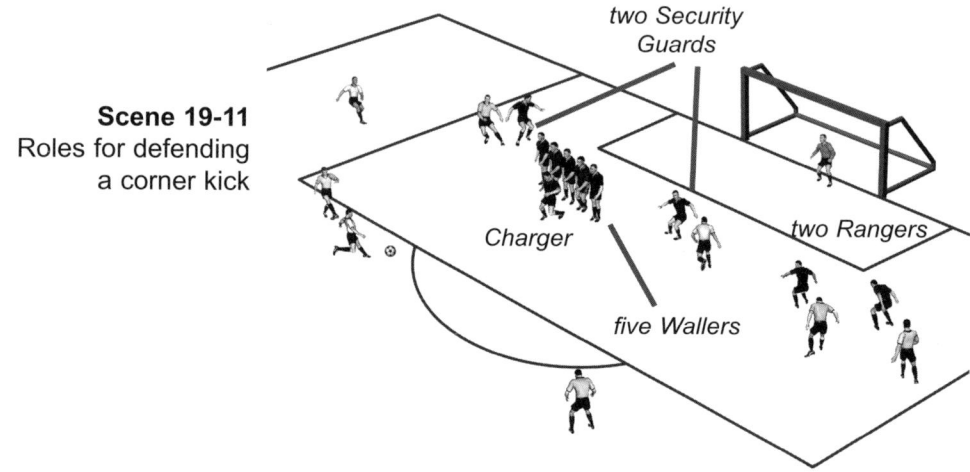

Scene 19-11
Roles for defending a corner kick

CHAPTER 19: AN OPTION APPROACH TO THE RESTART PART

- Five players serve as *Wallers*, creating a wall in front of the ball. The wall protects the near post, and extends a little beyond that post to discourage curved shots.

- Just in front of the wall is a *Charger*. This player charges the ball as soon as it's touched, to prevent trickery or block a shot.

- The Keeper calls out how many Wallers are needed and positions the wall. The Keeper can slide side-to-side before the kick, to keep a shooter guessing. But since the wall protects the near post somewhat, the Keeper's priority is the far post.

- Two *Security Guards* protect the space behind the wall. They start near the wall, but sag back as the ball is contacted. They guard zones rather than specific opponents.

- The remaining players serve as *Rangers*, ranging to other vulnerable spaces beyond the wall.

As Scene 19-12 shows, a free kick from the side requires fewer Wallers but more Rangers. The kick will probably be sent to the far post, and the Rangers must cover opponents there.

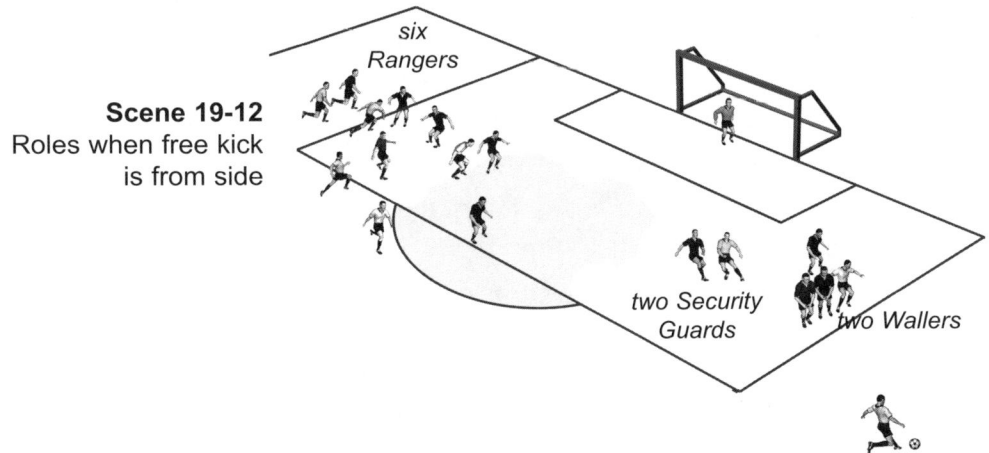

Scene 19-12
Roles when free kick is from side

Roles for Taking a Free Kick

The rules of soccer spell out two types of free kick. A direct kick, awarded for dastardly deeds, may be shot directly into the goal. An indirect kick, awarded for less dastardly deeds, must touch another player before going into the goal. With a minor adjustment here and there, the roles and options work with both kick types.

PART II: TEACHING SOCCER'S PARTS

Here are some roles to fill when your team is taking the free kick (Figure 19-13).

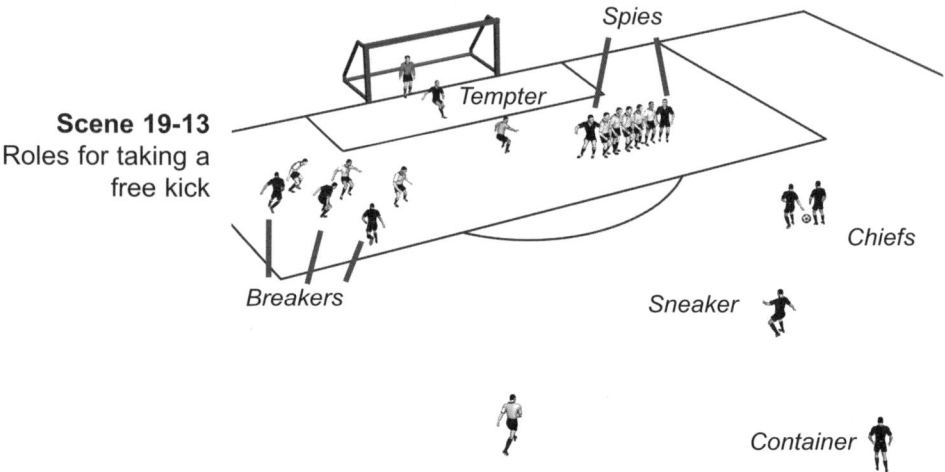

Scene 19-13
Roles for taking a free kick

- Two *Chiefs* hover over the ball. Either one might shoot, pass, or engage in trickery.

- Two *Spies* wedge their way into the wall. They interfere with the Keeper's view, and join the trickery.

- One *Tempter* begins in an offside position, tempting opponents to pull forward for an offside call. The Tempter gets back onside before the ball is struck, and is often uncovered.

- One *Sneaker* sneaks forward at the last moment for a shot around the wall.

- One *Container* stays back near midfield, to prevent a counterattack.

- The remaining players serve as *Breakers*. They break forward in a wave, hoping for a chip and a shot on goal.

A Free Kick Option Play

When your team earns a free kick, the first option is always a quick shot or pass—before the wall is in place. Otherwise, your players fill the required roles and consider the options below.

Shooting Options
If the Keeper or wall is poorly positioned, a Chief has the option of shooting (Scene 19-14). The shot can take several different routes:

- Around the wall to the near post, since the Keeper will usually be focusing on the far post

CHAPTER 19: AN OPTION APPROACH TO THE RESTART PART

- Over the wall
- Under the wall, if it has a habit of jumping
- At a Spy, who steps out of the wall at the last moment

The same shots are possible on an indirect kick, but one Chief must tap the ball to the other.

Scene 19-14
A shot around the wall

The Spy Peel

If space behind the wall looks vulnerable, the *Spy Peel* might lead to a goal (Scene 19-15). In the example, the Tempter comes back onside as a Chief makes a decoy run to the left of the wall. A gentle pass or chip is then placed to the right of the wall, where a Spy has peeled off. The Spy may either shoot the ball or cross it.

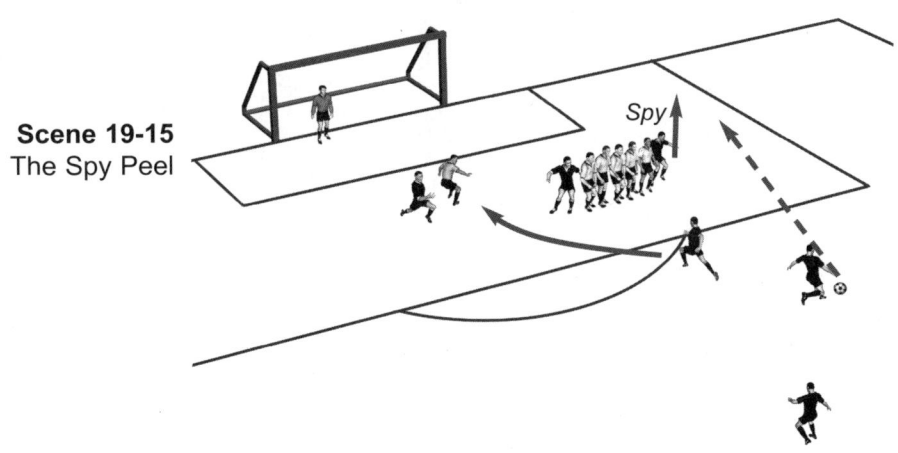

Scene 19-15
The Spy Peel

PART II: TEACHING SOCCER'S PARTS

The Spy Buster

The *Spy Buster* works in a similar way (Scene 19-16). A Chief runs over the ball and around the wall, this time to receive a pass. A low-speed shot is directed into the wall. A Spy there one-touches the ball to the Chief going by. The Chief may either shoot or cross the ball.

Scene 19-16
The Spy Buster

The Tempter's Choice

In the *Tempter's Choice*, the Tempter gets to touch the ball (Scene 19-17). The play begins like the Spy Pass, with a Chief running over and around the ball as the Tempter returns onside. The ball goes to the Tempter, though, who either one-touches a pass behind the wall, or shoots.

Scene 19-17
The Tempter's Choice

The Sneaker Play

A final trick to consider is the *Sneaker Play* (Figure 19-18). After distracting runs and fake shots by other players, the Sneaker comes forward to an open area. A Chief passes, and the Sneaker shoots around the wall.

CHAPTER 19: AN OPTION APPROACH TO THE RESTART PART

Scene 19-18
The Sneaker Play

The Standard Chip

If the shots and tricks don't materialize, the *Standard Chip* is the option of choice (Figure 19-19). The ball is chipped to the far post as the Breakers break in. The Breaker reaching the ball first may either shoot, or pass to the opposite post—where a Spy and Chief should soon arrive.

Scene 19-19
The Standard Chip

A Method for Coaching Restarts

How can you bring these roles and options to life? The same basic method works for corner kicks and free kicks. Walk through the roles and options, then practice them in a Thoughtscrim.

During the walk through, teach each player a few different roles. Juliet won't always be in the match! Also, show players how to disguise their final destinations. And invite players to invent even more options.

PART II: TEACHING SOCCER'S PARTS

After the walk through, players can compete at *Mister Crafty*—a large-sided Thoughtscrim that guarantees corner kicks and free kicks. The female version is cleverly named *Miss Crafty*. Each end of the field needs a penalty area (Figure 19-20).

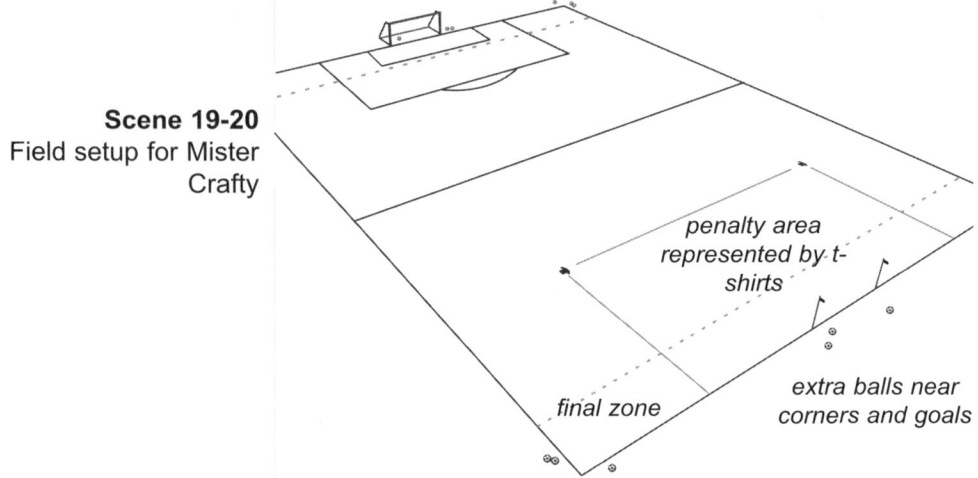

Scene 19-20
Field setup for Mister Crafty

penalty area represented by t-shirts

final zone

extra balls near corners and goals

Rules for Mister Crafty

Field Setup The field is as wide as a regular soccer field, but not as long. The exact size depends on the players per team. At each end of the field is a regulation-size goal and a penalty area. A final zone is marked with cones, five paces in from each goal line. Penalty areas may be marked with jerseys, if necessary.

Teams Two even teams are created, each with six to nine field players and a Keeper. A neutral player may participate, helping whichever team has the ball. If enough players are available, eleven-a-side teams may be used.

How the Game Proceeds As play begins, teams may score in any way they like. Regular soccer rules are in effect, including the offside rule. Corner kicks and free kicks are awarded in the usual ways, and in the additional ways described below.

Bonus Corner Kicks A team earns a bonus corner kick by:

- Taking a shot that is saved or travels over the goal line
- Making a crossing pass from the final zone, even if it doesn't result in a shot
- Scoring a goal

Due to the above conditions, a team will sometimes take several corner kicks in a row—provided those kicks result in goals or shots. However, a corner kick is not considered a crossing pass from the corner. A team may continue passing after earning a bonus corner kick. The kick isn't taken until possession is lost or the ball goes out of bounds.

CHAPTER 19: AN OPTION APPROACH TO THE RESTART PART

Bonus Free Kicks A team earns a bonus free kick by:
- Completing six consecutive passes in the attacking half of the field (the number may be adjusted to the experience level of the players)
- Winning the ball through an offside call
- Earning what would otherwise be a throw-in

A team may continue passing after earning a bonus free kick. The kick isn't taken until possession is lost or the ball goes out of bounds. The coach arbitrarily decides the type of free kick, direct or indirect, and the location.

If you spend an entire practice on corner kicks and free kicks, you might never get back to them. Frequent but brief work is better. Limit your first walk through and scrimmage to an hour. Then, an occasional game of Mr. Crafty will keep the options fresh.

Thinking for Themselves

Carefully scripted set plays rarely lead to goals. The ball never goes where it's supposed to. The players you need are never on the field together. And opponents are never where they're expected to be.

The option approach gets players thinking for themselves. It's simple enough for new players, but can fool experienced opponents. It allows players to invent their own options and to improvise. The Restart Part will leave you smiling!

---

[1] For a more detailed explanation of corner kicks and free kicks, see Mike Ditchfield and Walter Bahr, *Coaching Soccer the Progressive Way* (Englewood Cliffs, N.J.: Prentice Hall, Inc., 1988).

INDEX

A

Air Control 26-27
    rules for 27
Alligator River 27-28
    rules for 28

B

Back door 152, 166-167
Backup 125-128
    HISAs for teaching 126-128
Big Goal/Small Goal setup 77-78, 177
    scoring rules for 78
Bombs Away 28-29
    rules for 29
Box shot 36-37
Breakaway shot 36, 167-168
Breakthrough Part 102, 106-107,
   173-180, 181-192, 193-202
    combinations in 181-192
    counterattacks in 177-178
    indirect path in 177
    obstacles in 174

C

Chats, coaching
    halftime chat 88-89
    post-match chat 89
    pre-match chat 88
Check-to combination 188, 199
Check-to fake combination 188
Chest trap shot 38
Chipperoo shot 34-35
Chipping 5, 26-30
Coachable moments. *See* COMOs
Combinations 181-192
    check-to 188
    check-to fake 188
    creative runs in 184-186
    crossing 189-191
    dummy 186-187

give-and-go 183-184
run-on 182-183
takeover 186-187
Combo Bombs Away 190-191
    rules for 190-191
COMOs 91-98
    author's experience with vi
    corrective 93
    encouragement 93
    example of 93-94
    for combinations 192
    for offside rule 118-119
    in First-Time 96-97
    in large-sided scrimmage 97-98
    in Run the Gauntlet 98
    in Side-to-Side 97
    in Three-and-a-Drop 96
    number one mistake with 95
    steps in 95
Contain Part 102-103, 121-134
Corner Clear-Out 164
Corner kicks
    option play for 207-210
    problem with 107
    roles for defending 204-206
    roles for taking 206-207
Counterattack Exception 178
Counterattacks 177-178
Cover. *See* Backup
Creative runs 184-186
Crossing combinations 189-191
Cutthroat 80-81
    rules for 81

D

Defensive Halfback. *See* Stopper
Defensive systems 104, 143-158,
   193-202
    3-3-4 system 146
    breaking through 193-202
    Flat Back system 148-150

INDEX

for smaller numbers 155-157
importance of middle in 146
Marking Back system 147-148
possible systems 144-146
responsibilities in 145
staggering players in 145
Sweeper system 107, 131, 147, 195-198
teaching 157
Triangle Three system 150-154
Diagonal run 185-186
in Team Gauntlet 185-186
Directions, importance of v, 56-57
Distant Layers 127-128
rules for 128
Dizzy Miss Lizzy 168-170
rules for 169
Doctor Diagnoso 194-195
rules for 195
Donut Scrimmage 81-82
rules for 82
Dribble-by shot 34
Dribble-In 207
Dribbling 45-54
for possession 49-51
past defenders 47-48
through space 51-52
through offside line 116
warmup 46-47
Drills, problems with 15
Dummy combination 186-187
in Team Gauntlet 187

E

Evaluating players 83-84
Extra Fullback role 161, 167-170

F

Finish Part 102, 108
First-Time 68-70
benefits of 69
COMO in 96-97
concerns about 69
rules for 69
Flat Back system 148-150

attacking the 198-199
strengths of 149-150
triangle in 150
weaknesses of 149
Free kicks
option play for 212-215
problem with 107
roles for defending 210-212
roles for taking 211-212

G

Gate shot 33
Giant Slalom 51-52
rules for 52
Give-and-go 183-184
in Run the Gauntlet 183-184
Give-and-go shot 39
Glancing header 189
Goal types 76-78
Big Goal/Small Goal setup 77-78
big goals 76-77
small goals 77
Golden roller shot 38-39

H

Heading 25-26
crossing and 28-29, 189-191
diving headers 26
Headmaster 25-26
rules for 25
variations of 26
High Impact Skill Activities. *See* HISAs
HISAs
Air Control 26-27
Alligator River 27-28
Bombs Away 28-29
Combo Bombs Away 190-191
Distant Layers 127-128
Dizzy Miss Lizzy 168-170
Giant Slalom 51-52
One To Beat 124-125
One-Layer-Two 126-127
qualities of 15
Ride the Bronco 49-51
Run the Gauntlet 47-48

INDEX

Soccer Volley 21-24
Space Cowboy 175-176
Team Gauntlet 48-49

I

Indirect path 78

K

Keep-away games 62, 87
Keeper roles 105-106, 159-172
    Extra Fullback role 160, 167-170
    Possession Helper role 160, 162-163, 163-165
    Savemaker role 160, 170
    System Organizer role 160, 165-167

L

Layers, defensive 122, 167
    in Flat Back system 149, 198
    with larger numbers 133-134
    with one defender 123-125
    with three defenders 129-133
    with two defenders 125-128
Long Ball 72
    benefits of 72
    rules for 72
Loop Back 208
L-shot 33-34

M

Mambo Combo 191-192
    rules for 191
Man-to-man defense 136
    how to attack 200
    versus zone 122-123
Marking Back system
    weaknesses of 147-148
Mighty moe shot 35
Miniscrims 80-82
    Cutthroat 80-81
    Donut Scrimmage 81-82
Mister Crafty 216-217
    rules for 216-217

N

NAB rule. *See* No Aimless Booting rule

No Aimless Booting rule 63-66

O

Offside rule 103, 111-120
    ambiguities in 114-115, 118
    benefits for defenders 115
    communication code for 117-118
    explanation of 112-116
    imaginary offside line in 112
    offside position 113-114
    risks associated with 115-116
    sag/pull option in 116-117
    scrimmaging with 118-119
One Player on the Ball rule 64
One to Beat 124-125, 168
    on back-to-back goals 125
    rules for 124
One-hopper shot 39-40
One-Layer-Two 126-127
    rules for 127
One-touch play 57
OPOB rule. *See* One Player on the Ball
Options. *See also* Skills
    author's experience with v
    impact on practice 13-14
    on breakaway shot 36
    on restarts 203-218
    theory of v
    versus skills 13
    with offside rule 116-117
Organizing practice 4
    adjustments for skill level 16
    creating teams 78-80
    field size 76
    flexibility in 75-84
    long term impact of 16-17
    options and 13-14
    team colors 79-80
    team size 79
    time management and 14
    with larger numbers 82-84

INDEX

    Corner Clear-Out 164
    pass to corner 163
    Wave and Loop Trick 164-165
Overlap run 184-186
    in Team Gauntlet 185-186

P

Parts 101-110
    Breakthrough Part 102, 173-179, 181-192, 193-202
    Contain Part 102, 121-134
    Finish Part 102
    fixing broken 108-109
    Possession Part 55-60, 61-73, 102
    Pressure Part 102, 135-141
    Restart Part 102, 203-217
Pass-and-Move 71, 179, 188
    benefits of 71
    rules for 71
Passing. *See* Thoughtscrims
Paths to goal 177
Penalty Kick Game 41
Plan-to-Plan 139-140, 178
    rules for 139-140
Possession Helper role 160-161, 162-163
    groundrules for 162
    outlet passes in 163-165
Possession Part 55-60, 61-73, 102
Possession, secrets of 55-60
    directions 56-57
    open space 58
    pass length 58-59
    pass to space 59
    retreat 60
    touches 57
Pounder Play 209
Pressure. *See* Pressure Part
Pressure Cooker 138-139
    rules for 138-139
Pressure Part 102, 104, 135-141
    conditions for 137-138
    teaching the 138-139

Q

Quick-Start Rules 63-66

R

Receiving 21-24
Reset maneuver 60
Reset Thoughtscrim 70-71
    benefits of 70-71
    rules for 70
Response generalization iv
Restart Part 102, 107, 203-217
    coaching the 215-217
    problems with calling plays in 204
Ride the Bronco 49-51
    rules for 50
Rules
    Counterattack Exception 178
    for Air Control 27
    for Alligator River 28
    for arriving at match on time 88
    for Big Goal/Small Goal 78
    for Bombs Away 29
    for Combo Bombs Away 190-191
    for Cuthroat 81
    for Distant Layers 128
    for Dizzy Miss Lizzy 169
    for Doctor Diagnoso 195
    for Headmaster 25
    for Mambo Combo 191
    for Mister Crafty 216-217
    for One to Beat 124
    for One-Layer-Two 127
    for Pass-and-Move 71
    for Plan-to-Plan 139-140
    for Pressure Cooker 138-139
    for Reset 70
    for Ride the Bronco 50-53
    for Run the Gauntlet 47-48
    for Side-to-Side 67-68
    for Slalom Course 52
    for Soccer Volley 22-23
    for Soccer Volley Doubles 23
    for Space Cowboy 175-176
    for Team Gauntlet 48-49
    for Triangulation 132

INDEX

power of iv-v
Quick-Start Rules 63-66
Touch It Back 64-65
Run the Gauntlet 47-48
   COMO in 98
   give-and-go in
   rules for 47-48
   teaching backup with 126-128
Run-on 182-183, 198

S

Sag/pull option 116-117
Savemaker role 162, 170
Scrimmaging. *See also* Thoughtscrims
   Three Deadly Habits during 63
   versus skill work 14
   with offside rule 118-119
Set and Chip 208
Settlers 24
Shadow system
   attacking a 200-201
   defending with a 155
Shielding. *See* Dribbling for possession
Shooting 31-43
   from both sides 42
   on back-to-back goals 42-43
   response generalization and iv
   retrieving teams and 41-42
   in every practice 43
Shot food groups 32
   one-touch shots 38-41
   shots while dribbling 32-36
   two-touch shots 36-38
Shots
   box shot 36-37
   breakaway shot 36
   chest trap shot 38
   chipperoo shot 34-35
   dribble-by shot 34
   gate shot 33
   give-and-go shot 39
   golden roller shot 38-39
   L-Shot 33-34
   mighty moe shot 35
   one-hopper shot 39-40

penalty kick 41
volley 40
wide receiver shot 37
Side-to-Side 67-68
   benefits of 68
   COMO in 97
   rules for 67-68
Skill circuit 82-83
Skills
   body mechanics of iv, 4-5
   chipping 5, 26-27
   dribbling 45-54
   heading 25-26
   receiving 21-24
   passing. *See* Thoughtscrims
   shooting 31-44
   versus thought 5-6
Sneaker Play 214-215
Soccer Volley 21-24
   rule variations for 23-24
   rules for doubles 23
   rules for singles 22-23
Space Cowboy 175-176, 183
   rules for 175-176
Spaghetti system 156
Spy Buster 214
Spy Peel 213
Standard Chip
   on corner kicks 209-210
   on free kicks 215
Stopper 153
Support 96
Sweeper system
   attacking a 107, 195-198
   triangle with 131, 147
System Organizer role 161, 165-167

T

Takeover combination 186-187
   in Team Gauntlet 187
Teaching vi, 91-98
   wrong styles for 92-93
Team Gauntlet 48-49
   rules for 48-49
Tempter's Choice 214

INDEX

aggressiveness in 3, 73
method used in 4-5
name's meaning 3
picture used in 2-3
practice for two players 80-82
role of thought in 5-6
story of iii-viii
three-part practice in 108-109
two-part practice in 12
Thoughtscrims 62-74
   bread and butter 66-69
   development of v
   Doctor Diagnoso 194-195
   field lines for 63
   First-Time 68-70
   Long Ball 72
   Keeper participation in 162
   Mambo Combo 191-192
   Pass-and-Move 71
   Plan-to-Plan 139-140
   Pressure Cooker 138-139
   Reset 70-71
   Side-To-Side 67-68
   Three-and-a-Drop v, 66-67
   Triangulation 132
   versus keep-away games 62, 87
   with five players 79
Three Deadly Habits 63
Three-and-a-Drop 66-67
   benefits of 67
   Como in 96
   rules for 66-67
TIB. *See* Touch It Back rule
Time management 16, 42-43
Touch It Back rule 64-65
Triangle Three system 150-154
   attacking a 201-202
   Center Halfback in 153
   Forwards in 153
   Fullbacks in 151-152
   Outside Halfbacks in 152-153
   possession with 154
   Stoppers in 153
   variations of 154-155
   with Shadow 155
Triangles, defensive 129-133
   correct use of 129
   problems with 129-132, 166
   teaching 132-133
Triangulation 132-133
   COMOs during 133
   rules for 132

U

Unpredictability 3, 49, 170, 177

V

Values 85-90
   in pre-match chat 88
   list of recommended 86-87
Volley 40

W

Warmup for match 87-88
Wave and Loop Trick 164-165
Wide receiver shot 37

Z

Zone defense
   in Plan-to-Plan 139-140
   on corner kicks 204-206
   versus man-to-man 122-123

ABOUT THE AUTHOR AND THE ARTIST

Russ Carrington is a fulltime therapist and parttime soccer coach in St. Mary's County, Maryland. He developed Thoughtful Soccer while coaching his son's teams between 1987-98. When his son moved on to college soccer, Russ began conducting Thoughtful Soccer clinics for teams and coaches. He works with all age groups and ability levels. Helping brand new coaches is his specialty. Russ also coaches periodically at Middle States Soccer Camp (Richard Broad, Director). If you have Thoughtful Soccer questions or feedback, try emailing Russ at thoughtsoc@olg.com. A web site, thoughtfulsoccer.com, is also in the works.

Stan Waling is a fulltime freelance cartoonist/humorous illustator from Indianapolis, Indiana. His feature, DITHERED TWiTS, is syndicated nationally to collegiate papers and websites. Stan is also a contributing cartoonist for National Lampoon Dotcom. A four time ADDY award winner, his illustrations and designs have appeared in packaging and advertising as well as in books and on book covers. To view Stan's portfolio, visit his website at www.dtwits.com.